Linguistic Purism

Studies in language and linguistics

General editors: GEOFFREY LEECH & MICK SHORT
Lancaster University

Already published:

Women, men and language
JENNIFER COATES

A Dictionary of Stylistics
KATIE WALES

The Communicative Competence of Young Children
SUSAN H. FOSTER

Linguistic Purism
GEORGE THOMAS

LINGUISTIC PURISM

GEORGE THOMAS

Longman
London & New York

Longman Group UK Limited,
Longman House, Burnt Mill, Harlow,
Essex CM20 2JE, England
and Associated Companies throughout the world.

Published in the United States of America
by Longman Inc., New York

First published 1991

British Library Cataloguing in Publication Data
Thomas, George
   Linguistic purism. – (Studies in language and linguistics).
   1. Linguistics
   I. Title.   II. Series
   410
   ISBN 0-582-03743-3
   ISBN 0-582-03742-5 pbk

Library of Congress Cataloging-in-Publication Data
Thomas, George, 1945–
   Linguistic purism / George Thomas.
      p. cm. — (Studies in language and linguistics)
   Includes bibliographical references and index.
   ISBN 0-582-03743-3. — ISBN 0-582-03742-5 (pbk.)
   1. Language purism. I. Title. II. Series: Studies in language and
   linguistics (London, England)
   P40.5.L354T47   1991   90–20547
   410'. 1—dc20   CIP

Set in Palatino 9/11pt

Produced by Longman Singapore Publishers (Pte) Ltd.
Printed in Singapore

Contents

v

CONTENTS

Key to figures

Preface

My interest in linguistic purism now stretches back over a quarter of a century to my undergraduate days at the School of Slavonic and East European Studies at the University of London. It was from the late Professor Robert Auty that I first learned to appreciate its impact on the development of the Slavonic standard languages. Although many of my early publications dealt with loanwords, calques and problems of phonological and morphological adaptation, I was simultaneously collecting material on the resistance to the consequences of this language contact. Soon I began to treat purism as one of the factors involved in the revival before and after 1800 of the Slavonic standard languages. This in turn led me to compare the experience of ths Slavs with that of their neighbours.

During the early 1980s I was engaged in documenting the emergence of intellectual vocabulary in Croatian and I came to realise that many of the books and articles on purism did not satisfactorily answer the questions I had about the role of purism in this process. So I set about trying to find a theoretical framework in which purism in a single language could be fitted while at the same time endeavouring to uncover the possible motivations in the human psyche for an ideology which I was becoming convinced was shared at one time or another by speakers of most if not all of Europe's major languages. This resulted in a paper on the typology of purism in the Slavonic languages and an essay on the relationship between purism and nationalism. It was at this time that I first conceived the notion of a general monograph on purism, and this book was on its way. Research proceeded while on sabbatical leave in 1986–87 and the bulk of the book was written in the summers of 1988 and 1989. The manuscript was submitted early in 1990.

For an undertaking of this kind it is impossible to document adequately the help and advice I have received. Firstly, to all the scholars on whose work I have relied for languages for which I lack first-hand knowledge I extend my thanks and sincerely hope that I have not seriously distorted their views. Secondly, to all those people who have commented on the papers I have given on purism over the last 18 years in Hamilton, Ottawa, Toronto, London, Hull, Liverpool, Glasgow, Tübingen and Sofia, I should like to express my warm appreciation. Thirdly, I am endebted to those who have challenged me in correspondence or conversation to tighten my arguments: Robert Auty, Richard Bourhis, Dalibor Brozovic, Peter Herrity, Pavle Ivic, Rado Lencek, Thomas Magner, Tom Priestly. Finally, I should like to thank my colleagues at McMaster University Gerald Chapple, Gabriele Erasmi, Louis Greenspan, Magda Stroinska for reading early drafts of certain chapters. The thankless job of first non-specialist reader and general sounding-board went to my wife Margaret, who had right of veto on any phraseology she found incomprehensible or cumbersome. No words can express how deeply this and her uncomplaining and unselfish acceptance of my presence in body but not in mind over long periods of time were appreciated.

The faults which remain are, of course, mine alone. A work of this kind lays itself open to charges of pro-crusteanisation, Euro-centrism and over-generalisation. I hope that readers will excuse these and other possible shortcomings in the spirit that this book aims to break new ground. It is left to subsequent scholarship to reject in whole or part or alternatively to build on its foundations. In either case, this book will have fulfilled its aims to promote discussion of a controversial and elusive subject for linguistics.

The publication of this book was not directly supported by any granting agency but as it is the fruit of labours carried out in the Departments of Russian, Slavic Studies and Modern Languages at McMaster University, it would be churlish in the extreme if I did not acknowledge the considerable financial and moral support received from successive administrative officers of the institution where I have spent my entire academic career.

One of the best decisions I have made in my life was to offer this book to Longman for publication in their series *Studies in Language and Linguistics*. I should like to thank the editors of the series Geoffrey Leech and Mick Short for their invaluable advice on the content and style of the book.

I should like to end on a personal note. I began work on this book at the same time as I married my wife Margaret. The two projects have grown and matured contemporaneously and therefore will always be associated very closely in my mind. However, as my wife will well understand, even this association is overshadowed by another: between the two summers when the bulk of this book was written my father Russell Hambleton Thomas died after a long and courageous battle with cancer. He was no linguist – and certainly no purist – but as a displaced Anglo-Welshman living in the Thames basin he contributed in no small measure to developing in his son a sensitivity to questions of language usage which I hope is manifest in this book. I am sorry that he did not live to see the book published and in recognition of this I would like to dedicate it to my father's memory.

Hamilton, April 15, 1991

CHAPTER 1

Introduction

Introductory remarks

It is probable that mankind has always grumbled about the speech of his fellows: their high-falutin', their slipshod articulation, the breaking of taboos, or the intrusion of new words. At certain periods in human history, however, this rumbling discontent has grown into a chorus of concern about deteriorating standards or the unimpeded flow of alien elements into the language we cherish. The tendency to carp about any aspect of human behaviour is of course fundamental, but why are certain elements of language singled out for criticism and others not? What in any case makes us believe that we can, Canute-like, turn back the tide of linguistic development? Why do we come to revere Fowler, Robert, Duden, Vinogradov, Travníček, Maretić, Ben Yehuda and the countless other 'authorities' of language usage? Why are the books of René Étiemble in France or Edwin Newman in the United States so popular? These questions have no straightforward answers but they provide us nevertheless with a starting point for an investigation of what we may call linguistic purism.

In common parlance, a purist is a person who attempts to purify a language of certain undesirable features – be they unwanted foreign elements, vulgar colloquialisms, or some new-fangled popular jargon. Almost invariably such attempts at purification are treated by the observer – layman and linguist alike – with opprobrium or approval, scarcely ever with disinterested curiosity. From the very outset, therefore, we are confronted with a phenomenon which by its very nature is value-laden: some forms of purism are condoned, others condemned; some communities appear antagonistic to purism, others

1

receptive; even within a community attitudes may be sharply divided over the issue; or, it may be embraced with enthusiasm one minute and totally rejected the next.

Clearly, a first step must be to examine the substance of the puristic and anti-puristic points of view. Should the linguist take sides in the debate, or remain neutral? If the latter, should he be satisfied with cataloguing the crimes, excesses or successes of this puristic activity, or should he seek some justification for it in human nature or in the role that language plays in our lives? It is to answer such questions as these and to give as complete a picture as possible of purism as theory, process and effect that this book has been written.

The act of purification – whether consciously or unconsciously performed – is the result of individual or collective choice. Without minimising the role of the individual it is inevitable that purism is viewed primarily as a societal response to a particular concatenation of problems and as such can best be treated within the framework of socio-linguistics. At the same time, inasmuch as purism is an attitude towards language it also needs to be examined from the reference point of the social psychology of language. While it is true to say that in theory all linguistic communication – whether codified or not and whether in written or spoken form – may be subject to purism, it is also incontrovertible that puristic activity is usually associated with written, standard languages and indeed is often viewed as an intrinsic part of the process of codification. An important prerequisite for the study of purism, therefore, is a firm grasp of the theory and history of standard languages. Finally, there is a close connection between puristic attitudes and the cultural ethos of a speech community at various stages of its development. From this it follows that purism should also be studied within the framework of cultural and intellectual history.

This book sets out to provide the first broadly comparative and cross-cultural study of purism. Because puristic attitudes are so closely linked with other cultural values, the work should be of interest not only to the sociolinguist and the ethnographer of human communication but also to the social psychologist, the cultural and intellectual historian, the student of nationalism and ethnicity, as well as to the interested layman.

The remainder of this chapter provides a short report on the status of purism within linguistic theory, an examination of some special theoretical problems it raises, a survey of attempts to arrive at an adequate definition, a potted historiography and a brief statement of objectives.

The place of purism in linguistic theory

Before we can proceed further, it is essential that we address the problem of purism's place in linguistic theory. Without a proper understanding of the viewpoints adopted by various schools of linguistics it is impossible to evaluate the contributions made by individual scholars to a formal study of the subject.

Before the emergence of linguistics as an organised scholarly discipline, purism enjoyed an autonomous existence as a theory about what language should be like. Although continuing in some quarters until the present day, this prescriptivist view has come to be regarded with suspicion or repugnance by most serious linguists. Nevertheless, even within the mainstream of linguistics there is considerable variation in the treatment of purism. In particular, four main schools of linguistic thought need to be considered: historicism, descriptivism, functionalism and socio-linguistic empiricism.

Historicism

The neo-grammarians (or *Junggrammatiker*) of the nineteenth century were primarily interested in language from the point of view of its historical development and the possibilities this provided for genetic classification. In many respects their implicit model was a biological one, and they tended to see language as an organic process governed by immutable laws. For the linguist to try to stem this tide was, according to this view, a pointless exercise. Jakob Grimm, for example, attacked contemporary purists for their one-sidedly synchronic, ahistorical view of language (Kirkness 1975: 280). It is also instructive that the letter of complaint sent in 1889 to the *Allgemeiner Deutscher Sprachverein*, the self-appointed body to oversee the purity of the German language, was signed by Delbrück and other leading lights of the neo-grammarian school (Kirkness 1975: 386–8). The force of the historicist argument can be further demonstrated by the fact that even active purists, like the Czech Josef Jungmann, stressed the organic nature of language and the foolishness of trying to halt the process (Jungmann 1829: 77–8).

On the other hand, this very historicism exposed neo-grammarians to the danger of confounding synchronic and diachronic approaches to language. As von Polenz (1967: 105) has pointed out, this preoccupation with questions of etymology and origins could lead to the exclusion of so-called Jewish words in Nazi Germany without reference to their synchronic function. Indeed von Polenz has gone so far as to claim that: 'Der ganze Sprachpurismus beruht auf dem methodologischen Irrtum der Vermischung von Diachronie und Synchronie.'[1]

Jakob Grimm and his followers were deeply influenced by the Romantic Movement. One of the consequences of this Romanticism was the interest accorded dialects and other vernaculars. Standard languages were seen as artificial creations affording the linguist less information than language in its natural state. From this followed not only a heightened profile for dialectalisms but also a diminished interest in the national language and its attendant problems of cultivation, enrichment, standardisation and purification.

On the other hand, the comparative-historical method allied with rigorous philological analysis increased the awareness of the lexical treasures formerly available to a language or preserved in cognate languages whether dead or alive. For example, the lectures given in London by Max Müller on Germanic philology confirmed William Barnes' recognition of the 'impoverishment' of English compared with Gothic, Old Norse and Anglo-Saxon and led directly to the latter's attempts to purify English (Jacobs 1952: 17). The growth of interest in Finno-Ugric led to a similar impulse among Finnish, Estonian and Hungarian purists to use the resources of cognate languages of this group.

Descriptivism

Descriptivism was in many ways a reaction to the historicism of the neo-grammarians. By its insistence on the distinction between synchrony and diachrony it robbed purism – if we take von Polenz's view to its logical conclusion – of its very *raison d'être*. In point of fact, descriptivism devoted most of its attention to synchronic studies. Thus, questions of origins were pushed into the background. The phoneme, not etymology, emerged as the central focus of interest. In this atomistic search for the essence of language, questions of purism inevitably came to appear trivial and irrelevant.

Linguists of the descriptivist schools also parted company with their predecessors by playing down genetic relationships between languages and by exploring instead their typological similarities and

---

[1] The whole of linguistic purism is based on the methodological mistake of confusing diachrony and synchrony.

contrasts. This down-playing of genetic relationships had as a natural corollary a diminished interest in what constituted the inherited, native element in a given language. As we shall see later, this interest – not to say obsession – is at the very heart of purism. The typological approach in turn led to the study of exotic and hitherto overlooked languages, not just the great languages of civilisation with their long and rich textual traditions.

The descriptivists did share with the neo-grammarians an interest in dialects and a corresponding disinterest in standard languages. As before, this was based on the dichotomy between the natural and the artificial, but for somewhat different reasons: the descriptivists saw any intervention in language as an obstacle to their own empirical investigations. Furthermore, they were firmly set against the prevailing trend of prescriptivism, which sought to legislate language usage (for a detailed history of this battle in American linguistics, see Drake 1977). The legacy of this aversion to all forms of human intervention in language is still strong today. Surprisingly, however, this view, so prevalent among professional linguists, has been largely rejected by the general public – not only perhaps because it is counterintuitive but also because it undermines confidence in man's ability to control his own linguistic destiny. Nevertheless, for our purposes, it is sufficient to underline the fact that the theoretical standpoint of the descriptivists was fundamentally opposed to purism as an aspect of human intervention in language. This of course did not stop them writing about purism and challenging its precepts. Indeed, this critical attitude to purism is probably their greatest contribution to the development of a well-founded, comprehensive theory of purism.

Neither historicism nor descriptivism could provide a theoretical base for purism: the historicists, on the one hand, simply ignored it, while the descriptivists, on the other, explicitly excluded it from the canon of linguistics. Purism was reduced to being treated as an extralinguistic factor or, worse, as an inadmissible approach to language. Some fresh theory was required to rescue it from this state of limbo.

Functionalism

Those linguists who, dissatisfied with the atomism and empiricism of the descriptivist approach, began to explore questions of the functioning of language as a system, still retained a basic antagonism towards purism. Take for example the following statement by Horálek (1948: 65), quoted by Vachek (1960: 42) as one of only two representative pronouncements on purism by members of the Prague School, perhaps the most coherent group of functionalists: 'Le purisme se manifeste comme une tendance qui, au fond, n'est pas extralinguistique, mais qui interprète la langue d'une façon erronée.'[2] Indeed, the Prague School became embroiled in a fierce polemic with their puristic compatriots (Ševčík 1974–5; Jelínek 1971; Rothstein 1976; Salzmann 1989), but like all good disputations, it helped to refine the two positions and led ultimately to a higher synthesis.

The Prague School linguists (see particularly Jakobson 1932; Weingart 1932, 1934; and Mathesius 1932, 1933, 1947) argued that in their zeal to protect their language from unwanted influences the purists had not only wrongly identified non-Czech elements but more importantly ignored the communicative and stylistic functions of foreign words. They viewed the purists' concept of the 'spirit' of a language – an idea which goes back to the German idealist philosopher Herder – as vague and dangerously prone to subjective interpretation. The functionalist approach to the various elements of a language was to judge them solely on the criterion of how they function in the system. In this connection, the Prague School evolved a theory of standard languages based on four inviolable principles: elasticity, stability, prestige and polyvalency (Mathesius 1947). Standard languages required care and cultivation if none of these principles was to be violated. Questions of language cultivation were regarded as 'an important component of general linguistics' (Jakobson 1932: 85). Within language cultivation (G. *Sprachpflege*, Pol. *kultura języka*, etc.) purism might also have a part to play particularly with respect to the stability and prestige principles. This incorporation of purism within a linguistic theory – albeit in a radically reduced capacity – was the first step towards its legitimation and constitutes therefore an important stage in the professional linguist's attitude to it.

Some of the later adherents of functionalism came to realise that it did not pay sufficient attention to the social and psychological impulses shaping attitudes to language. Not only did the functionalists ignore these seemingly irrational factors, but were guilty at times of not giving due regard to one of their own principles – prestige. Nevertheless, the new synthesis at least provided a theoretical position from which purism could be discussed as an intralinguistic phenomenon. In both its original and somewhat modified forms it

---

[2] Purism is manifested as a tendency which is basically not extralinguistic but which interprets language in an erroneous way.

has won widespread support in many parts of the world but especially – as one might expect – in central and eastern Europe.

Socio-linguistic empiricism

The spark for socio-linguistics was provided by such figures as de Saussure, Schuchardt, Baudouin de Courtenay, Sapir and Polivanov. Kindled by a growing dissatisfaction with the limitations of descriptivism, from which, significantly, many of its earliest adherents were in fact renegades, and fuelled by the introduction of theories and methodologies taken from the social sciences, sociolinguistics was inflamed by the deliberate neglect of questions of language performance in transformational generativism, the most influential prevailing linguistic theory. It has since won respect and interest throughout the world as a legitimate attempt to view language objectively as a form of social communication. This new objective approach has paved the way for a detailed analysis of the very sociological and psychological impulses in language variation which functionalism had tended to ignore. Purism could now be treated as a socio-linguistic factor to be taken into consideration in any proper analysis of a given language situation. Socio-linguistics has also further elaborated the functionalist theory of standard languages. In this scheme, language cultivation has become an aspect of language planning, a term which covers all rational and purposeful intervention in language and the social situations in which it operates, and purification has been identified by Nahir (1977) as one the five possible objectives of such planning.

The contribution of socio-linguistics to the study of purism is, then, of crucial importance. It provides:

1. A forum for the objective study of purism.
2. A theoretical framework.
3. A legitimate role for purification among the objectives of planned language intervention.

The theoretical status quo

Although the four basic positions have been presented in chronological order, we should not suppose that there has been a linear development in the treatment of purism: conflicting views have coexisted and even interacted, and continue to do so. Indeed, even today it would not be difficult to find adherents of at least the last

7

three of these positions, as the various definitions of purism in contemporary linguistics discussed below will illustrate. Nevertheless, they do allow us to identify five stages in the development of theories about purism:

1. Purism as an autonomous theory of language.
2. A sceptical or disinterested attitude to purism.
3. The exclusion of purism from linguistic theory.
4. The qualified acceptance of purism within a theory of language cultivation.
5. The incorporation of purism into a theory about the social and psychological impulses which affect language use, language attitudes and language planning.

These five stages may be presented in the form of a graph (Figure 1) depicting the status of purism at each successive stage.

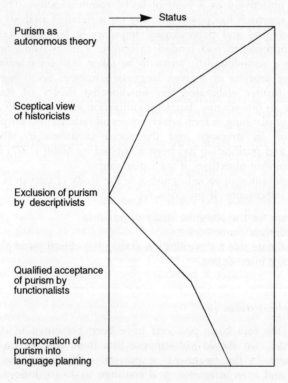

Figure 1: The status of purism in linguistic theory

Some further theoretical problems

Many recent investigators of purism have noted the absence of an adequate theory of purism (Thomas 1988b: 97). This theoretical poverty embraces not only questions of taxonomy and typology but even basic motivations. Moreover, there has been no attempt to study purism in the framework of a general theory of purity and purification in the human experience. Another neglected problem is the interplay of intra- and extralinguistic factors. Even more basic is the paucity of objective studies of attitudes to loanwords, one of the principal targets of purism. However, the empirical work of Tejnor and his associates (1971) on attitudes to loanwords in Czech and the theoretical work of his compatriot Daneš (1968, 1982, 1987) on language values and attitudes suggest some promising paths of enquiry, which will be explored in Chapter 3.

The primary desideratum of a book on purism is that it present a descriptive narrative of the origins, operation and results of purism in a wide variety of languages differing not only in their typologies but also in the social situations in which they are spoken. However valuable such a narrative may be – and nothing similar, as we shall see presently, has been attempted to date – there are surely some basic ontological and phenomenological questions which need to be addressed if we are to avoid the pitfall of describing purism without properly explaining it.

Let us look first at some of the ontological questions. While a purist is clearly an actor with a certain set of attitudes and certain intentions stemming from these attitudes, purification is the activity in which he is involved, and purity is the quality thought desirable by him, what exactly do we mean by purism? Does the word even have any significance when applied to language? Can we talk about purism without reference to some concrete manifestation of puristic activity or intent? For example, does such an entity as 'Hebrew purism' exist, or would it be more proper to talk of the attitudes of a particular individual or group at a particular point in time? Can we talk of 'Baroque purism' as a way of generalising about certain common features in quite separate languages, or should we not limit ourselves to expressions such as 'purism in the age of the Baroque'? Are we justified in using purism as a blanket term to describe differing phenomena in a whole range of languages? Even if in the final analysis we are able to answer all these questions affirmatively, they do demonstrate some of the theoretical difficulties we face when trying to pin down an abstraction like purism.

The phenomenological questions are no less perplexing. Does purism have an absolute or relative value? A maiden can be more or less virtuous, but can she be more or less pure? Do similar restraints exist when speaking of the purity of a language? Does purism have a single nature or many? And if many, how many? Can we equate English purism, which is peripheral to the development of English, with Estonian purism, where it is central? Can purism be applied both to the insistence in Serbian on words in popular usage (even if they are of foreign origin) and to the rejection in Croatian of words of foreign origin (often the very words admitted in Serbian)? Is purism a language universal or is its existence determined by a certain concatenation of circumstances?

Clearly, no treatise on purism can afford to ignore such fundamental problems as these. The rhetorical questions aired here should, if nothing else, have prepared the way for an examination of some of the available definitions of purism.

Some definitions

One of the basic problems in discussing purism is that there is so little agreement about what it is. Not only are we faced with the old Humpty-Dumpty syndrome of a word meaning what each scholar wishes it to mean, but the years of its exclusion from mainstream linguistics and a long history of lay usage have taken their toll: purism has simply not been terminologised.

We may begin our survey of definitions of purism with a succinct statement from 1854 by the English purist William Barnes: 'A language is called purer inasmuch as more of its words are formed from its own roots' (Jacobs 1952: 16). The core of the definition carries several assumptions which are widespread in the literature on purism: only the lexicon is concerned; the absence of words of non-native origin is the only criterion of purity. Implicit in the statement is the relative, as opposed to absolute, nature of linguistic purity.

A recent description of purism may serve as an elegant modernisation and extension of Barnes: '[Purism is] the attempt to remove from a given language elements that are foreign or deemed to be foreign and replace them by elements of a native, national character' (Auty 1973: 335). This definition makes reference to purism as a two-fold activity (involving removal and replacement), which may or may not be crowned with success. It also extends purism to include all levels of language. Furthermore, Auty draws our attention to the possibility that the identification of these foreign elements might not be justified.

Many scholars (for example, Urbančič 1972: 43; Moskov 1976: 7) have widened the scope of purism to include not only an opposition to foreign elements but also to dialectalisms and jargon. These views of purism have been neatly brought together in the following definition:

> The word purism is associated primarily with the antipathy to foreign words and the resulting attempt to expel them from the language. . . The purist's anathema can however also be aimed at the social and territorial variants of its own language area, because they do not conform to the articulatory, morphological, syntactical or lexical norms of the standard language (or his notion of the latter). (Keipert 1977b: 286)

As representative of the descriptivist school, I have selected this definition, taken from Robert Hall's excellent book on the *Questione della lingua* in Italian:

> Purism, in its essential nature, consists of considering one type of language (a given dialect, or the speech of a given social class or of a certain epoch etc.) as 'purer' than and therefore 'superior' to other types. (Hall 1942: 4)

It is immediately noticeable that purism is presented here as a prescriptive attitude, the indictment of which is signalled by the presence of quotation marks. Furthermore, the focus of attention has shifted from the origins of the word-stock to the selection of a particular language code as deserving of more prestige than any other. Such a broadening of the definition of purism robs it of much of its illocutionary force. Nevertheless, it is in this sense, as a virtual synonym of élitist prescriptivism, that the term is most often used today.

Two recent dictionaries of linguistic terms appear to be trying to weld a viewpoint similar to Hall's with a more traditional one:

> [Purism is] the struggle against neologisms, against the introduction into usage of loan and international words etc., not based on a scientific study of the developmental tendencies of a given language and the activity of people attempting to protect their native language from foreign influence. (Axmanova 1966)

> [Purism is] an attitude towards language which disapproves of deviations

11

from certain grammatical rules, or neologisms and borrowings from other languages. Often purists make a vain attempt to preserve the status quo of a language. (Hartmann and Stork 1972)

The cleavage between the two viewpoints embedded in each of these definitions is clearly marked by the punctuation and the awkwardness of the syntax.

As a representative of the functionalist viewpoint we may cite the following:

[Purism is] an assemblage of views regulating the codification and cultivation of the literary language in accordance with an ideal model of a 'pure' language by the elimination of elements, which are at variance with this model. (Ševčík 1974–5: 56)

Purism has been reduced here to an aspect of the codification of literary languages, but gone too is the highly critical attitude to it. We may also note that the definition does not equate purism with a rejection of foreign elements only. Ševčík's definition does not touch on the processes whereby the elimination is achieved, nor does it say anything about the social circumstances of purism.

Finally, here is a modern socio-linguistic statement about purism:

The concept of purism comprises different forms of language cultivation and language planning, which have the common aim of ridding. . .[a] language of, or keeping it free from, foreign influences. (Gerdener 1986: 20)

We might have anticipated the explicit reference to language planning, but less predictable perhaps is the return to a concentration simply on foreign elements. This is not, however, representative of all socio-linguistic treatments of purism.

While not without merit, all of these definitions have some shortcomings, which stem for the most part from the outlook of the school of linguistics with which they are associated. While it would be clearly premature to offer one of my own at this stage, it may be useful to propose a working definition which seeks as far as possible to combine the best features of all the definitions discussed above:

Purism is the manifestation of a desire on the part of a speech community (or some section of it) to preserve a language from, or rid it of, putative foreign elements or other elements held to be undesirable (including those originating in dialects, sociolects and styles of the same language). It may be directed at all linguistic levels but primarily the lexicon. Above all, purism is an aspect of the codification, cultivation and planning of standard languages.

A review of previous study

While purism in one form or another is probably coterminous with language, the study of the phenomenon thankfully covers a much shorter time-span. The first serious attempts to plot the course of purism belong to the last two decades of the nineteenth and the first decade of the twentieth century and are limited to the German experience. The inter-war years brought not only renewed interest in purism but a widening of perspective to include other languages (Hungarian, Czech, English, Dutch, Danish and Swedish). After the war came important treatments of the role of purism in Hebrew, Turkish, Estonian, Ukrainian, Belorussian, Bulgarian and, more recently still, the languages of the developing world. In other words, what had appeared to earlier investigators to be a feature of a single language was now revealed as little short of a universal characteristic. Yet it is precisely the comparative aspect of purism, which has been so thoroughly neglected. As Auty (1973: 335) has pointed out, 'there is a lack of studies analyzing purism as a general linguistic (or sociolinguistic) factor or attempting to draw conclusions as to its causes, characteristics and influence'. Serious as this deficiency obviously is, there are some other more disturbing features of the historiography of purism: (1) the national perspective, (2) subjectivity, (3) diffuseness, (4) lack of theoretical perspective, and (5) absence of methodological principles. The consequences of each of these shortcomings need to be faced before we can return to a proper examination of Auty's contention.

Most of the early studies of purism are concerned with the investigator's native language. Unfortunately, while he is likely to have a more extensive and more intimate knowledge than the outsider, this advantage is more than offset by the bias which often accompanies writing about one's own culture. This is especially evident in cases where purism is part of the national myth and a nationalist orientation provides the impulse for studying it. For example, in the years 1885–1912, a period which begins with the founding of the *Allgemeiner Deutscher Sprachverein* and coincides with the intense nationalism of Wilhelmine Germany, no fewer than nine theses and essays were produced dealing with German purism (Blume 1967: 21). Similarly, the fiercely patriotic period following the First World War in Czechoslovakia saw the publication of Lisický's detailed but nationalistically coloured study of the long Czech struggle against Germanisms (Lisický 1919, 1920). Gradually, however, the tide began to turn. In 1909, for instance, a German

13

dissertation (Prein 1909) was devoted to puristic trends in sixteenth-century English. This was followed in 1928 by a scholarly account of the English puristic attitudes giving rise to abortive efforts to form a language academy (Flasdieck 1928). Since then, with ever-increasing frequency, scholars have written about languages other than their own, and even those writing from within their own national culture have expressly distanced themselves from nationalist positions (Blume 1967: 21). Nevertheless, with some rare exceptions (Auty 1973, Fodor 1983b), studies of purism tend to be longitudinal rather than comparative.

Throughout most, if not all, of its recorded history, purism has had a strong ideological component. Not surprisingly, therefore, much that is written about purism is coloured by the author's attitude to this ideology. In many cases the marshalling of evidence and the concomitant manipulation of our sensibilities are performed with great subtlety. How can these biases be reliably identified and corrected for? To what extent, if any, is subjective evidence admissible? Or worse, is it a delusion to suppose that purism is open to objective examination at all?

Of course, used with caution the evidence of some of these value-laden studies (Schultz 1888; Dunger 1910; Lisický 1916, 1919, 1920) is not necessarily invalidated. Nevertheless, we are bound to favour those works which are relatively free of such biases. The post-war period which has brought greater objectivity to the study of purism has produced admirable monographs for Belorussian and Ukrainian (Wexler 1974), Bulgarian (Moskov 1958, 1976), Turkish (Heyd 1954), German (Blume 1967, Kirkness 1975), and Norwegian (Gerdener 1986), as well as a plethora of valuable journal articles for a wide range of languages. Not only have these works provided sketches of individual puristic movements but in certain cases (most notably Kirkness 1975) they have supplied the necessary documentary evidence against which the reliability of the historical sketch can be calibrated. Furthermore, the incorporation of purism into a body of linguistic theory – be it functionalist or socio-linguistic – has helped enormously to remove the worst abuses of subjectivity. In sum, despite some vivid contra-indications, this century has witnessed a gradual professionalisation of the study of purism.

Nevertheless, it is worth bearing in mind that even those works which subjectivity has robbed of their value as history retain their worth as evidence for purism. For example, Dunger's account of the history of the *Allgemeiner Deutscher Sprachverein* (Dunger 1910) tells us as much about his own puristic attitudes as about its ostensible subject-matter. In other words, while the store of secondary literature may be diminished, there is a compensatory increase in the availability and quality of the primary sources. A survey of Brang and Züllig (1981), a bibliographical guide to Slavonic sociolinguistics, for instance, reveals that of the huge number of entries indexed under purism only a very low percentage are scholarly accounts; the rest are essentially apologias for or against a particular brand of purism.

Many of the early works treated purism as an isolated phenomenon, while later ones tended to integrate it into more wide-ranging studies. These include above all language histories (Bach 1970; Havránek 1936; Skautrup 1944–68; Sauvageot 1971, 1973; Hakulinen 1961; Vince 1978), monographs on language academies (e.g. Hall 1942; Bellamy 1939; Otto 1972), the awakening of national consciousness (Tolnai 1929; Becker 1948a; Jedlička 1948), and, more recently, language reform (Fodor and Hagège 1983). Nearly all the essays in the last-named work touch on purism at some point, and for some it is the main focus. Since the range of languages treated is also extremely broad, one gains from it a clear perception of purism as a component of the reforming, modernising and intellectualising aspect of written languages.

These varied perspectives on purism produce a picture which is at once unfocused and refracted. On the other hand, this prismatic effect has the virtue of allowing us to see more clearly the different types and varied functions of purism. It would be quite wrong, for example, to equate instances of purism produced under quite different sociolinguistic conditions without making explicit reference to the language situations which engendered them. To do so would be to produce a typology which would be so flat as to be valueless.

We have already discussed at length the shortcomings of the available definitions and the intellectual poverty both of purism itself and of much of the writing about it. This all stems from the lack of a general theoretical perspective – a failure, for example, to address the very ontological and phenomenological questions raised earlier; a failure to produce hypotheses about the causation and motivation of purism; and, finally, a failure to recognise that, as an attitude to language, purism needs to be treated within a theory of values.

The first serious attempt to examine values in language was Ray (1961). This short but seminal article suggested a number of evaluative scales: economy/richness, transparence and logicality of word-formation, comprehensibility, opening (or semiotic and semantic accommodation and assimilation) and closure (or semiotic uniformity and semantic solidarity). These scales may to some extent be applicable to purism but they do not provide a rigorous scheme of language values into which purism can be neatly fitted. However, a scheme for examining value-orientations in language elaborated by Daneš (1968, 1982, 1987) on the basis of Talcott Parsons' theory of social values (Parsons 1951) opens up the possibility for purism to be discussed on an altogether more elevated theoretical plane.

The methods used to study purism are predominantly those of the philologist: dictionary work, the collection of evidence from primary sources, the analysis of textual material, attention to cultural values and literary poetics, consideration of the purist's knowledge of the etymology and word-formation of his native language. Without this painstaking, documentary approach there would be no study of purism. Nevertheless, such studies are often marred by a number of methodological shortcomings: an over-reliance on personal intuition and *a priori* reasoning, an unwillingness to use quantitative methods, and the lack of a rigorous comparative, typological framework. Among the questions to which these studies fail to provide adequate answers are the following: How do we know purism has had an effect on a language? How can we measure this effect? Is it indeed measurable? By what criteria can we say one language is purer than another? Can we even compare one instance of purism with another quantitatively and qualitatively? How can we resolve the problem of circularity in the arguments about the influence of cultural values on purism when purism itself is one such cultural value? How is it that identical cultural conditions can produce a dichotomy of attitudes to purism?

None of these questions has a straightforward answer, particularly those pertaining to measurement, which, as we shall see, present difficult problems of interpretation and evaluation. Nevertheless, they would all seem to be perfectly legitimate and, even if not explicitly posed, should at least underlie the description of any individual instance of purism.

Several of the more recent works on purism are alive to some of these methodological problems. Among those works to discuss the problematics of quantification and attempt some statistical analysis of purism are the following: Heyd (1954) for Turkish, Zvelebil (1983) for Tamil, Şerban (1983) for Romanian, Zaidi (1983) for Urdu, Gerdener (1986) for Nynorsk. Problems of typology are addressed in Ševčík (1974–5), Moskov (1976), and, at greater length, in Wexler (1974), but the first attempt to suggest a systematic typology (solely on the basis of the Slavonic languages) is Thomas (1988b).

We have painted a bleak picture of the historiography of purism. It not only confirms Auty's viewpoint but suggests some other shortcomings as well. Moreover, the five major inadequacies should not be seen in isolation but rather as overlapping and mutually reinforcing. Thus, for example, nationalism of outlook strengthens the tendency towards subjectivity and vice versa. The diffuseness of the literature fuels both the lack of theoretical perspective and the methodological inadequacies. Clearly too, there cannot be a methodology without a theory. Finally, subjectivity is both a conditioning factor as well as the result of this lack of a proper theory of purism.

It should be pointed out, however, that in many respects contemporary scholarship is aware of the deficiencies of the past and is well on the way to correcting them. The anchoring of purism in linguistic theory and the professionalisation and international profile of this scholarship should ensure a more dispassionate, a more intellectually rigorous as well as a more broadly comparative approach to the problem in the future.

Statement of objectives

This book aims to provide as comprehensive an introduction to the study of purism as space allows. The emphasis throughout is on the comparative and contrastive aspects of purism rather than on the *minutiae* of puristic activity in individual languages. References to individual instances of purism are intended to be merely illustrative of general statements about purism.

Each chapter in turn examines the problem from a distinct perspective. The first two chapters are exploratory in nature. Chapter 2 attempts to come to grips with the notions of 'pure', 'purity', 'purification', on which a definition of 'purism' inevitably depends. Chapter 3 offers a theoretical framework for understanding the motivations of purism.

The next two chapters provide a basic taxonomy of puristic intervention. Chapter 4 offers a typological framework for examining all instances of purism. Chapter 5 examines the process of purification itself.

The next three chapters are concerned with the circumstances in which purism occurs. Chapter 6 discusses the identity of the purist, the role of institutions and the social environment of the purificational process. Chapter 7 discusses the particular types of language situation which give rise to purism. Chapter 8 deals with the extralinguistic factors which determine the form that purism takes. The next two chapters are concerned with the changes wrought by puristic intervention. Chapter 9 discusses purism from the point of view of historical development within a single language tradition, and Chapter 10 seeks to analyse the ways in which purism has effected language development and attitudes within a speech community.

The two concluding chapters seek to provide a synthesis of the arguments provided in the earlier chapters. Chapter 11 attempts to weave the material of the book into a core definition of purism, which can serve as a basis for the development of several working hypotheses about purism as a factor in human intellectual development. Chapter 12 seeks to examine the possible applications of the conclusions reached about purism to the theory and practice of language planning.

CHAPTER 2

The imagery of purism

Introduction

We have defined purism as an attitude to language which labels certain elements as 'pure' (therefore desirable) and others as 'impure' (therefore undesirable). For the professional linguist of course even this basic distinction is questionable. Equally dubious is the assertion that to remove the 'impure' elements is to render the language 'pure'. The question is, however, not whether purists are right or wrong to structure their thinking about language in this way, but rather why they do so, and what actions stem from this thinking.

In order to understand something of this mentality, it is essential to look at the problem with the eyes of the purist by examining in some detail the imagery with which his ideology is expressed. First we shall examine aspects of his self-image, then the notion of purity, and finally the possible paradigms these offer for understanding linguistic purism.

The purist's self-image

Of all the images conjured up by purists themselves to provide a framework for their mentality and activities the most prominent are: (1) the miller, (2) the gardener, (3) the metallurgist, (4) the grinder, (5) the physician, (6) the genealogist and geneticist, and (7) the priest. We shall examine each of them in turn.

19

The miller

The Florentine *Accademia della Crusca* founded in 1572 was not only the first language academy to grace Europe but was also the most influential. It derived its name from the separation of the *crusca* 'bran, husk' from the wheat in the milling process. In those distant days long before the merits of 'roughage' or 'fibre' were recognised, it was considered desirable to use for baking only wheat 'purified' of all its non-nutritious elements. The quality of the flour produced would depend on the success obtained in removing these elements.

Language purism was seen, therefore, as a process of separating the useless, undesirable elements from the truly useful ones. Purification was simply a matter of refining. Significantly, while it is possible to distinguish wheat from bran without difficulty, this image offers no guidance to recognising which elements are useful to a language. Not only did this open the door to subjective judgement, but, more importantly, it was inevitable, in the context of Florentine society in particular and Italian humanism in general, that the image of refining should support an élitist and archaising viewpoint (Hall 1942: 27, 53–5).

The 'wheat and bran' image had one further important corollary for the development of puristic thinking. Obviously, just as the higher the proportion of pure grain to bran, the better the flour was considered to be, so too a 'purer' language was necessarily 'superior'. Thus began that long association between the notions of purity and superiority, which has plagued so many of the attitudes about language ever since.

The gardener

A somewhat different image is that used by the most prominent of the German language societies of the seventeenth century – the *Fruchtbringende Gesellschaft*. Like the Florentines, these purists saw language in nutritional terms, but for them the essential task was pruning the fruit-bearing tree to promote growth and fertility. Associated with this image too was the idea of removing choking weeds. While even weeding requires fundamental knowledge, it is pruning which calls for the higher skills of the seasoned gardener.

As with milling, the image is based on the process of selection. It also fails to offer criteria for this selection. How should we recognise the weeds in a language? How do we know what should be pruned and what growth should be promoted? It does not necessarily follow, for example, that foreign words should have been the target of pruning, nor that these German purists should have attacked in the process words which a more intimate acquaintance with etymology would have revealed as not foreign at all.

Nevertheless, this image of language as a garden in need of careful cultivation is one of the more popular themes in the apologetics of purism. Moreover, as we saw in Chapter 1, it has been incorporated into linguistic theory as a fundamental aspect both of the Prague School theory of standard languages and of modern language planning.

The metallurgist

A frequent image used in puristic writing is the recovery of metals from their ore and their subsequent refining. This simile suggests that language in its raw, natural state must be freed from impurities before it can be used. As with the images of the miller and the gardener, the purist as metallurgist is faced with the task of revealing the true nature of language by removing extraneous elements. But once again the image provides no guidance as to how the impurities are to be identified or removed.

It is also instructive that the purists chose not to draw attention to the fact that certain metals like gold and silver are usable only in combination with copper, nor that the production and the examination of the physical properties of alloys is an essential aspect of metallurgy. But of course this would have robbed the image of its illocutionary force.

The grinder

The use of another image associated with metals is limited to the history of Czech purism. In 1674 the Czech grammarian Jiří Konstanc published a bilingual work *Lima linguae bohemicae* or *Brus jazyka českého* about the plight of the Czech language. Concerned about the contemporary deficiencies of his native language, Konstanc sought to sharpen it on a *brus* or whetstone. This image was revived in the 1870s and 1880s by Czech purists, and its derivatives *brusič* 'grinder' and *brusičství* 'grinding' became synonymous with purism, particularly of the overly zealous variety. Today, as a result of severe criticisms of excessive purism by the Prague School, this group of words carries a decidedly negative connotation.

Despite its national limitations and its negative associations, the image of the whetstone has several points in its favour. Firstly, it suggests a critical attitude towards language usage, a sharpening of

21

its communicative tools. At the same time, it makes no explicit reference to the removal of undesirable elements but rather to an improvement of what is already there.

The physician

Purists are keen to see themselves as physicians administering to the afflictions of the body of language. Some anti-purists would see them as quacks, but, as we shall see soon, perhaps they come closer to fulfilling the functions of a shaman. The procedures to which purists allude are those time-honoured methods of the physician's craft: surgery and administering physic. The cutting of diseased portions of the anatomy in order to prevent further infection and thus promote the well-being of the healthy parts is readily transferable to the intentions of language purism. So too is the administering of a purgative to provoke the evacuation of impurities.

Like the tree-pruning image, the surgical remedy suggests that we are able to distinguish that which should be retained from that which should be removed. Moreover, the body must go on functioning despite its losses. How successfully it continues to do so may depend on how radical the surgery was. In linguistic terms, the expressive capabilities of a language may be severely hampered by the removal of elements thought detrimental to its well-being. We may well ask, in any case, whether all language surgery is not simply cosmetic.

The fact that the evacuation of the bowels following the administering of an aperient removes substances which were foreign to the body in the first place makes purging an altogether more satisfactory image for understanding purism. Moreover, the feeling of well-being which results from such catharsis comes close to one of the self-avowed aims of the linguistic purist: the restoration of vigour and vitality to the language in question.

The genealogist and geneticist

We have already identified the preoccupation with genetic relationships as one of the chief characteristics of the purist. To pronounce on the bloodlines, the pedigree and the legitimacy of an element in a language is one of his main concerns. It is not surprising, therefore, that the image of genetic or genealogical purity should be invoked so constantly in puristic writings. Indeed, it is precisely this obsession with etymological justification which leads to the identification of foreign elements and substandard usage as the primary targets of puristic activity. In other words, purism is essentially a campaign waged against the perceived 'bastardisation' or 'hybridisation' of a language.

The genealogist can only investigate and pronounce upon the bloodlines of linguistic elements. But it is somehow implicit in these investigations and pronouncements that there is some inherent virtue in being a thoroughbred rather than a mongrel, legitimate rather than a bastard. The applications of genetics in selective breeding and, more recently, in biogenetic engineering, however, offer a further implementational dimension to the image of the genealogist and geneticist for linguistic purism.

The priest

The first organisation to concern itself with the purity of modern Hebrew was the Pure Language Society (*Śafah Berurah*), a name based on a passage in Zephaniah 3:9 about the removal of the curse of Babel (Saulson 1977: 22). This apparent reference to purists as instruments of God's will may be isolated, but the attribution to the purist of sacerdotal functions of ritual cleansing is widespread. This flattering self-image confers on the purist not only an inspired source for his pronouncements but stresses their quasi-sacramental character. Furthermore, at times there is a suggestion in puristic writings that the aim is merely to rectify the manifold corruptions which have defiled the language as created by God. Perhaps more than anything else, the adoption of this priestly image goes some way to explaining the somewhat sanctimonious tone taken by many purists through the ages.

Few will deny the close association of godliness and cleanliness, or holiness and purity. Indeed, priestly functions often include acts of linguistic purification. Consider, for example, the iconicity of language in all forms of religious ritual. Perhaps then, of all the self-images the sacerdotal comes closest to capturing the true essence of the purist's role.

The composite image of the purist

Each of these images reveals an important aspect of the purist's character: the self-styled physical or spiritual healer, the critical pedant, the essayer and guardian of a language's treasures. In what way do these different aspects of his character cohere?

A shared feature of all these images is the implicit recognition that the purist knows what is best for a language. Whether this knowledge comes to him from the long practice of a craft comparable to pruning trees, cutting off limbs, grinding knives, essaying metals, breeding animals or from divine inspiration matters little. The purist, then, applies this knowledge to make judgements about the elements which rightfully belong to a language and those which do not. These judgements then form the basis for some radical action of separating the desirable from the undesirable elements.

Admittedly, some of the images allow for gradations of purity (for example the flour, the metal ingot, the pruned fruit tree, the radicality of the surgery), but in all but the knife-grinding image the purist's view of language, on which his judgements, pronouncements and actions are to be based, is dualistic: some elements belong, others do not.

It is perhaps surprising in view of the fact that purism is so often associated with the opposition to foreign words, that most of the images say nothing about the nature of the elements to be removed. The major exception, of course, is the genealogical image which strongly suggests that the basis for pronouncing elements undesirable is their etymological (or genetic) origin.

The images also tell us something of the purist's motivation. It is clear that he intends, by his actions, to improve the quality, the physical or spiritual health, the value, the usefulness and the productivity of the language in question, even if that means reducing the inventory of expressive means available to it. In other words, a purer language must necessarily be a superior language.

To sum up: a purist is, on his own admission, one who maintains a dualistic view of language as containing desirable and undesirable elements, who feels able to recognise these elements in a given language and who, prompted by a desire to promote the well-being and prestige of the language in question, seeks to remove those elements he deems undesirable. In this context, the tasks of this book are two-fold: to provide an accurate assessment of the veracity of this self-image and, more profoundly, to examine whether a dualistic view of language and the actions stemming from it are indeed justified. Before dealing with these issues, however, we should say something of this purity which is the purist's avowed concern.

The notion of purity

The central image of linguistic purism is of course the notion of purity. Yet it is a remarkable fact that no study of linguistic purism as far as I am aware, makes the slightest reference to purity as a general notion.

All languages are teeming with words and phrases alluding to the purity or impurity of a referent. In English, for example, while the groundstrokes of Françoise Durr may be described as 'not for the purist', those of Rod Laver may be referred to as 'out of the textbook'; the wicket-keeping style of John Murray of Middlesex and England has been described as 'immaculate', that of his contemporary Wally Grout of Queensland and Australia has not; mathematics may be 'pure' or 'applied'; Harry Truman's reputation may be 'unblemished' or 'undefiled', but Richard Nixon's certainly is not; our lakes and rivers may be 'polluted', or not; a beer may be 'adulterated', or not; a look may be 'virginal' or not; morals may be 'corrupt', or not; beauty may be 'pristine'; Coca-Cola may be 'the real thing' or now even 'classic'; a car may have 'pure' or 'classic' lines; Maggie Smith's performance may have been 'pure gold', the audience reaction to it 'pure, unadulterated joy'.

Despite their specific meanings and collocations, all these words and phrases are clustered around the notion of purity. Yet these examples show purity to be characteristic of a wide range of persons, objects, activities and abstractions. At the same time, it is noticeable that the various synonyms for purity betray their origin as metaphors. Interestingly, these metaphors are taken from some of the very fields of human activity, which the purists refer to in their self-imaging: metallurgy, genetics and religion. However, one important source of metaphors is not covered in the purists' self-assessment: the field of aesthetics. We shall now briefly examine in turn the fields from which these metaphors are taken to see whether they can be reduced to a unitary notion of purity.

Genetic and genealogical purity

The breeding of animals and the selection of cereal grains is what distinguishes the farmer from the hunter-gatherer. The recognition of the importance of maintaining the purity of bloodlines and the possibilities of cross-fertilisation have been among mankind's longest-lived concerns. Their importance is evident in the prominence and widespread distribution of words like *mongrel, pure-breed, cross-breed, hybrid*, and the need to produce 'pedigrees'.

These concerns have spread to include a preoccupation with man's own genetic make-up – his genealogy and his racial affiliation – as well as the legitimation of his lineage. Concerns about racial purity have produced concepts like *coloured*, *pure-breed*, *half-breed*, *methi*, *quadroon* and *octoroon*. Several of these words even attempt, however imprecisely, to fractionalise the racial purity of the individual. Even though the preoccupation with racial purity is now widely stigmatised, and attempts at defining racial characteristics largely abandoned, the link between racialism and linguistic purism has sometimes been painfully close.

With regard to legitimacy of lineage the central concept is, of course, *bastardy*, which does not mean 'being born out of wedlock' but 'not legal progeny'. Thus, when Jane Seymour became Henry VIII's third wife, all three of Henry's known off-springs were technically bastards: Mary by Act of Parliament; Elizabeth because her parents' marriage had been declared to have been null and void following Anne Boleyn's execution; and Henry Fitzroy because he was born out of wedlock. It was within Henry's powers, however, to declare any or all of them legitimate heirs, and hence no longer bastards. In other words, bastardy is an arbitrary category, definable only at law.

An important secondary concept in questions of genealogy is the inviolate chastity, or virginity, of the bride. At first sight, virginity would seem to be a clearcut matter, but even here there are age-old problems of definition. What is the nature of the proof? Can horse-riding, for example, deprive a woman of her virginity? These are murky waters indeed, but it is worth remembering that sexual purity is still often equated with virginity.

Many of the referents employed in this section are encountered frequently in the puristic literature. Indeed it is hard to imagine a puristic tract without words like *pedigree*, *hybrid*, *bastardised* and *adulterated*. They are among the most potent and emotive images available to the purist. Nevertheless, their use is based on arbitrary systems of classification. Genetic purity has nothing to do with the modern science of genetics and the operation of the DNA molecule but with some rather older and murkier concerns of mankind.

This notion of purity deals in absolute, non-quantifiable values: you cannot be half a virgin, or half a bastard. Even the fractionalisations which do exist are misleading: our dog is not really half Lhasa Abso and half Cairn Terrier (even though I might loosely describe him as such); rather, he is simply the product of a union between parents of a lineage guaranteed by a pedigree. Furthermore, genetic purity cannot be restored when once it is lost. Even though one can make a vow of chastity at any time of one's life, one cannot return to the virginal state.

Metallurgical purity

It may be thought that metallurgy is a strange bed-fellow for religion, aesthetics and genetics, but the notion of metallurgical purity sheds considerable light on the imagery of purism. Metals, if they are to be used, must be recovered from the ore, in which they naturally occur. This recovery and the subsequent refining of the metal by physical and chemical means may render it 'pure', i.e. free from an admixture of any other elements. Metals may also be mixed with each other in varying quantities to form alloys, which combine the physical properties of their constituents. Gold and silver, for example, are never used in their pure state but are always alloyed with copper, sterling silver being 92.5 percent pure silver, 18 carat gold being 75 percent pure.

As metallurgy has progressed from art to science it has learned to establish the purity of a metal by experimentation. Furthermore, it can now provide exact measurement of the degree of purity, whereas formerly the constituents of a coin could be established only by weight, colour or acoustic properties. Where once purity was 'essayed', it is now measured. Even so the practice of 'hall-marking' provided a standard of purity before the era of accurate measurement. Indeed, we no longer consider the baser metals in these alloys as 'impurities' but as essential components, without which the gold and silver sample would be unusable.

Purity in the metallurgical sense differs, then, from the genetic notion of purity in that it is not an abstract, arbitrarily determined commodity but a concrete, experimentally determinable fact. Furthermore, the purity of certain samples, as for instance the 'lead' in your pencil or the 'gold' in your fountain-pen, is relative and can be calibrated on a generally agreed scale of measurement.

The notion of purity in metallurgy is still polarised as in genetics but the relativity of the former means that we are no longer dealing with a dualistic view. Some metal samples are purer than others, but they are not necessarily better for being so: the 12,000 or more available alloys far outweigh in importance the 70 or so pure metals.

Aesthetic purity

The artistic productions of mankind as well as his perception of the world around him seem to be governed by two clusters of polarised aesthetic values. At one pole are ranged: subjectivity, dramaticality, expressivity, emotionality, dynamicity, naturalness, unpredictability; at the other, proportion, symmetry, simplicity, stability, abstraction, predictability, objectivity. These two clusters coincide with two of the basic polarities of human nature – the emotional and the cerebral and are subsumed under the headings 'romantic' and 'classical' respectively. As an aesthetic value purity belongs with the latter, as a brief examination of the artistic credo of the Dutch De Stijl School (Jaffe 1967: 20–4) will reveal.

Like their fellow-countryman Spinoza, the De Stijl artists sought a transcendence of nature and personal arbitrariness in the application of geometrical principles. Theirs was a striving towards the elemental, the absolute. They stressed harmony and plasticity, restricted their palate to primary colours, and reduced objects to rectilinear, rectangular, two-dimensional shapes. This restriction of expressive means was aimed at a 'purification of the arts', their liberation from the bonds of nature. To its detractors, the art of the De Stijl School has a certain sterility (the negative correlative of purity), but for Jaffe the beauty of their works 'arises from their immaculate purity' (Jaffe 1967: 20). It is not perhaps coincidental, as Jaffe himself points out, that the word *schoon* in Dutch has two meanings: 'beautiful' and 'pure'. He also draws our attention to some important parallels between the aesthetics of De Stijl and Dutch puritanism, including 'their rectilinear and rectangular principles and the rigidity of religious orthodoxy'.

One aspect of classicism is, however, absent from the De Stijl philosophy: the importance of following acceptable iconographical models. The faithfulness with which the example set by these models is followed is closely related to a notion of purity. The importance attributed to paradigms in classical art leads to an abhorrence of deviations from them and a correspondingly high evaluation of those works which manage to follow them correctly. This reverence for old models is also closely associated with a need to return to primal values untainted by modern corruptions. A measure of the connection between the reverence for the primal state and purity is provided by the evidence of the word *pristine* in English. In the OED it is given in the meaning 'former, original, primitive', while the Supplement adds a new meaning of American origin: 'unmarred, unspoilt, untouched, virginal, pure, spotless, good as new, brand-new'.

Purity, then, occupies a crucial position within the cluster of values associated with the classical aesthetic. It has close links with the search for the absolute, the abstract, the universal and elemental, the predeliction for simplicity and geometricality of form, the reduction of expressive means, and a reverence for the values and models of the past. In this context, a purist is one who prefers clean, uncluttered lines and has a high regard for traditional values ('When it comes to

Bach, I must admit I'm a bit of a purist – viola da gambas, clavichords, valveless trumpets and all the repeats played'). Purification means an attempt to remove modern encrustations, to turn back the clock, to resuscitate old values, to revive old techniques and to create works of art according to established models. Purism, then, is the attitude, which responds to the stimulus of modern adornments by looking back with longing to these primal traditions and paradigms.

In aesthetics just as in metallurgy, purity does not imply a dualistic viewpoint. Furthermore, it is not defined by reference to impurity but stands as an autonomous value. This can be demonstrated by the fact that the antonym for 'pure' in aesthetics is often not 'impure' but a word which invests an extra meaning like 'corrupt' or 'complicated'.

Aesthetic purity cannot be absolute: it can only be relative. We can say, for example, that Kiri Te Kanawa's tone in the rendition of a Mozart religious aria is pure, but we might rate Elly Ameling's sound purer, and Emma Kirkby's purer still. Similarly, few would argue that Ken Collyer's conception of dixieland is somehow purer than Chris Barber's.

Nor is the degree of aesthetic purity amenable to direct measurement. This is not to say that we cannot measure some of the indicators of purity, like, for example, the presence of overtones or tonal modulations in the vibration of the human voice. But it should be borne in mind that even the choice of these measurable criteria is predicated on the value system of the appraisal process. It is therefore an inescapable fact that, however objective their intent, all statements about aesthetic purity are effectively appraisive judgements.

Religious purity

Where it is only one notion among many in aesthetics, genetics and metallurgy, in religion purity assumes central importance. In all religions, it would seem, certain actions together with the objects and actors associated with them may under certain conditions be pronounced unclean and subject to some form of taboo: defecation, micturition, copulation, menstruation, child-birth, spitting, incest, diet, personal hygiene. Indeed, the regulation of these actions may well be one of the prime causes for the rise of religion.

At first glance, the reasons for pronouncing some acts, places, objects and persons unclean and others not appears quite arbitrary. Consider, for example, the elaborate dietary restrictions called for by Hinduism and Judaism, or the churching of women after child-birth in the Anglican Church. These taboos, as Mary Douglas (1966) and other structural anthropologists have conclusively shown, are not as arbitrary as they might appear but are explicable within the framework of man's basic needs to make sense of the world around him and to ward off the dangers which threaten his well-being. Their effect is to maintain a strict dualism by sharply dividing the clean from the unclean.

In many cases, religions will be content to condemn that which they consider unclean. If, however, such impurities are seen to be a hindrance to religious practice by threatening to defile the sanctity of some person, object, place or act, they must be annulled through a ritual act of cleansing, often involving some form of purging, sacrifice or penance. These ritual acts of purification have a cathartic value: that which was unclean is made clean; and the threat to the sanctity of the object, person, place or act is removed. Purification, then, is a ritualistic response to undo the effects of unclean elements, which threaten the margins of the religious system.

An interesting feature of religious purity is its competitive nature: purists try to outdo each other in the strictness of their observance. Moreover, this competition follows an infinite regression: however extreme a purist may be, there is always someone lurking in the bushes ready to condemn him for his compromises. This infinitely regressive nature of purism is also explicable within Douglas' conceptual framework:

> The final paradox of the search for purity is that it is an attempt to force experience into logical categories of non-contradiction. But experience is not amenable and those who make the attempt find themselves led into contradiction. (Douglas 1966: 162)

Towards a unitary notion of purity

The various notions of purity may be organised according to five dichotomies: dualistic/non-dualistic, absolute/relative, central/peripheral, quantifiable/non-quantifiable, arbitrary/non-arbitrary. These dichotomies do not, at first glance, offer much promise of finding a unitary notion of purity.

Much of the problem stems from the nature of the subject-matter involved in each notion of purity. Some referents can only be characterised as absolutely pure, some only as relatively pure, and others as both. Consider, for example, the purity of a vestal virgin, the purity of a voice, and the purity of a metal ingot.

Equally dependent on the subject matter is the meaning of purity:

to attribute purity to a voice cannot be equated with attributing purity to a breed of dog, a vestal virgin, or a gold ingot. As Aschenbrenner (1971: 119–20) points out appraisives are rarely reducible to straightforward dictionary definitions. This is certainly confirmed by the OED which, apart from defining purity as the condition of being pure, merely provides an incomplete catalogue of such conditions.

Perhaps we can agree that purity is an appraisive of positive valence which refers to such characteristics as 'wholeness', 'unitariness', 'homogeneity', 'originalness', 'inviolateness', 'true or original essence', 'simplicity' and 'correctness'. Does this imply, however, that these characteristics form a composite identity, or are they just possible components of purity? As we have seen, it is the identity of the referent and its semantic properties that determine which of the components of the core meaning will apply.

Some paradigms for linguistic purism

From the earlier sections of this chapter we can extract the following statements:

1. A 'purist' is one who maintains a dualistic view of a referent as containing desirable and undesirable elements, who feels able to recognise these elements in a given referent and who, prompted by a desire to promote its well-being and prestige, seeks to remove those elements he deems undesirable.
2. 'Purity', the condition of being 'pure', is an appraisive term of positive valence, which refers to a set of core meanings, including 'homogeneity', 'wholeness', and 'oneness'. The meaning of 'purity' as well as its relativity or absoluteness is partially determined by the semantic characteristics of the referent.
3. 'Purism' is the totality of the attitude of concern about the 'purity' of some referent together with the behaviour which stems from it.

These statements reveal that it is possible to define 'purism', 'purity' and 'purist' by reference to 'pure', but that there is no unitary notion of 'purity'. Furthermore, we have established that the notion of 'purity' is dependent on its referent. What kind of referent is 'language'? Can a language be absolutely or only relatively pure? Can the elements in it be absolutely or relatively pure? Before answering these questions, let us consider what components of the core meaning the 'purity' of a language refers to.

Firstly, a language may or may not be 'whole' in the sense that it is not divided into parts of itself. It may or may not be 'unitary' in the sense that it is recognisable as a single unit. It may or may not be 'homogeneous' in the sense that its elements are freely mixed. As we shall see in Chapter 3, these three characteristics are concerned with the solidarity or unifying function of language. Since the absence of these characteristics may severely handicap a language in carrying out its social functions, any concern about them on the part of any individual would be legitimate.

Secondly, a language may be 'original' in the sense that it has been preserved in an unchanged state, though there are no empirical data to support such a suggestion. Indeed, except in the case of artificial languages, there is no way of knowing the origin of a language. Nevertheless, the maintenance of a close relationship with earlier stages of a language is founded in the stability criterion of standard languages, and as such may be a legitimate concern.

Thirdly, a language may be 'inviolate', 'unitary' or 'homogeneous' in the sense that it has not incorporated elements not of itself, but again we have no evidence that any known language has ever failed to incorporate some element from outside its own repertoire. Nevertheless, concerns about the violated state of a language have been frequently voiced by speakers in a wide range of languages.

Finally, although reference is often made to the notion of 'simplicity' and 'correctness', these are not characteristics that professional linguists are comfortable about using as characterisations of a language. To have any relevance, both notions would need to be arbitrarily defined for each known language. Nevertheless, a concern about correctness is a widespread component of the attitudes to codified languages.

We see that all of the core components of the meaning of 'purity' have been applied to languages. It is therefore justifiable to use 'linguistic purism' as a blanket term to cover any of these concerns about language, irrespective of their legitimacy or their rationality. It is in this sense that we shall use the term henceforth.

When applied to the pedigree of a dog or the chemical composition of a metal ingot, 'purity' is a descriptive term, but for a referent like 'language' it can only be appraisive: a language can be characterised as pure but not described as such. Furthermore, this characterisation has relative not absolute value. German might be characterised as 'pure' – and certainly as 'purer' than English – but might not be as 'pure' as Icelandic. The problem comes at the opposite end of the scale: can a language like English be legitimately characterised as 'impure', any more than the voice of Julie Andrews can?

An appraisal of the 'purity' of a language is based on an assessment of the 'purity' of the individual elements of its repertoire. When referring to these elements of language, the term 'purity' is therefore descriptive not appraisive. Of course, inasmuch as the description may be based on false criteria, on faulty language knowledge, or on incorrect linguistic assumptions, it may be invalid. Nevertheless, it remains a description not a characterisation. The character of the referent determines that only a binary description is possible. An individual element can be described as 'pure' or 'impure' but not 'fairly pure' or 'very pure' or 'not pure enough'.

Since the purity of a language can only be appraised, it is not subject to direct empirical verification. This exposes statements about the purity of a language to the danger that the evaluation may be shaped, coloured, distorted or exaggerated by the prejudicial attitudes of the assessor, be he puristically or antipuristically inclined. Furthermore, measurement of the purity of a language can only be indirect: the proportion of 'impure' elements to 'pure' elements could serve as indicators of a language's purity. If, for example, we were to compile a 'purity index' of a particular text or dictionary from the percentage of the 'impure' words it contained we would not be in a position to state that the language in question was such and such percent pure. Strictly speaking, we would simply be in possession of an indirect measure with which to flesh out our evaluation of the language's purity.

According to Mary Douglas (1966: 35), the distinction between clean and dirty rises out of a basic human need to make sense of the chaos around us: 'Dirt is the by-product of a systematic ordering and classification of matter, in so far as ordering involves rejecting inappropriate elements.' In other words: 'When something is firmly classed as anomalous, the outline of the set in which it is not a member is clarified' (Douglas 1966: 38). She concludes: '. . . our pollution behaviour is the reaction which condemns any object or idea likely to confuse or contradict cherished classifications' (Douglas 1966: 36). Whether or not this theory offers a satisfactory explanation of taboo and pollution and their relationship to religion and magic, there is no question that it provides a promising paradigm for understanding linguistic purism: that which is classified as part of the system is 'pure'; that which is anomalous, inappropriate and therefore to be rejected is classified as 'impure'.

This theory would not necessarily be invalidated even if purists were not to see their actions in this way, since this is an area where post-rationalisations are commonplace (Douglas 1966: 31–2). But in fact, the dualistic, systematising viewpoint is inherent in the very images used by purists themselves: the wheat and the chaff, the fruit and the pruned branches, the bastard and the legitimate heir, the diseased and healthy parts of the body.

One commonsense objection to Mary Douglas' contention that dirt is relative is that there may be a limited number of objects or actions which all human beings find intrinsically dirty, irrespective of any classification of matter (e.g. faeces, rotting food, and the action of eating either of the above). Are there linguistic elements which provoke a similar, universal abhorrence? Does this perhaps explain why foreign elements are the primary targets of purism? Are we repelled by their transgression of the our/their boundary? This subject will be taken up in greater detail in the next chapter.

The anomalies in classificatory systems may be treated by humans in a number of ways: (1) they can go unnoticed, (2) they can be ignored, (3) they can be condemned, or (4) they can be confronted and be made part of a new pattern of reality. The first two treatments may be called apuristic and correspond to the viewpoints of the neo-grammarians and the descriptivists respectively; the third is puristic; and the fourth anti-puristic.

Mary Douglas's work sheds some light on the personality of the purist: he abides strictly by a set of rules and regulations, abhors grey areas, and condemns the actions of those who transgress the rules. His essentially dualistic viewpoint draws very clear distinctions between categories. As Douglas (1966: 162) points out: 'Purity is the enemy of change, of ambiguity and compromise.' The purist may be characterised, then, as strictly orthodox in his beliefs, unyielding to change, intolerant of the transgression of others, and fiercely repressive of any desires within himself to cross the same bounds. Freudians, of course, would immediately recognise these as typical traits of the anal-retentive personality. Indeed, whether or not one accepts the tenets of Freudianism, one cannot ignore the fact that purism combines within itself all three elements of the anal-retentive triad: obsessive obstinacy, orderliness and parsimony. We shall return to the personality of the purist in Chapter 6. Our immediate task, meanwhile, is to investigate the motivations for purism in more detail.

CHAPTER 3

The theoretical foundations of purism

Introduction

We have determined that purism is predicated on the following perceptions about a language:

1. That it can be divided into acceptable and unacceptable elements.
2. That these elements can be labelled 'pure' or 'impure' respectively.
3. That a language characterised as 'pure' is one which is relatively free of 'impure' elements.
4. That this concern about the 'purity' of a language can and indeed should be translated into some form of intervention which renders the language in question purer.

Of course, none of these perceptions can be substantiated by the principles of descriptive linguistics. Rather, their theoretical foundation must be sought in an approach which views linguistic events from the point of view of the speech community. As we saw in Chapter 1, such an approach must seek to reconcile a socio-linguistic concern with language situations and the interest of the social psychologist in attitudes to variation in language usage. Furthermore, the close association between purism and standard languages demands that the theoretical framework also incorporates theories about the functioning of standard languages. In my view, the work of František Daneš (1968, 1982, 1987) provides just such an overarching thesis about the operation of language values in a speech community.

Theoretical framework

According to Daneš (1982: 93–5), all linguistic behaviour is motivated in some way by one or more of the following attitudes: (1)

instrumental (or pragmatic), (2) ethical, (3) affective, (4) traditional. Instrumentally determined behaviour (which chooses the means for achieving some goal from the point of view of effectivity and expediency) and ethically determined behaviour (which is motivated by a recognition of norms which allow integration of the whole speech community) are rationally based, whereas the affective attitudes (which are controlled by emotional factors) and the traditional attitudes (based on a reverence for custom) have a non-rational basis.

In Daneš's view, this distinction between rational and non-rational orientations is of great importance despite the admitted difficulty in certain cases of separating ethical and affective considerations. The rational orientation emphasises the instrumental character of language and evaluates linguistic means according to the criterion of functional adequacy, effectivity, economy and the binding force of collective norms. The non-rational orientation, on the other hand, is expressed in an attitude which is motivated by national and aesthetic factors. The coexistence of these two orientations produces a tension, which must be resolved by a motivational model, valid only for a particular speech community at a particular time. There is no ideal model which would be valid for all languages at all times.

The resolution of this tension is based on the interplay of five antinomies introduced by Talcott Parsons (1951: 67) to explain the value-orientations which motivate social behaviour

1. The gratification-discipline dilemma leading to affectivity versus affective neutrality.
2. The private-collective interest dilemma, that is, self-orientation versus collectivity-orientation.
3. The choice between types of value-orientation standard, that is, particularism versus universalism.
4. The choice between modalities of the social object; that is ascription versus achievement.
5. The definition of scope of interest in the object, that is specificity versus diffuseness.

A speech community may embrace all the first items in the antinomical pairs (Set A), all the second items (Set B) or any combination of them. The employment of criteria from a single set represents a polarised orientation, while a mixture of items from both sets is characteristic of a balanced viewpoint. The orientation may also be modulated by a differential weighting given to one or other of these evaluative criteria. Furthermore, attitudes may be located at various points on a scale between each antinomical polarity.

Various questions now arise: How does purism fit into the theoretical framework proposed here? Which of the four attitudes to language does it embrace? Does it have a rational or non-rational basis? If rationally based, what instrumental features does it encompass? If non-rationally based, by what factors is it motivated? Finally, how does purism relate to the sets of value-orientations?

Rational and non-rational bases

The four attitudes to language intervention outlined in Daneš's schema can be organised into two sets of binary oppositions:

1. The instrumental versus the affective.
2. The ethical versus the traditional.

In both sets a pragmatic, rational approach is counterposed by a non-rational, idealistic one. Furthermore, we may note that the first element in these binary oppositions is unmarked, while the second is marked. The effect of the non-rational set of attitudes is to emphasise specificity, limitation, and rigidity, while the rational attitudes are associated with universality, freedom, and tolerance.

We have seen already that puristic attitudes are prompted by a dualistic perception of the natural world, by an abhorrence of grey areas, and by a desire to force reality into classificatory systems. It should not be surprising, therefore, to find that linguistic purism is governed primarily by the non-rational member of these binary oppositions. Indeed, the two main thrusts of purism – an opposition to foreign influences on the native language and a striving to retain the language in an unchanged traditional form – may be subsumed under the affective and the traditional attitudes respectively. For example, from the instrumental point of view, it matters not at all whether Croatians use *historija* or *povijest* for 'history', but some Croatian purists might want to opt for the latter on the ground that it is composed of native morphemes. Similarly, while there may be equal merit from an ethical point of view in insisting on the spelling *nite* or *night*, a traditionalist might argue for the latter on the grounds that it is the customary form. The effect of non-rationally based purism, then, is intolerance and a closure to certain linguistic elements, and hence a limitation of choice in language variation.

This should not be taken to mean that purists have totally ignored the rational attitudes to language intervention. Most purists, for example, retain a vision of their native language as a tool of communication uniting in its observation of an agreed system of linguistic norms all their compatriots. Indeed, it is the willingness to compromise the non-rational attitudes for the rational ones which characterises a moderating tendency in linguistic purism. For example, the leading Turkish purist Gökalp was not opposed to modernisation and Europeanisation of his language in the scientific sphere provided that the core of the vocabulary, the syntax and the orthography remained untouched (Fishman 1973: 75).

Moreover, it can be argued that purism is not only moderated by rational attitudes but to some extent is actually controlled by them. For example, the exclusion of certain unwanted elements may be perceived as helping to differentiate the language from some other, to consolidate it as a communicative tool and to heighten its prestige in the estimation of the speech community. These rationales for purism correspond to the separating, solidarity and prestige functions of standard languages.

It follows from the above that establishing the foundations of purism requires an examination of both the non-rational motivations and the rational factors involved. Only when we have looked at each of them separately can we return to an examination of their interaction.

Before we leave the rational/non-rational antinomy, however, a cautionary note must be sounded. According to Daneš (1982: 99) the antinomy is associated with two contradictions, which, as it turns out, have some importance for purism:

1. The contradiction between actual language behaviour of the members of a language community and their expressed views about the language in question.
2. The contradiction between the proclaimed and publicly recognised motives for their language behaviour and the actual reasons and motives.

Purists may be either conscious or unconscious of these contradictions. If conscious, they are guilty, at best, of rationalisation and, at worst, of hypocrisy; if unconscious, they are subject to serious self-deception. As we explore the various explanations and motivations given by purists for their conduct, these contradictions must be kept firmly in mind.

Non-rational motivations

Aesthetic considerations

'Purity', as we have seen, is an aesthetic notion closely associated with such values as 'wholeness', 'oneness', 'homogeneity', 'pristineness', 'correctness'. It is used as an appraisive to provide positive characterisations of a referent. Linguistic purism, then, is a language attitude prompted by some perception of a shortcoming with respect to one or more of the values associated with 'purity'. It is motivated by the implicit assumption that purification confers superiority.

There is one aesthetic principle which dwarfs all others – nationalism. The nationalist aesthetic is primarily concerned with defining what are the characteristic features of the national culture. This is accomplished by stressing those elements which distinguish the national culture from other cultures and minimising or ignoring their common features. In other words, the nationalist aesthetic involves a binary classification into 'national' and 'non-national'. It is based not so much on the proposition that the native language is better than any other but that it is unique and irreplaceable, a notion first formulated by von Humboldt (Ray 1961: 225). According to this aesthetic, that which is 'national' is identified as 'pure', that which is 'non-national' is 'impure'.

Apart from the essentially dualistic perception and attitude to the facts of language alluded to above and the overwhelming importance of the nationalist orientation, there is little which supports the notion that purism is governed by a single set of aesthetic principles. Indeed all the evidence points to the opposite conclusion, namely that each type of purism has its own aesthetic basis and must be treated as *sui generis*. We shall return to this problem in Chapter 8.

Social factors

The two dominant sociocultural determinants of attitudes to variation are standardisation and vitality (Ryan *et al.* 1982: 3–4). Both factors are evident in various aspects of purism: standardisation in the desire to conserve what is best of the past and vitality in the need to remove unwanted elements and revitalise the expressive capabilities of the language. The degree to which these two determinants co-occur in a particular language situation affects the form purism takes. The effects of these two determinants will be examined in greater detail in the next chapter.

There are two main evaluative dimensions of language attitudes: social status and group solidarity (Ryan *et al.* 1982: 8–9). Social status is reflected, for example, in the snobbery of some puristic attitudes and the inverted snobbery of others. This provides us with one of the basic distinctions in purist ideologies: élitism and populism (for more details, see Chapter 4). We shall also presently see that group solidarity in the form of national identity and pride is a crucial motivation of puristic attitudes.

Purism is very much concerned with limiting and determining lexical choices by praising some words and dispraising others. Among the dimensions affecting lexical choice suggested by Bradac (1982: 101–3) are two which are relevant to purism: familiarity and goodness.

In language, familiarity far from breeding contempt induces a positive attitude leading at times to a word's acceptance even before its meaning has been learned. The relevance of this for purism is twofold. Firstly, it is not uncommon for a word introduced by an innovating purist to be subjected to ridicule on its first appearance only to become so familiar later that it comes to be accepted by an entire language community (Becker 1948a: 91). Secondly, the familiarity of a word may preserve it from that puristic censure, to which because of its etymology it might otherwise have been subject. Indeed, as we shall see, the insistence by purists on removing words already familiar to the speech community and replacing them by words totally unfamiliar can provide a gauge of puristic intensity and serve as one of the components to be used in devising a profile of a particular purist movement. Finally, the familiar/unfamiliar distinction may, according to Bradac, 'increase cohesion or solidarity by increasing members' perceptions of their group distinctiveness'.

The concept of 'goodness' and 'badness' is tied to the existence of linguistic taboos, individual preferences about words, and the evaluation of the appropriateness of a word in a particular context. Clearly, purism is intimately concerned in pronouncing taboos on certain words and in stating individual preferences and seeking to manipulate the linguistic choices of others. Just as important for purism, however, is the recognition of the stylistic or contextual appropriateness of a given lexical item. A word may be subject to puristic disapproval only in particular stylistic registers and certain social contexts.

The repertoire of languages has rarely been subjected to public opinion survey. An exception is a study of attitudes to loanwords in the Czech population conducted by Tejnor and associates (1971). A group of 635 respondents, proportionally representative in terms of age, sex and social status of the overall Czech population, was first asked its opinion about the use of foreign words in the media; 43 percent said they noticed them often, 51 percent sometimes, 6 percent never. The survey reveals that awareness of foreign words increases with the age of informants but that there is little differentiation by sex (p. 64). The majority (56 percent) of the respondents demonstrated some resentment towards users of foreign words. Typical answers were: 'tries to show off', 'thinks a lot of himself', 'doesn't want to lower himself to the common people', 'is an uneducated person' (p.11).

Scores vary for the use of foreign words in different spheres of activity (p. 65). The lowest negative reaction was in the technological and health sphere; sport and music were in the middle range; the most negative reaction was in the field of politics and economics (pp. 17–18). However, the response to the question on the choice of terms to be used in school textbooks showed a 13 percent preference for international words, 55 percent for domestic words, while 29 percent preferred domestic and international words to be used interchangeably.

Perhaps the key question for our purposes was 'Does the loaning of words enrich or spoil the language?' It elicited the following response: 8 percent said it 'enriches', 29 percent 'mostly enriches', 35 percent 'mostly spoils', 11 percent 'spoils' (p. 12). The concentration of scores in the middle range suggests a generally tolerant attitude especially among young people and those with good education.

The attitude to loanwords from specific languages (pp. 67-9) showed considerable variation: for Graeco-Latin words 60 percent were positive, 22 percent negative, 18 percent didn't know (100 percent of those with university education approved of Graeco-Latinisms). For German, 21 percent approved, 65 percent disapproved, 14 percent didn't know (there was little variation by age, education, sex or occupation). For 'Western' languages – a coy form of words probably designed not to identify attitudes to English – approval was 30 percent, disapproval 48 percent, don't knows 22 percent (approval increased for those with university education). For 'Russian and other Slavic languages' – again coyly worded, possibly to forestall the expression of anti-Russian sentiments – 34 percent responded approvingly, 46 percent disapprovingly, 20 percent didn't know (approval of loanwords from this source drops with education).

A number of questions dealt with the intelligibility of foreign words and the role of such factors as language knowledge and

41

readiness to use dictionaries and similar reference materials. Respondents were also asked to give domestic equivalents for a series of internationalisms. The results varied widely from word to word, but for several of them the numbers of incorrect answers and don't knows were in the majority. The fact that the number of correct answers were higher among those who use foreign words frequently (p. 32) suggests that the answers reflect the intelligibility of the foreign word rather than knowledge of a suitable native equivalent.

This spontaneous dislike of foreign words does not necessarily translate into an avoidance of them. This is demonstrated by the fact that 48 percent of the respondents thought that the loaning of words is inevitable and that 89 percent didn't think it worthwhile looking for domestic equivalents. Furthermore, 43 percent believed that the use of foreign words was defensible on the grounds that it fostered international understanding. In mentalistic terms, then, the attitude can be understood as mediating between the stimulus (dislike of certain linguistic items motivated by aesthetic and psychological considerations) and the reaction (a resolve to use or not to use, to replace or not to replace, a given linguistic item).

When asked whether they themselves used foreign words, 4 percent responded 'often', 32 percent 'sometimes', 62 percent 'little', 2 percent 'don't know' (p. 21). Obviously, as so often in the condemnation of human behaviour, the use of foreign words is something only other people do! The low level of don't knows reflects an unwarranted degree of certainty in the respondents. It is also revealing that those informants with less education tended to report fewer foreign words. Conceivably, this could be attributable to actual language usage but more probably reflects unconcious under-reporting by less well educated respondents. More revealing of actual practice was the question whether informants gave preference to a domestic word over a foreign word: 51 percent replied that they did, 5 percent that they did not, but interestingly 38 percent said that it depended on the circumstances. In other words, there was a contextual variable operating in personal choice of vocabulary. Tejnor concludes that the attitude to foreign words is distinctly rational in concrete situations even if the speakers could not themselves formulate the rationale explicitly:

> Above all, they do not accept those foreign words, which have a fairly exact domestic synonym and which do not at the same time serve for specialist expression and which do not introduce expressive possibilities of distinguishing the meanings of words more precisely. (p. 52)

Clearly, the attitudes discussed here are determined to some extent by the socio-cultural and socio-linguistic experience of the Czech people. Nevertheless, it seems safe to extrapolate from these data certain general observations about the operation of social factors on purism:

1. Puristic attitudes are not absolute but are subject to a number of variables, including the age and educational profile of the speech community, social situation, stylistic register, subject-matter, and the identity of the source of the lexical item. Blanket condemnation of all 'impurities' in all circumstances is extremely rare.
2. Acceptance of items otherwise subject to puristic censure may be predicated on rationally based functional considerations.
3. A negative attitude to certain linguistic items does not necessarily correlate with banishing them from personal use or, still less, with seeking some native replacement.

The role of national consciousness

So important is the role of national consciousness in the formation of purism that it is often assumed – by layman and scholar alike – that purism is little more than an epiphenomenon of nationalism (Thomas 1989a: 6–8). Not only do periods of strong national sentiment tend to co-occur with purism, but where associated with xenophobia they almost invariably share the same targets. While there are such languages as English and Polish, where national fervour and pronounced xenophobia did not on the whole lead to a puristic movement, it is hard to think of an instance of purism which is not motivated by some form of cultural or political nationalism.

We have seen already that the nationalist aesthetic is based on the notion that the national culture is unique and irreplaceable. According to the nationalist viewpoint, only the national language can adequately serve as a symbol of self-identification with this national culture. Our native language is that form of speech which we recognise as 'ours'. That is why in some societies, where linguistic nationalism has developed only recently, it is not uncommon to use no more specific name for the language than 'ours' (Lencek 1989: 108).

Since the native language, as a component of this national culture, serves as a card of national identity, it must be carefully differentiated from any other. In the process a national language, with which its speakers can identify, is created. As we have seen already, this differentiation can be achieved through purism. In other words,

43

purism can be motivated by a search for, or the need to preserve, national identity.

Examples of this search for national identity abound, but two illustrations of it will suffice. For Aasen, the most important activist for a new national language for Norwegians, it was a national duty to pass on to one's successors a language which provided possibilities for the self-expression of the nation (Gerdener 1986: 36). This was to be achieved by distancing Nynorsk as much as possible from Dano-Norwegian (Gerdener 1986: 299). As a result, many of the words to be replaced in Nynorsk were to be found in city speech, where the influence of Dano-Norwegian was strongest (Gerdener 1986: 22). In nineteenth-century Bulgarian, the distancing from Turkish and, to a lesser extent, Greek was directly tied to the question of the spiritual independence of the Bulgarian people: 'Die Abgrenzung von der türkischen Sprache wurde von einer zielbewussten Begrenzung der türkischen Sprachelemente im gesellschaftlich-kulturellen Leben begleitet'[3] (Georgieva and Lilov 1983: 122). Interestingly, this disavowal of Greek and Turkish was also attributable to the fact that these languages were identified with the outmoded cultural life of the Ottoman Empire and consequently lacked the prestige to serve the needs of a people undergoing a renewal of national culture.

The need to preserve national linguistic identity by differentiating and distancing the language from its competitors finds a ready explanation in the pollution theories of Mary Douglas. The system is defined by pronouncing certain elements as not belonging or impure. Any transgression of these defining boundaries comes to be viewed as a threat to the system as a whole. Puristic ritual expresses anxiety about the need to protect the 'orifices', the sociological counterpart of which is the 'care to protect the political and cultural unity of a minority group' (Douglas 1966: 124). A nice illustration of the differentiating and distancing function of purism is offered by the language reforms of Noah Webster. His aims were not only to provide a guide to usage which could unite all Americans but to distance this usage as much as possible from what Samuel Johnson had laid down for usage in England. The decision, for example, to prefer spellings like *fervor* was predicated on the fact that Johnson had chosen *fervour*.

In other words, purism focuses attention on the very elements of the national language, which pose a threat to its own identity and the identity of the culture of which it is both a manifestation and a

[3] The differentiation from Turkish was accompanied by a conscious limitation of the Turkish language elements in socio-cultural life.

symbol. It is not surprising, therefore, that the targets of puristic activity can often be identified with precisely that culture which is deemed to pose a threat to the national culture; compare the attack on so-called Yiddishisms in German as a feature of Nazi anti-Semitism, or, its inverse, the condemnation by Jews at the end of the nineteenth century of 'daytshmerish', the highly Germanised version of Yiddish, as an expression of a fear of Jewish secularisation and deracination.

Einar Haugen has sagely remarked: 'While the argument is often advanced that . . . purism preserves the characteristic structure of the borrowing language, a more powerful motive is probably the sense of pride which derives from "doing it yourself"' (Haugen 1966: 23). Countless examples of purism spurred on by national pride spring to mind. No apologia for the elevation of an idiom to the status of standard language is complete without a ritual reference to qualities, in which it is said to equal or indeed surpass all others. Indeed, many a puristic tract swells with pride at the contribution that purification has made to the prestige of the language concerned.

These proud claims are pressed so often, and with such vigour, that one may be excused for suspecting them to be a mask for insecurity. This suspicion is strengthened into a certainty once we examine the basis of the claims in more detail. Indeed, while we may argue that national pride may be the outcome of 'successful' purification of a language, it is more likely that it is its obverse – shame, insecurity and a collective inferiority complex about the blemishes and inadequacies of the national language – which has provided the motivation for linguistic purism in the first place.

The reaction to the intrusion of unwanted linguistic elements, then, is often closely associated with some deeply felt insecurity. This insecurity may be fuelled by the mirthful reaction of foreign observers to a language apparently inundated with foreign expressions. Indeed, a fear of looking ridiculous in the eyes of foreigners has drawn comment from several observers of nationalism (Minogue 1967: 67, Kohn 1944: 300). As Noah Webster has written: 'Nothing can be more ridiculous, than a servile imitation of the manners, language, and the vices of foreigners' (Kohn 1944: 300).

An excellent example of the effects of foreign ridicule is given by Josef Dobrovský, who says that his Czech contemporary, the purist Václav Pohl, felt obliged to create large numbers of neologisms because the German-speaking courtiers of the Emperor Josef II laughed at all the German words in his Czech (Lisický 1920: 168). The fact that Germans later also laughed at the foreign words in English (Schultz 1888: 59) without provoking a similar reaction should not mislead us into minimising the role of foreign ridicule. English was not fighting for its survival against German competition as Czech was; its status in British life and as the bearer of a long literary tradition was assured while that of eighteenth-century Czech decidedly was not. To laugh at the supposed shortcomings of someone else's language is probably universal; but to take this ridicule seriously is confined to those language situations where speakers are beset by insecurities about the status and prestige of their language.

Further insight into these and similar insecurities is provided by the observations of ethnolinguistic fieldwork. In one of the best accounts of this kind, dealing with the demise of Gaelic in East Sutherland, Nancy Dorian writes:

> The use of recognizably English loanwords in Gaelic is currently a touchy matter in East Sutherland. English monolinguals, rather than giving credit to the bilinguals for command of two languages, frequently mock the bilinguals' Gaelic because of the English loanwords which they can perceive embedded in it. . . .The bilinguals are self-conscious about the matter of loanwords and frequently check each other for use of an English word, as when one Embo bilingual corrected his wife's borrowing of *tiun* 'tune' to *port*, the Gaelic equivalent. Precisely because everyone uses such loanwords, and because there is considerable self-consciousness about it, the number of loanwords in a verbal performance seems to have become a matter of degree of formality in [East Sutherland Gaelic]. In a relaxed and casual performance, the number of lexical borrowings will rise (most of them, as usual, well integrated into the Gaelic framework). On the other hand, the more formal the performance – for example, established narrative routines reproduced for tape-recording – the lower the number of lexical borrowings and the greater the likelihood that some of those which appear will be accompanied by lead-in phrases like 'as we would say'. (Dorian 1981: 101)

Here we gain a revealing glimpse of the sensitivity and insecurity of the speakers of a language containing too many loanwords: the embarrassment at being found using them, the lame attempt to sanction their use by means of a framing device, the censorship and correction of language usage by neighbours and close relatives. It is somewhat ironical perhaps that in Dorian's scenario the wife should be the victim of paternalistic criticism, since women are more often credited with being the vessels of linguistic purity – yes, even the morality of language operates on a double standard! Finally, the differentiation Dorian describes between formal speech, in which censorship purism is functioning, and a more casual discourse, where it is not, is symptomatic of the fact that the more consciously mediated the language performance the greater the likelihood that national pride will enter into the equation.

Psychological impulses

Purists themselves advance two sets of explanations for their language attitudes:

1. The need for intelligibility.
2. The need to protect the language as part of the native culture from outside threat or internal disintegration.

The first is not widely promoted but, at first sight at least, offers a rational justification of puristic activity. We shall examine its validity, therefore, as one of the rational foundations of purism. The second, on the other hand, is generally accepted as – indeed often assumed to be – the main motivating force behind linguistic purism. But what psychological impulses are responsible for the development of this point of view?

The view that the language is exposed to a threat posed by some external source or from internal disintegration is based on the us/them, our/their dichotomies, which are at the very basis of our earliest perception of the world around us and our place in it, even though there is considerable variability and subjectivity in interpreting what precisely is 'ours' (Fishman 1983: 5). There are four attitudes about the value of something which does not belong to us:

1. It is better than what we have.
2. It is worse than what we have.
3. It is no better or no worse than what we have.
4. We don't care whether it's better or worse than what we have.

The last two points of view are essentially apuristic and need not concern us further, but the clash of the first two viewpoints is the crux of the puristic debate.

The first attitude – based on the 'grass is greener' hypothesis – can lead to a repudiation of one's own culture and an exaggerated respect for and imitation of an alternative culture or cultures. Purism – the antithesis of this view – not only affirms the superiority of one's own native culture but is also a defensive reaction to the admiration of an alternative culture. Strictly speaking, then, purism is directed not so much at the alien culture itself as against the use of elements of that culture by persons who belong to one's own group. As Jean Genet has sagely remarked in the debate about the inundation of French by

English, one should perhaps excoriate not Anglo-Saxons for exporting 'franglais' but the French for importing it (Gordon 1978: 44–5).

The dialectic between these antithetical views may take the form of a public debate, a polemic between members of the intellectual élite, or an internal conflict for an individual. A compelling model for understanding the outcomes of this interaction is provided by Leon Festinger's theory of *cognitive dissonance* (Festinger 1957):

1. The polemic between the purists and anti-purists may continue unresolved, resulting in an ever firmer conviction on both sides of the rightness of their point of view.
2. There may be oscillation between the two positions, either in the individual or in society at large.
3. The interaction may result in ambivalence as manifested in a public disavowal coupled with covert admiration: hence the contradiction between theory and practice alluded to earlier.
4. The debate may lead to a higher synthesis incorporating features from both positions: an acceptance, for example, of the benefits provided by a foreign model coupled with a resolve to utilise as many elements of the native language as possible and to maintain a rigorous and critical stance towards further incursions of non-native material.

These four outcomes are of great importance for describing the social organisation and the diachronic development of purism (see Chapters 6 and 9 respectively).

The threat posed to the national language by elements from an external source is almost always predicated on a fear of foreign domination – primarily, of course, linguistic, but secondarily also cultural, political or religious. The general absence of such a threat explains why purism has never taken hold in English despite statements by such prominent figures as Dryden, Defoe and Addison that English has too many foreign words (Flasdieck 1928). A similar case is that of Serbian, where puristic activity in the second half of the nineteenth century has left hardly any traces in the contemporary standard language (Herrity 1978: 223). In some cultures, the fear of linguistic domination, valid enough in itself, may become morbid or excessive. Any exposition of purism should try – despite the obvious difficulties involved – to distinguish between purism motivated by a healthy concern about the language's well-being and future vitality on the one hand and purism emanating from a morbid anxiety about the ability of a language to survive on the other. There is, for example, a world of difference between the threnodial tone (laced, it is true, with black humour) of René Étiemble and the healthy, vitalising attitude of such puristically inclined language reformers as Jungmann for Czech, Aavik for Estonian, Gökalp for Turkish, or, perhaps most remarkable of all, Ben Yehuda for Hebrew.

Summary

The threat to a language posed by certain external or internal elements may go unnoticed, may be ignored, may be dismissed or – the puristic response – may be acted upon. The cognitive dissonance inherent in the choice to accept or reject the threatening elements may in turn lead to several outcomes: oscillation, ambivalence, polemic, or resolution by compromise. The perception of the threat is conditioned by a number of environmental variables (social values, aesthetic and ethical considerations) and by the collective or individual mind-set. The threat looms larger for groups or individuals with a preference for maintaining strict classificatory systems and with feelings of insecurity about the fate of their language. Where this anxiety exceeds the magnitude of the threat posed it may be characterised as pathological and obsessive.

For Robert Hall (1974: 174), the prevailing characteristics of linguistic purism are the three 'i's – insecurity, ignorance and insensitivity. According to him, purism may be reduced to the following narrative: out of ignorance or *naïveté* about linguistic facts and fed by insecurities about their own language, purists feel duty-bound to bring dissenters to adhere to their perception of linguistic orthodoxy. This may be an unnecessarily harsh point of view but it does have the merit of exposing some of the grimmer realities of the non-rational basis of purism.

Rational explanations

The intelligibility argument

Some purists contend that language elements unknown to the broad masses should be avoided on the grounds that they hamper intelligibility. This was the guiding principle for such widely different figures as Malherbe for French (Hall 1974: 174) and Lenin for Russian (Rothstein 1976: 63), both of whom were content simply to press for a reduction of the lexical and syntactical resources of their native language. An opposition to words of foreign elements could be similarly motivated: Dr S. Ali Bilgirami, the leading light of the movement to remove English words from Urdu literature, wished to alleviate comprehension for wide sectors of the population (Zaidi 1983: 420). Similarly, Bogorov, a leading Bulgarian purist of the nineteenth century, based his opposition to Russian influences partly on the lack of comprehension they induce in the youth (Moskov 1958: 26). In certain Iranian circles, too, it was considered that the use of foreign words rendered Persian 'stiff and vague' (Jazayery 1983: 255). Much more comprehensively motivated by the intelligibility argument was Aasen's plan for Nynorsk (Gerdener 1986: 33).

The intelligibility argument is often applied to word-formation: natively formed words are considered to be more comprehensible than foreign-based compounds. Furthermore, etymological connectibility in word-formation may lead to transparence and logicality (Ray 1961: 222). For example Sauvageot (1971: 262) claims that it is easier for a Hungarian to understand the meaning of *szemeszel* than for a Francophone to know the meaning of *ophthalmologie* without recourse to a dictionary. This was also the motivation for the society formed in Copenhagen to promote the purity of Icelandic. It used Old Icelandic as a model on the grounds that knowledge of word-building structures rendered the language more intelligible (Groenke 1983: 145). Disquiet about the incomprehension of his parishioners was the chief reason given by one of the earliest European purists, the Czech religious reformer Jan Hus, for creating native replacements for archaic and foreign words (Němec 1970: 315–16).

A similar motivation prompted William Barnes to purify his English, but in his case there was also a pedagogical dimension. As he wrote in 1854:

> While a thousand compound words from English single words would bear, to English minds, their own meanings in their own elements, a thousand words borrowed from another tongue would need a thousand learnings to be understood . . . and the large share of Latin and Greek words in English makes it so much less handy than purer English would be for the teaching of the poor by sermons and books. (Jacobs 1952: 16)

For Barnes, this incomprehension was not only a liability for appreciating the Word of God but was a serious barrier to social unity. Purism was perceived as a necessary antidote to political and social subjugation.

This socio-political theme is touched on elsewhere in puristic writings. For example, Gerdener (1986: 162) notes for modern Nynorsk: 'Das Austauschen von Fremdwörtern gegen norw. würde zu einer Demokratisierung der Sprache beitragen, da es nicht so leicht möglich wäre, die Sprache als Machtmittel zu missbrauchen.'[4] More extreme, perhaps, was the notion of the Soviet dissident Dmitry Panin, prototype for Sologdin in Solzhenitsyn's *First Circle*, that the incomprehensibility of foreign words in Russian could lead to language manipulation. He proposed to guarantee clarity by forming all words in Russian from 100 elementary words used in combination (Keipert 1977b: 301), a kind of 'Basic Russian'. Panin's fears of language manipulation are not so far fetched when we recollect that in Nazi Germany foreign words were often favoured precisely because their opacity of meaning could promote their usefulness as euphemisms. For example, *Sterilisation* might be preferable to *Entmannung* or *Unfruchtbarmachung* (von Polenz 1967: 84; for further examples see Seidel and Seidel-Slotty 1961).

What unites all the examples we have discussed so far is a 'democratic' or 'populist' orientation. Indeed, the intelligibility argument is an important factor in what I shall call *ethnographic* or *populist purism* (for more details, see Chapter 4). Despite the importance of the intelligibility argument in this brand of purism, it must be pointed out that the perceived need for intelligibility is really a mask for a motivation based on a desire for national solidarity by removing barriers to social unity. We are reminded here of Gellner's assertion that, strictly speaking, nationalism is a crisis in the intelligentsia, 'a class which is alienated from its society by the very fact of its education' (quoted in Smith 1971: 132–3). To restore intercomprehensibility between the élite and the uneducated masses removes a cause of alienation.

The force of this is made clear if we extend the intelligibility argument beyond national boundaries. If a Norwegian chose to plan his native language on the principle that it should be intelligible to Danes and Swedes he would be expressing an adherence to internationalist or at least pan-Scandinavian sentiments. To be concerned about communicating with his fellow Norwegians alone is to be guided by national sentiments.

The problem of incomprehension can, of course, be tackled on a completely different front – by launching a campaign of education in the use and meanings of the foreign words. Indeed, this approach to the problem has been vigorously propounded by opponents to purism and even by some moderate purists. Its success, however, unlike purism, depends on the level of popular education. In this

[4] The replacement of foreign words by Norwegian ones would contribute to a democratisation of the language, since it would not be so easy to misuse the language as means of authority.

context, purism might have a significant role to play before the necessary educational infrastructure has been created to explain to the population at large the meanings of loanwords. For example, in the early years following the social upheaval of the Russian revolution, widespread folk-etymologies and surveys of soldiers and peasants revealed alarming ignorance of the meanings of even prominent, well-established loanwords like *kooperativ*, *revoljucija*, *ser'joznyj*, *sistema* (Comrie and Stone 1978: 136–9). In view of this incomprehension on the part of large sectors of the population, as yet unexposed to massive literacy programmes, Soviet journalists were strongly advised, as far as possible, to avoid foreign words.

The fact remains, however, that the intelligibility argument is based on an unproven hypothesis. Although the Czech survey of attitudes to loanwords revealed that their use is perceived as making the Czech language less comprehensible and therefore spoiled (Tejnor *et al.* 1971: 10), we simply do not know whether it is in fact easier to understand – much less to learn – words whose meanings are derivable from their word-building structure. As Fodor (1983b: 466–7) has pointed out, it would be very useful to conduct a psychological study to determine whether the purists' claims are indeed justified.

In other words, the intelligibility argument is in most cases a rationalisation of nationalistically motivated purism. Where it is based on legitimate concerns for maintaining the language as a communicative tool for all its speakers, however, there are grounds for subsuming it under a more general rational criterion: the solidarity function of language.

As a footnote to the intelligibility argument, it is perhaps worth pointing out that very occasionally purism may be motivated by a desire to make a break with the philosophical associations of established words. Instead of a familiar loanword, which is etymologically opaque and therefore neutral with respect to the native language, an etymologically transparent neologism is proposed. The effect of this laying bare of the 'philosophical content' of a word by means of etymology is defamiliarisation, in the Shklovskian sense. An example of this form of purism is to be found in the work of the aptly named German Wolke, who wanted to transform sentences like *Die Poesie ist in ihren freien Dichtungen über alle Moralität erhaben* [Poetry in its free verses is elevated above all morality] into *Die Lebeinbildung* [lit. life-imagining] *ist in ihren freien Ewiglebdarstellungen* [lit. eternal life-presentations] *über alle Eigenwesenlebgesetzlichkeit* [own-being-life-legitimation] *erhaben* (Kirkness 1975: 224). However, the argument that Wolke's brand of purism renders the statement more intelligible would be hard to sustain!

Socio-linguistic functional criteria

All language has two social functions:

1. To make possible communication between members of a group (the solidarity function).
2. To exclude non-members of the group from communication (the separating function).

As a bulwark against domination by some other tongue, a language – this is especially true of a standard idiom – must have prestige in the eyes of its native speakers (the prestige function). The less its prestige, the greater the danger of linguistic domination. All language is governed by norms of usage, but in standard languages these norms are codified according to the twin principles of elasticity and stability (Mathesius 1947), that is to say that a language must be able paradoxically to resist change while at the same time being capable of modification. A standard language must also be capable of expanding its repertoire in order to fulfil all the social functions which it is required to carry out (the polyvalency criterion). These three criteria (elasticity, stability and polyvalency) are therefore inextricably linked to the prestige function. It is now time to examine the role played by these three functions in the rise of purism.

THE SOLIDARITY FUNCTION

We have already seen that the intelligibility argument used by purists themselves to justify their opposition to foreign words in a language may be based on the solidarity function: foreign words divide the speech community, whereas domestic words allegedly unite it. This viewpoint, it should be reiterated, is characteristic of a populist or democratising form of purism.

The solidarity function also plays a role as a determinant of élitist purism: dialectal usage or elements restricted to a particular segment or stratum of a speech community should be excluded on the grounds that they would promote linguistic disunity. Purism may also be concerned with coming to terms with the past: seeking to preserve the link with some past golden age. This conservative purism is also determined by the solidarity function inasmuch as it is guided by the principle that a speech community should retain maximal solidarity with the previous speakers of a language, as represented by a corpus of literary tradition.

The solidarity function may operate not only within individual languages but also among groups of languages united by genetic ties. As we have seen, such pan-nationalist groupings may promote a particular variety of purism. In other words, interlanguage solidarity may be a factor in pan-national purism.

THE SEPARATING FUNCTION

We have already determined that purism is concerned with a threat to the well-being of the language, prompted by a fear primarily of linguistic and secondarily of cultural, political or religious domination. We have further demonstrated that one of the goals of the nationalistically inspired puristic aesthetic is to differentiate and distance the language from all others. This concentration on *differentiae* is firmly rooted in the separating function of language. A few examples will serve to illustrate this point.

In Yiddish, according to Schaechter (1983: 214), there are 33 synonyms for 'now', of which *yetst* has the widest distribution. Nevertheless, the modern literary language has rejected this word because of its similarity to German. In its place, the language reformers have chosen six words, none of which is shared with German.

Opposition to Danish words in Nynorsk was justified by Aasen on the grounds that they have replaced genuine Norwegian elements and are, therefore, difficult to recognise (Gerdener 1986: 54). A more cogent reason for his dislike of these elements, as Gerdener says, is 'dass die nn. Schriftsprache, sich möglichst deutlich vom Dän. abheben muss, ihre Existenzberechtigung nachzuweisen'.[5]

Contemporary Croatian purism is mostly concerned with maintaining the differences between the two literary codes of Serbo-Croatian (the western or Croatian variant and the eastern or Serbian variant) (Thomas 1978a). This is because a threat of 'Serbification' of Croatian would deprive it of its *raison d'être* as an autonomous code. As a result, purists in Croatia keep a watchful eye on a sensitive core of synonyms which are held to differentiate the two codes. In the early 1970s during a period of mounting Croatian nationalism, the Croatian *Matica* – a patriotic organisation responsible for cultivation of the language – withdrew its cooperation in a venture to publish a joint dictionary of the two standard codes on the grounds that it failed to distinguish Croatian from Serbian usage.

[5] That the Nynorsk standard language must be contrasted as clearly as possible from Danish in order to demonstrate its right to exist.

The threat posed by the inability to maintain such differences is the loss of a language's identity. As Gerdener (1986: 21) puts it: 'Der Grund für das Entstehen puristischer Bestrebungen ist oft die Befürchtung, die eigene Sprache könnte durch Ueberfremdung ihre Identität verlieren.'[6] This is particularly true of closely related languages, where a cogent argument could be advanced for their amalgamation (e.g. Czech and Slovak, Serbian and Croatian, Nynorsk and Dano-Norwegian, Urdu and Hindi, the Katharevousa and Dimotiki varieties of Greek) or for the promotion of the dominant language for another speech community (Spanish for Catalan, Serbo-Croatian for Slovene, Dutch for Friesian). The overabundance of words from a threatening non-related language may also pose a threat to the autonomy, if not the continued existence, of the dominated language by ensuring enrichment of the linguistic repertoire from one source only (compare the Russification of the non-Slavonic languages of the Soviet Union, the Germanification of the Sorbian languages of Lusatia, the Sanskritisation of Tamil, and the Anglicisation of Welsh).

THE PRESTIGE FUNCTION

We have noted that the presence of foreign words in a language can provoke mirth and ridicule. This reaction is a direct response to the diminished prestige of the language in question. As Dostál (1982: 112) writes, the introduction of foreign words 'belittles one's own literary language and weakens its position with respect to the neighbouring languages'. In Icelandic too, the 'puristic policy is considered a dam against foreign influences that might threaten the autonomy of the language . . .' (Haugen 1976: 33). Yet it is not only foreign words which pose a threat to a language but also, at least from the perspective of élitists, the introduction of substandard elements. In essence, this involves a redefinition of the norms of the language concerned. In this connection, it is also legitimate to question whether the presence of certain elements is appropriate in a particular stylistic register. Rational arguments of this kind are frequently advanced within the framework of language cultivation. Provided the élitists do not impose rigidity but are mindful of the need for elasticity, such insistence on stable norms does not put excessively narrow limitations on linguistic expression. If it did, this would itself threaten the prestige of the language. Indeed, this is essentially the

[6] The reason for the rise of puristic efforts is often the fear that the native language could lose its identity as a result of foreign influence.

claim of writers like Solzhenitsyn about the purism produced by the editor's blue pencil (Keipert 1977b: 297).

Purism, then, serves as an antidote to loss not only of autonomy and identity but also prestige. Once a language loses prestige, its socio-communicative functions are likely to be usurped by a more prestigious idiom. For example, the Czech standard language had been codified in the age of humanism. This form of the language enjoyed enormous prestige; any deviations from the norms of the humanist ideal – be they outrageous neologisms, countless German loanwords, syntactical constructions based on German, or elements from the vernacular – were regarded as pollutants (Ševčík 1974–5: 49–50). Only purification of the language could restore its prestige, provide a justification for the Czech intelligentsia to turn back from German to Czech, and thus eliminate the threat to its continued existence. Most, if not all, of the languages of Europe faced similar dilemmas at some point in their literary development.

If this is true of a language which has a tradition of codified written usage behind it, how much more valid must it be for a language which is either freshly embarking on a career as a written language or is being totally recodified. Languages such as Yiddish had to compete for prestige with Russian, German, Aramaic and Hebrew (Schaechter 1983: 197–8). Yet these are the very languages from which it is most likely to borrow words. Recourse to any source of lexical enrichment other than internal resources or native word-building mechanisms would certainly jeopardise any remaining prestige. Such diverse newly codified or recodified languages as Hebrew, Afrikaans, Irish, Swahili, Hausa, Faroese or Estonian faced similar problems. What would be the point, the purist would argue, of codifying the grammar of a language if its lexico-semantic repertoire were almost entirely derived from foreign sources?

An important factor in the attitude to elements from a particular language is the prestige of this source in the eyes of the speech community borrowing the elements. Any fluctuations in this prestige are likely to result in a change in openness or closure to enrichment from this source. For example, the languages of the Balkans turned away from Turkish and Greek as sources of enrichment as both of them had lost prestige in the disintegrating Rumelian province of the Ottoman Empire. For the Turks themselves, Arabic and Persian, which had enjoyed a long tradition as prestigious languages of culture and as sources for high-style, religious and abstract vocabulary, came to be associated with an outdated past. Some Iranian purists like Behruz turned against Arabic words, because they said that Arabic is more suited to desert life while Persian is more at home in the urban setting (Jazayery 1983: 255). The Bulgarian purist Bogorov based his rejection of Russianisms partly on the fact that Russian itself was already corrupted by German, French and Tartar words (Moskov 1958: 26).

The diminution of prestige might be the result of intralinguistic factors (the unsuitability of the language as a source for enrichment or as a model for copying, or the abundance of loanwords in it) or extralinguistic associations. In either case, the continued borrowing by a speech community of elements from a language which had lost prestige in its eyes would be unlikely to enhance the prestige of its own tongue.

Structural arguments

The phonological and morphological structures of languages differ widely. The borrowing of a word from one language to another requires some form of phonological and morphological adaptation, in some cases trivial in others radical. Can the difficulties of adaptation provide a rational basis for purism? There is certainly some evidence in support. For example, Kramer (1983: 314) states categorically:

> It must be emphasised that the aversion of Italian to foreign elements and their far-reaching Italianization is by no means to be ascribed to any degree of national chauvinism: it is simply the result of morphological necessity which makes foreign elements awkward to handle in Italian.

In Hungarian, the principle of vowel harmony and other phonological constraints may cause a loanword to be so distorted as to be unrecognisable, e.g. G *Frühstück* 'breakfast' entered Hungarian as *fölöstököm* (Simonyi 1907: 69). Lauri Hakulinen (1961: 286) in part attributes the low number of primary loanwords in Finnish (1,350 by his reckoning) to its phonological structure. By way of illustration, he points out that Latin *structura* would have to be rendered in Finnish as **ruhtuuri*. The meaning would be opaque and any obvious etymological connection with the Latin cognate would be lost. In conditions such as these, loaning would serve no purpose and the language would be better off with a native coining.

In some languages the difficulty of adaptation leads to the exclusion of foreign words from the phonological or morphological system of the borrowing language. These words may contain sounds or combinations of sounds which are absent or marginal in the main system. They are, therefore, marked off from the main system and assigned to a subsystem of foreign words. In Russian, for example, foreign words do not always follow the usual constraint that the vowel /e/ is preceded by the palatalised member of a palatalised/non-palatalised pair of consonants, thus [t'en'i] 'shades' but [ten'is] 'tennis' (for a full discussion of this problem, see Waight 1980). In some languages, the special status of foreign words may be marked by special graphemes or even by the use of an alternative script. In other languages such as Tamil, reluctance to adapt loanwords to the native system is reflected in widespread code-switching, which has the effect of keeping the languages carefully apart (Zvelebil 1983: 435-6). Such instances seem to be motivated not by structural differences but by nationally orientated aesthetic concerns.

An interesting case is the morphological treatment of loanwords ending in a vowel in the various Slavic languages (Thomas 1983). In all these languages there operates the constraint that no stem may end in a vowel. A foreign noun ending in a vowel must therefore be treated in one of three ways:

1. It may be morphologically reinterpreted as a stem ending in a consonant followed by a vowel desinence.
2. The morphophonemic constraint may be lifted.
3. The word may remain uninflected.

The first treatment may be classed as non-puristic in the sense that it does not distinguish loanwords from the main body of the vocabulary; the second is marginally puristic inasmuch as it suspends the rules for a special group of words; while the third is more obviously puristic in the sense that it excludes a class of loanwords from the native system. Each of the Slavic languages shows different tendencies: Serbo-Croatian and Slovene favour the first type but show increasing evidence of the second; Czech and Polish employ the first option where the vowel fits into a native paradigm and where not the third; and Russian almost always tends towards the third option. In these five languages with their virtually identical morphophonemic systems, then, the response to precisely the same structural dilemma is radically different. In other words, the different treatment of these loanwords is determined not by structural considerations but by taste and habit. In Russian this is amply demonstrated by the fact that there is wide variation between the vernacular, which assimilates them into the paradigms followed by the native vocabulary, and the standard, which excludes them.

In the past, contact between languages possessing vastly different structures has resulted in widespread borrowing. There is no evidence that the structural differences between them have substantially affected the extent to which they have been ready to accept words into their systems. The avoidance of words displaying difficulties for adaptation seems, therefore, to be predicated primarily on aesthetic values. The structural questions are at best secondary and may in certain cases be little more than rationalisations of attitudes motivated by other factors. Indeed, the structural arguments for purism are not unlike the practice of a country which, despite free trade, refuses the importation of some article on the grounds that it does not conform to its own (possibly arbitrary) standards of production as in the case of the exclusion of British beer from the West German market because it does not meet the requirements of the aptly named *Reinheitsgebot* of 1516. Nevertheless, an argument can be made for the desirability of a 'filter' between closely related languages to shut out certain phonological structures, word-building elements or lexico-semantic models (Horecký 1967: 44).

Summary

The intelligibility and structural arguments cannot be regarded as primary rational bases for purism. In both cases, they are either secondary manifestations or rationalisations of aesthetically or nationally inspired attitudes. The primary rationale for puristic attitudes and behaviour is provided by three socio-linguistic criteria: the solidarity, separating and prestige functions of language.

The solidarity and separating functions combine to define the limits of the language in question. Purism serves these functions by acting as a principle of what is acceptable and what is unacceptable in a given language: unacceptable elements diminish the prestige of a language; acceptable ones enhance it. This prestige is maintained by the elasticity, stability and polyvalency requirements, in all of which purism also has a possible part to play.

The interplay of rational and non-rational factors

It must be immediately obvious that rational and non-rational factors in purism are not necessarily at variance. For example, the separating and solidarity functions are closely related to the nationally orientated puristic aesthetic, to problems of national identity and to the psychological distinction between 'ours' and 'theirs'. The non-rational factors supply a principle for deciding on what features the definition of the language's corpus is to be based. Similarly, the prestige function is paralleled by national pride, the perception that what is 'ours' is or should be superior, and the belief that purity confers superiority. Again, the non-rational factors supply a set of assumptions on which the prestige of a language can be evaluated. Nevertheless, it is possible for the socio-linguistic functions to be served in ways which have nothing to do with purism. In other words, purism is only one of several possible responses to these three functional criteria. It is impossible, therefore, to explain purism without reference to non-rational motivations.

Indeed, it is not difficult to find instances where purism is motivated by non-rational or pseudo-rational factors alone. Compare, for example, the following statements from totally different language situations:

> Original primitive languages are superior to composite, derived languages. . . . German is an original language, its speech must be cleansed of foreign accretions and borrowings, since the purer the language, the more natural it becomes for a nation to realize itself and to increase its freedom. (Fichte 1808 as quoted in translation by Fishman 1973: 67) . . . consistent and intelligent modernization of their national languages would enable the Malaysians, the Indonesians and the Filipinos to overtake and eventually surpass in science and technology the Western nations, whose national languages are burdened with large numbers of terms derived from Latin and Greek, combining forms which are no longer consistent with home and community languages spoken by their children. (Rosario 1968)

What unites them is their idealism, their programmatic nature and their reliance on value-judgements which have no linguistic basis. It is important to remember, however, that even non-rational statements like these may in fact lead to outcomes which are not incompatible with a rationally based purism. Most puristic attitudes, however, fall somewhere between the pragmatic, rational principles and the idealism of Fichte or Rosario.

Purism, then, involves a resolution of the clash between the rational and non-rational orientations to language intervention. On the one hand, wholly idealist purism embraces Set A of Parsons' antinomies:

1. Such purists tend to be emotionally committed to their goals.
2. They tend to display subjectivity in identifying their own usage with what is desirable for the collective.
3. Their brand of purism is concerned with foregrounding what is specific to a particular language and downplaying universal characteristics.

4. Such purism is prone to identify wrongs without reference to what righting these wrongs may achieve.
5. Such purism is often a single-issue ideology: it seeks a specific, short-term solution to a perceived shortcoming in a language.

The compromising forms of purism, on the other hand, involve recognition of the merits of one or more of the members of Set B:

1. Objective purism is distinguished from subjective purism by its affective neutrality.
2. Purism guided by the solidarity function differs from idiosyncratic purism by stressing the collectivity orientation (compare the pragmatic though radical aims of William Barnes and the equally radical, but totally imbecilic intentions of Wolke).
3. Purism tinged with cosmopolitanism or pan-national sentiments demonstrates a willingness to recognise the merits of some universal features even at the expense of the particular features of its own linguistic idiom.
4. Purism governed by the three functional criteria is essentially achievement-oriented rather than being an end in itself.
5. Lastly, purism which has developed as part of an integrated interventionary response to the functional needs of a language demonstrates diffuseness as opposed to the specificity of purism operating as a single-issue ideology.

Compromises in purism involve not only espousal of one or other of the B Set of value orientations but also occupation of a non-polarised position with respect to a particular antinomy. Further modulation in puristic attitudes is made possible by differential weighting of the various antinomies.

The complex interplay of these various value orientations allows for a comprehensive framework in which purism can be described in all its variety. Finally, since all purism is motivated to some extent by non-rational factors whereas only some instances of purism have a rational explanation, non-rational (that is, purely idealistic) purism is the unmarked attitude, whereas purism moderated to some extent by rational criteria is marked.

CHAPTER 4

A typological framework

Introduction

Thus far we have looked at purism as if it were a single, unified approach to language – the reaction to the presence of certain undesirable elements in a language. In fact, as we might expect, the situation is much more complex. Purism comes in different shapes and sizes; furthermore, it is espoused by groups and individuals imbued with quite different ideas of linguistic purity. In this chapter we shall examine the linguistic levels affected by purism, explore the selection of targets for puristic concern and offer a taxonomy of puristic orientations.

Linguistic levels

Potentially at least, purism may operate on all linguistic levels. Interestingly, though, purism on one level does not necessarily presuppose purism on another. We shall briefly examine in turn the ways that purism can affect the various levels of language before suggesting a possible descriptive framework.

Phonology

Opposition to the introduction of sounds from dialects or sociolects of the same diasystem is in all probability a universal of standard languages. It is the basis of such concepts as *received pronunciation* in English or *orfoèpija* in Russian. It is preferable, however, to treat this opposition not as purism but as an aspect of language cultivation, designed to protect the norms of the standard language. Nevertheless, there is an obvious link with purism in the way that such language cultivation also supports the prestige and solidarity functions of the standard language.

If we exclude normative attitudes to pronunciation, purism on the phonological level is a relatively rare phenomenon. For example, opposition to the introduction of phonemes from foreign languages is poorly represented, though it is worth noting that the inability of alphabets or graphemic systems to deal with sounds not of the domestic phonemic pattern can foreground the foreignness of the words in which they are found. For example, the Latinisation of Turkish was designed specifically to deal with the native sound-pattern; the large numbers of Persian and Arabic elements which did not fit with this sound-pattern were thus automatically rendered 'foreign' (Tachau 1964: 195).

Some languages like Russian employ a phonemic subsystem to deal with words of foreign origin. If this subsystem serves to separate these words from the native lexical repertoire by labelling them as + foreign (Waight 1980), then it is appropriate to view this as puristic intervention.

Morphology

As in phonology, so in flexional morphology most potential cases of purism can best be regarded as instances of language cultivation. Nevertheless, where the advocacy of certain morphemes is motivated by the wholesale acceptance or rejection of the morphological system of a dialect, an earlier stage of a language or the adoption of morphemes from a foreign language then purism may be said to be involved. For example, the diglossia between Katharevousa and Dimotiki is maintained in part by a puristic attitude to the incorporation of morphemes from the other literary code. The refusal of Russian to inflect certain loanwords is attributable, as we have seen, to an essentially puristic attitude (Thomas 1983). The most severely puristic period in the history of Czech (1870–90) was characterised by an archaistic insistence on strictly maintaining the morphology of sixteenth-century Czech (Mathesius 1933: 75; Dostál 1982: 110). But perhaps the most radical example of morphological purism is that of the Estonian language reformer Aavik (Kurman 1968: 58).

Derivational morphology is, however, another matter: puristic reaction to undesirable word-forming morphemes is widespread. The Bulgarian purist Bogorov, for example, objected to the introduction of words using the agentive suffix *-tel* from Russian, preferring to substitute what he regarded as domestic suffixes *-ač, -ar, -arnik, -nik* (Moskov 1958: 50–1). The Slovak journal *Slovenská Reč* insisted that Slovak should not blindly employ word-formational morphemes borrowed from Czech (Fryščák 1978: 347). In Yiddish, too, there was a negative reaction to certain German affixes, e.g. *-bar, -haft, -loz, er-, -ismus, selbst-* (for which the respective replacements *-lekh/-evdik, -(d)ik/-ish, on-, -izm, aleyn-/zikh-* were suggested, e.g. *Zikhlibe* for *Selbstliebe* 'egoism', *Aleynbildung* for *Selbstbildung* 'self-education') (Schaechter 1983: 214). Perhaps the most thoroughgoing rejection of foreign word-building morphemes is Aasen's attitude to the German (usually Low German) affixes (*be-, er-, -else*), which, though widespread in Swedish and Danish (and in consequence also in Bokmål), were in his view unacceptable for Nynorsk (Gerdener 1986: 54). It is instructive that in all these instances the morphemes to be rejected belonged to closely related languages. The separate identity and autonomy of the language were threatened if it followed the word-building elements of a related idiom too closely.

Syntax

Most cases of syntactic purism constitute a negative reaction to innovation or importation of substandard usage in a standard language and as such, like similar instances of phonological and morphological purism, can best be treated as aspects of language cultivation.

The syntax of most standard languages is modelled to some extent on some foreign exemplar. Purists seem to take exception to this modelling only where it is excessive or seriously violates the syntactic system of the language. For example, in Czech there has been a long tradition, initiated by Dobrovský and Tomsa and developed by Jungmann, to oppose the use of constructions modelled on German (Havránek 1936: 89). Indeed, this obsession with the syntactical 'Germanisms' in their language was the focal point of the famous polemic between the purists and the Prague Linguistic Circle. The presence of Indo-European syntactic structures in Finno-Ugric languages such as Estonian, Finnish and Hungarian has also provoked puristic reaction (Kurman 1968: 58; Becker 1948a; Sauvageot 1971, 1983).

Lexico-semantics

Puristic reaction to certain lexical elements is so widespread as to be almost universal. It is important to remember that this reaction may concern not only foreign elements (loanwords or calques) but also dialectal material, neologisms and professionalisms. Somewhat less frequent as a subject of puristic concern is the semantic element – established words changing their meaning as a result of innovation or foreign influence. An instance of the latter is noted by van Haeringen (1960: 70):

> The influence of German on Netherlandic is to be perceived, not so much in words directly borrowed from German and recognizable as foreign, as in peculiarities of word-formation and semantic nuance where Netherlandic follows or imitates German in a way contrary to its own idiom. . . .'

Phraseology

If set phrases like *point of view* or *take into consideration* – in contradistinction to collocations – are lexicalisations, i.e. they function in a sentence as if they were lexical items, then it is not surprising that they should come in for puristic opposition in much the same way that words do. Furthermore, since so much phraseology is freely borrowed from one language to another, the suspicion that a phrase is of foreign origin may be sufficient to bring down puristically motivated criticism upon it.

Orthography

As we have seen, graphemic systems – especially phonemic ones – may serve to highlight words which do not fit easily into the native phonological system. This is particularly evident when some large-scale spelling reform is underway or – even more strikingly – where a fresh alphabet or writing system is adopted. The same objective is served in languages like German, which formerly used the so-called Gothic script (*Fraktur*) for domestic words and the Roman script for words of foreign origin. A similar case is Japanese where *katakana* is used exclusively for onomastics and for words of foreign origin, while *kanji*, the Japanese adaptation of Chinese characters, is never used for non-native lexical items.

Furthermore, an orthography can be used to maximise the distance between one code and another. The Belorussian orthography, for example, has succeeded in providing the language with a surface appearance quite unlike that of Russian. In Norway, there has been a long-standing battle – now somewhat relaxed – between the spelling conventions of Nynorsk and Bokmal (Haugen 1966). Even in English, Noah Webster's primary intention was to give Americans a spelling system which would make it markedly different from that advocated by Samuel Johnson for use in England.

On the other hand, orthographic purism is often associated with a traditionalist attitude to language. Such was the situation with the Czech *brusíči* of the late nineteenth century (Mathesius 1933: 75). Even the introduction of a single alien grapheme like the latinic *j* employed in Vuk Karadžić's new Serbian Cyrillic orthography of 1818 was enough to provoke a considerable puristic outcry, particularly from the conservative clergy. Vuk's own followers roundly rejected the introduction into the latinic version of Serbo-Croatian the grapheme *ě*, introduced by the Croat Ljudevit Gaj from Czech as an etymological rendition of what was pronounced in various dialects as [i], [je], [ije], [e], on the grounds that it broke with the strictly phonological principle on which their orthography was based. But examples of this kind are quite overshadowed by the role of orthographic purism in Chinese, where the prestige and the stability of the writing system are synonymous with linguistic nationalism (de Francis 1950). Indeed, the alphabet or graphic system may itself be such an evocative national symbol that its revocation or replacement may be greeted with a puristic response. The Turkic languages of the Soviet Union have experienced this trauma twice in this century, first following a switch from Arabic to Latin and then a further switch to Cyrillic. Conversely, the retention of an alphabet other than that used by a closely related code may serve to reinforce the differences between them. Such is the case of Moldavian with its Cyrillic as opposed to Romanian with its Latin script.

A descriptive framework

While examples of purism can be found on all linguistic levels, it would be manifestly misleading to give them equal weight in any descriptive framework. In order to separate the archetypal from the exceptional, it is imperative that the various levels be presented not serially but hierarchically.

The primary distinction is between purism operating at the level of the lexis (unmarked) and that operating at the levels of smaller or larger linguistic segments (marked). Lexical purism may be further divided into that which is concerned with the surface manifestation of the words themselves and their underlying semantic structures.

Purists may object to the words in themselves (the lexical repertoire) or to some aspect of their formation. Such word-formational purism may be directed at the word-building elements (morphology) or the manner in which they are combined (syntax).

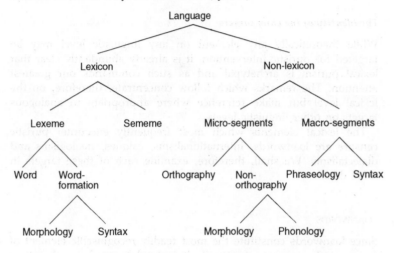

Figure 2: A hierarchy of linguistic levels

Non-lexical purism may be divided into that which pertains to macrosegments and microsegments. Macrosegmental purism may be further subdivided into phraseological and syntactic varieties. Microsegmental purism may be divided into orthographic and non-orthographic types (Figure 2). The latter comprise phonological and morphological purism.

The selection of targets

We have already determined that the concept of purity as applied to language has an appraisive not a descriptive force, and a relative not an absolute value. Not surprisingly, therefore, purists, whatever they may say to the contrary, are generally only concerned with elements which they see as posing a threat to the homogeneity, the autonomy or the prestige of the linguistic system, that is to say would, if left unattended, violate the solidarity, separating or prestige functions of the language concerned. In other words, as a general rule, purism is not applied blanket-fashion but is *targeted* at those elements threatening in some way to harm the status of the language (Daneš 1982: 102).

The identity of the chief targets

While theoretically any element on any linguistic level may be targeted for puristic intervention, it is already abundantly clear that lexical purism is archetypal and as such commands our greatest attention. The remarks which follow concentrate, therefore, on the lexical level but make reference where appropriate to analogous targets on other linguistic levels.

The lexical elements which most frequently encounter puristic censure are loanwords, internationalisms, calques, neologisms and dialectalisms. We shall, therefore, examine each of these targets in more detail.

LOANWORDS

Since loanwords constitute the most readily recognisable element of foreign influence in a language, it is hardly surprising that they should be the most prone to puristic intervention. However, several factors may serve to mitigate this puristic concern:

1. Their integration into the phonological and morphological system is so complete that their foreign origin could be revealed only by etymological analysis.
2. They have long been accepted as occupying an important niche in the lexico-semantic system.
3. They are represented in a wide variety of languages.
4. They are not borrowed from neighbouring or competing languages.
5. They are borrowed from languages of the same language family particularly at a time of pan-national solidarity.
6. There is no native synonym to replace them.

These factors may be mutually reinforcing: French words in Romanian are borrowed from a distant, prestigious, related language and are likely to be widely represented in other languages, be fully integrated and occupy a niche in the lexico-semantic system. Alternatively, they may counteract each other as when a related language is also a competing or neighbouring language as is Finnish for Estonian, Czech for Slovak, German for Dutch. In any case, the interplay of these six factors plays a large part in determining the profile of a given instance of purism.

INTERNATIONALISMS

Internationalisms do not pose an intense or immediate threat to the autonomy or integrity of a language (Thomas 1988b: 104). Furthermore, they perform an important role in the formation of scientific terminology and as a bridge to international communication as in the case of Nynorsk where Danish loanwords are viewed as an impoverishment but internationalisms as advantageous (Gerdener 1986: 42). Slovene and Slovak purists have voiced similar sentiments in their opposition to domination from Serbo-Croatian and Czech respectively (Auty 1973).

Nevertheless, there are also plenty of examples of purism directed at internationalisms. Such purism is supported by one or more of the following motivations:

1. A conviction that a language should have its own domestically produced terminology.
2. The possible incomprehensibility of internationalisms for the masses.
3. The source language of the internationalisms is too closely identified with a dominating, often colonialist power.
4. The internationalisms are adopted in a form which clearly betrays the mediation of a language which threatens to dominate the language concerned, as is the case with languages of the Soviet Union where internationalisms are perceived as a form of Russification.

Unfortunately, there is lack of agreement about what exactly constitutes an internationalism (for further discussion, see Wexler 1969; Akulenko 1972; Mistrík 1973). Much of the thinking on this subject tends to be unashamedly Eurocentric: Graeco-Latinisms together with a number of items from the major west European languages.

An interesting case where there has been considerable debate about internationalisms in language planning circles is Hebrew (Masson 1983: 459–60), where it is now commonly accepted that a word common to Russian, German and Yiddish – the three main languages with which Hebrew has had to compete – is international. Since the main motivation for Hebrew purism is the danger of national assimilation, such internationalisms were deemed acceptable: 'on s'explique ainsi la présence massive des éléments paneuropéens en hébreu moderne: ils sont sentis comme supra-nationaux et, en quelque sorte, le bien commun de toute nation, juive ou non[7] (Masson 1983: 464–5).

CALQUES

Calques (or loan translations) are often tolerated where loanwords from the very same language are inadmissible. In Tamil, a language quite inhospitable to western loans and even internationalisms, for example, calques based on European models abound: *ulamnūl* 'psychology' (lit.: mind-science), *tolai-pēci* 'telephone' (lit.: far-sound), *tolaik-kāṭci* 'television' (lit.: far-sight), *nīrāvik-kappal* 'steamship' (Zvelebil 1983: 434). Similarly, in Hebrew a prominent part of the vocabulary comprises calques from German and Russian, languages from which Hebrew is reluctant to borrow directly (Masson 1983: 467–8). The Nynorsk language reformer Aasen too did not shy away from calquing words from German although rejecting loans from the same source, e.g. *orskot* 'committee' (from G *Ausschuss*) (Gerdener 1986: 55). Such varied languages as Turkish, Danish, Icelandic, Persian, Hungarian, Czech, Croatian, Yiddish, German and even Latin offer further proof of the acceptability of calquing as a means of replacing loanwords from the same source (Heyd 1954: 94–5; Karker 1983: 286; Haugen 1976: 33; Jazayery 1983: 247; Fodor 1983a: 74; Thomas 1975, 1978a, 1978b; Schaechter 1983: 210; Kamb-Spiess 1962; Efremov 1960: 20). This acceptability is partially attributable to the fact that the foreign impulse behind loan translations, even if consciously formed to replace loanwords, remains discretely hidden from view. Alternatively, it can be explained by the readiness on the part of purists to make compromises (Fishman 1983: 7):

> The calque then serves as a healthy compromise between linguistic chauvinism on the one hand and the unnecessary use of modish foreign words on the other. To sum up, one can say that the calque satisfies aesthetically and functionally, being national in its outer form, yet supra-(and often inter-) national in semantic content (Thomas 1975: 23)

Nevertheless, for many, calques were unacceptable. Indeed for some, because of the restructuring of the word-formational, syntactical, phraseological or semantic system which calques may incur, they constituted a greater danger than loanwords, whose presence did not pose a threat at the grammatical level.

[7] This is how the massive presence of pan-European elements in modern Hebrew is explained: they are felt as supranational and in some way the common property of every nation, Jewish or not.

Such was the position of the Czech language reformer Josef Dobrovský, who wrote: 'Zudem sind die meisten neuerfundenen Wörter nach der deutschen Etymologie ängstlich geschmiedet, gerade, als wären die deutschen Zusammensetzungen zum Muster vorgestellt'[8] (Dobrovský 1779: 331). On another occasion he criticised *bratrovraždení*, a contemporary calque of G *Brudermord* by asking rhetorically: 'Wer hat es zum Gesetze gemacht, dass es die Böhmen den Deutschen in ihren Zusammensetzungen der Wörter nachmachen sollen?'[9] (Dobrovský 1780: 94). In Dobrovský's opinion such calquing could have serious consequences for the Czech language: 'Wenn man so fortfährt, so wird man nicht mehr böhmisch, sondern mit böhmischen Wörtern Deutsch schreiben'[10] (Dobrovský 1780: 100). So hostile to this rash of calques was Dobrovský, that he would often prefer a loanword like *jarmark* 'market' (from G *Jahrmarkt*) to *roční trh* (a German-based calque) (Dobrovský 1799: 67). He recommends the creators of these calques to read the German philologist Adelung, who held similar reservations about calques, and compare the latter's condemnation of *Gemeinplatz* for Lat. *locus communis* (Kirkness 1975: 61).

Some extreme nineteenth-century German purists were also opposed to calquing, a method which had reached a new peak in the *Verdeutschungsbücher* of Joachim von Campe of 1814. Prominent among them was Jahn, who 'betrachtet die Uebersetzung der ausländischen Wortform als ein schlechtes Hilfsmittel. Die Lehnübersetzung verwirft er völlig und hält sie nicht nur eine von Campes Schwächen'[11] (Kirkness 1975: 202).

As with loanwords, calquing may be reflected in a whole chain of languages. In such cases, a language adopting a calque may be deemed not to be subservient to the lexico-semantic system of one particular language posing a possible threat but simply following the example of a whole series of languages, which together often formed a *Sprachbund* (Becker 1948b). Indeed, this is precisely one of the points made by the Prague Linguistic Circle in its polemic with the purists.

[8] Moreover, most of the newly invented words are forged in timid imitation of German etymology, just as if the German compounds had been presented as a model.

[9] Who has made it a rule that the Czechs in their compounds must imitate the Germans?

[10] If we continue in this vein we shall not be writing Czech any more but German with Czech words.

[11] views the translation of the foreign word form as a poor remedy. The calque he rejects totally and considers it just one of Campe's weaknesses.

When considering attitudes to calques, it is also important to distinguish between conscious, literary creations and spontaneous, vernacular ones (Unbegaun 1932). For, while literary calques may be justified as part of the enrichment and intellectualisation of a language (the polyvalency factor), vernacular calques may indicate the extent of foreign domination (Thomas 1988b: 106).

Werner Betz makes another crucial distinction: between two types of calques *Lehnübersetzungen* ('die genaue Glied-für-Glied Uebersetzung des Vorbildes') and *Lehnübertragungen* ('die freiere Teil-Uebersetzung des fremden Vorbildes')[12] (Betz 1944). While the former may appear to be slavish imitations or may violate structural constraints, the latter provide an opportunity for more creative freedom (Thomas 1988b: 106).

To sum up, calques provide the purist with a dilemma: on the one hand, they may be welcomed as an acceptable alternative to a loanword or a clumsy neologism; on the other, they represent an intrusion from a foreign source at a much deeper level than any loanword. 'Indeed, precisely because of their compromising nature, calques offer an excellent litmus test of the intensity of puristic feeling' (Thomas 1988b: 106).

NEOLOGISMS

The ability to create new words from internal resources independently of any foreign model is an important desideratum for any autonomous standard language (Shevelov 1977: 238, 255). It would be surprising, therefore, if purists were opposed to neologisms in their native language. Indeed, most of them not only accept but actively encourage the coining of neologisms. Nevertheless, there is hostility to neologisms which either violate strictures on word-building or risk incomprehensibility because of poor semantic motivation.

As well as the familiar compounding and derivation neologisms include truncations, back-formations, deformations of foreign words and even creating words *ex nihilo* (for some Icelandic, Hungarian, Finnish and Estonian examples, see Groenke 1983; Sauvageot 1971, 1983; Ross 1938). Some purists strongly object to the artificiality and idiosyncrasy of such procedures. Others operate a double standard: neologising is acceptable if carried out unconsciously in a dialect setting but is unacceptable if performed consciously by an urban intellectual.

---

[12] 'the exact element-for-element translation of the model';
'the freer partial translation of the foreign model'

DIALECTALISMS

Enrichment from dialects and sociolects of the same language is often a welcome procedure for purists' particularly where it can be shown that the language has hidden riches in its own back garden and does not need to have recourse to foreign material. Nevertheless, there are some, who would point out that substandard language and elements confined to a small section of society are inappropriate to the dignity of a standard language. This response may greet not only the introduction of lexical items but also phonological, morphological or syntactic features of a non-standard variety.

Descriptive framework

The various targets of lexical purism form themselves into a hierarchical arrangement, which is presented in Figure 3 in the form of a tree diagram. It will be seen that at the first node foreign targets

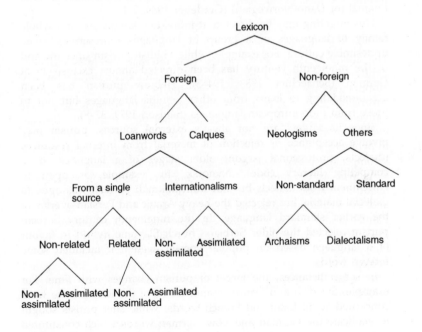

Figure 3: A hierarchy of lexical targets

are distinguished from all others. Furthermore, from the puristic perspective foreign items are the unmarked member, thus reversing the apuristic marking (Ivir 1989).

The notion of opening and closure

The targeting of purism involves a language being *open* to some sources but *closed* to others. Urdu is closed to Sanskrit words but open to Persian ones, whereas in Hindi the reverse is true (Fishman 1973: 67). In the Balkans, closure to Turkish (and to a lesser extent Greek) led in the nineteenth century to renewed openness to enrichment from Romance languages (Italian, Latin and French) in Romanian, and Slavonic languages (Russian, Czech, Church Slavonic) in Bulgarian and Serbian (Hill 1975: 122). Czech, Hungarian and Sorbian purism were all directed primarily at a single target – Germanisms (Ševčík 1974–5: 53; Czigany 1974: 329; Stone 1968: 152). In the Nynorsk (or Landsmål) form of Norwegian, the principal target of purism has been those Danish elements which are characteristic of Bokmål (or Dano-Norwegian) (Gerdener 1986: 22).

This targeting may be directed at individual languages, at a whole family of languages or a group of languages representing some undesirable culture. For example, while Yiddish purism since the end of the nineteenth century has been directed almost exclusively at German (Schaechter 1983: 194–5), Hebrew purism has been accommodating to loans from other Semitic languages but not to those from Indo-European languages (Saulson 1979: 37–8).

Since its targets are not always external sources, purism may involve acceptance or rejection of material from internal resources (dialects, professional jargon, older stages of a language, or a competing literary code). Nynorsk, for example, is open to enrichment from dialects but not from Bokmål; Turkish was open to dialectal material but rejected the heavy Arabic and Persian overlay of the earlier standard language. In the nineteenth century Serbian purism rejected the older Serbian/Church Slavonic hybrid in favour of a language based on popular speech even if it included some foreign words.

In some instances, the target of purism changes with time. For example, Swedish and Danish grammarians of the Renaissance were concerned about Latin and French words, while later purists sought to eradicate the German and Low German words which constituted such a large part of the abstract vocabulary of these two languages

(Karker 1983: 286). Where in the nineteenth century Turkish had been opposed to western elements, the chief target in this century has been Persian and Arabic (Heyd 1954). To take a contrary example, Jazayery (1983: 265) predicted that the overthrow of the Shah in Iran would result in an opposition to western influences and a renewed openness to Arabic, to which earlier purists had sought to close Persian.

There are also instances where a language faces a threat on two fronts simultaneously: some individuals may perceive the threat from one direction while opening the language to influences from another; other individuals may seek to do precisely the reverse. In both Belorussian and Ukrainian, for example, Polish elements were seen as a threat by some and by others as a welcome remedy against Russification; at the same time, there were those who were ready to accept Russian words at the expense of Polish influence (Wexler 1975). For the majority of Bulgarian purists, Russianisms were readily accepted in the place of Turkisms, while others fought against their introduction (Moskov 1958).

Finally, there may be different degrees of *opening* and *closure*. Serbian, for example, was more open (or tolerant) towards Turkisms than neighbouring Bulgarian (Hill 1975: 123). Within a language too there may be variation from time to time in the degree of openness to certain items.

The various degrees of openness and closure, the consistency with which they are applied, the ranking of the various alternatives for enrichment and the compromises which these choices bring with them are founded on differing attitudes to purism. Consequently, this complex interplay of choices and preferences provides a promising starting point for examining the various puristic orientations.

A taxonomy of puristic orientations

One of the problems in dealing with purism has been the absence of a systematic typology (Wexler 1974). Some scholars, like Moskov (1976: 7–8), have used the targets of purism as the basis for a typology. Since it may be directed at several targets simultaneously, this does not seem to be a very promising procedure. A more satisfactory approach has been offered by Ševčík (1974–5: 56), who proposes a two-tier classification. Firstly, on the basis of the identity of the *targets* he identifies the following types:

1. Geographic: concerned with dialectalisms.
2. Social: directed at elements from certain sociolects.
3. Xenophobic: directed indiscriminately at all foreign elements.
4. X-phobic: directed at material from a specific language.
5. Historical: directed at elements threatening the language's historical continuity.
6. Aesthetic: at odds with a particular literary poetic.

Secondly, on the basis of *goals*, he divides it thus:

1. Unificatory: to satisfy the solidarity criterion of standard languages.
2. Prestige: to satisfy the prestige function.
3. Defensive: to deal with nonrational concerns about the threat a language faces.
4. Delimiting: to satisfy the separating function.

Ševčík's two-tier typology allows for a separation of concrete manifestations and sociolinguistic foundations of purism and accounts for most forms of purism encountered in a large number of languages – even though it was developed to deal with Czech purism exclusively. Nevertheless, several of his categories seem redundant: all purism is to a great extent defensive, delimiting and aesthetic. Furthermore, it misses the point that purism is as much about opening as it is about closure. Therefore, despite the undoubted merits of Ševčík's scheme I would like to propose an alternative based on the overall orientation of the puristic intervention (for an earlier version, see Thomas 1988b: 101–4). We shall review these orientations in turn and then attempt to fit them into a framework.

Archaising purism

As we have already seen, reverence for the past is an important aspect of purism. It can be manifested in an attempt to resuscitate the linguistic material of a past golden age, an exaggerated respect for past literary models, an excessive conservatism towards innovations or a recognition of the importance of literary tradition. It corresponds, therefore, not only to Ševčík's historical purism but also in part to his unificatory, aesthetic and defensive categories.

In Hindi this 'purity of the past' (Fishman 1973: 69) takes the form of Sanskritisation (Fishman 1973: 140). In both Icelandic and, to a lesser extent, Nynorsk it is evident in a desire to go back to words of Old Norse (Old Icelandic), some of which are still to be found in the dialects of the respective languages (Groenke 1972, 1983; Gerdener 1986: 23). French purism too 'fondé sur le culte d'une langue fixée par les modèles (Racine, Pascal, Bossuet, Bouffon ou Voltaire) dans un "état de perfection" dira-t-on même parfois'[13] (Quemada 1983: 98). Purism in Czech from the 1870s onwards, building on the historicising attitudes of the language historian Jan Gebauer, was also essentially archaising (Ševčík 1974–5; Mathesius 1933: 75).

Perhaps the most striking example of archaising purism though is to be found in Arabic:

> Arabs are conservative classicists even purists in all that concerns their language. They do not want to facilitate the rules of grammar, they do not welcome foreign words, even those which have a modern scientific meaning. They invent words from Arabic roots for vitamins, hormones, automobiles . . . This purism is the result of . . . more than thirteen hundred years of literary religious memories. (Moussa 1955: 41–2)

Ethnographic purism

Anthony D. Smith (1971: 63) has noted that while 'nationalistic movements are all urban-based . . . their imagery is full of nostalgia and idealisation for the countryside and folk virtues'. Similarly, the notion that the rural dialects are somehow purer than city speech or the standard is commonly encountered as a form of linguistic nationalism. As a result, purists have often looked to folk poetry, proverbs and popular sayings as a source of lexical enrichment. This form of purism may be called, after Wexler (1974: 114), *ethnographic*. While partially intersecting with Ševčík's unificatory purism, ethnographic purism is largely omitted from his scheme.

In Nynorsk and Icelandic, as we have seen, the dialects were surveyed for words which had been preserved from Old Norse times. In Finnish too the dialects have been the main source for making up the deficiencies caused by the refusal to borrow foreign words (especially in the crucial period between 1820 and 1914): 'Ainsi, la langue commune a pris un caractère de plus en plus "national" et naturellement "populaire" puisque la nationalité finnoise s'exprimait

---

[13] 'founded on the cult of a language fixed by models (Racine . . .) in a "state of perfection" one might say sometimes'.

avant tout dans les dialectes'[14] (Sauvageot 1983: 186). Other examples of pronounced ethnographic purism are Serbian, Ukrainian, Belorussian, Slovak, Turkish and Dimotiki.

There are also a number of instances of languages where individuals have advocated a populist approach against the general trend: Żeromski for Polish (Rothstein 1976: 70–1), Bogorov for Bulgarian (Moskov 1958: 25–6). However, perhaps the most colourful figure in this regard was the English would-be language reformer William Barnes, who believed that the Dorset dialect could serve as a guide to standard English in its use of affixes like *-some, for-*. Furthermore, he tabulated words that had been lost in English except among the poor and rural population, e.g. *earthtillage* (*agriculture*), *fairhood* (*beauty*), *forewit* (*caution*), *bodeword* (*commandment*), *outskirts* (*environs*), *kindle* (*ignite*), *spell* (*incantation*), *freedom* (*liberty*), *bookroom*, *bookcove* (*library*), *maze* (*labyrinth*), *wondertoken* (*miracle*), *chapman* (*merchant*), *upbraid* (*reprimand*), *commonwealth* (*republic*), *upshot* (*conclusion*), *inwit* (*conscience*), *neighbourhood* (*vicinity*) (Jacobs 1952: 27, 36). This is a curious list: items like *spell*, *outskirts*, *kindle*, *freedom*, *maze*, *commonwealth* and *neighbourhood* were and remain part of the standard language repertoire; all the others do indeed go back at least to Middle English; according to OED *upshot* became particularly frequent from about 1830, i.e. before Barnes' literary activity; the others had already become obsolete in standard English (significantly, usually during the Renaissance) but were retained in the dialects. None of them has been reinstated in the standard language.

One of the characteristic features of ethnographic purism is the extent to which only certain dialects are recognised as suitable sources of words. Sometimes the preferred dialects are those which have been least subjected to external influence; in other instances, as in the case of Barnes, the native dialect is selected presumably on grounds of familiarity.

Élitist purism

If ethnographic and archaising purism stress the virtues of the countryside and the past respectively, élitist purism embodies a negative, proscriptive attitude to substandard and regional usage. It corresponds somewhat to Ševčík's prestige and aesthetic purism. It is

---

[14] Thus, the common language has taken on a more and more 'national' and naturally 'popular' character since Finnish nationality was expressed above all in the dialects.

also closely linked with that aspect of archaising purism which venerates models, inasmuch as it is often based on the notion that a language is perfectible.

Élitist purism is perhaps most often associated with the language of court, for which Versailles can be viewed as the paragon. Yet it should also be remembered that most modern standard languages display a liberal dose of élitism, particularly where prestige has to be defended against the democratising force of an army of newly literate speakers. In Soviet Russian, for example, there has been a high degree of closure to colloquial elements in the language – no doubt the result of a need to shore up the standard language following the loss of so many 'norm-bearers' after the Revolution and their replacement by a new élite which emerged from the massive literacy campaigns of the immediate post-revolutionary years (Comrie and Stone 1978: 3–21; Perelmuter 1974; Keipert 1977b).

An interesting example of élitist purism in a non-European context is eighteenth-century Urdu. Formerly there had been a trend of naturalising and hence accommodating Arabic and Persian words in Urdu writing. Now a new movement, reaching its peak at the seat of the Nawab of Oudh in Lucknow, fought to retain the original pronunciation and spelling of Persian and Arabic words, to open Urdu up to fresh importation of Persian words and to purge it of words from neighbouring dialects (Zakir 1983: 426).

Reformist purism

Purism is an important constituent of the conscious efforts to reform, regenerate, renew or resuscitate a language. Not surprisingly, therefore, reformist purism is a salient feature of most of the language renewals of the nineteenth century as well as the more recent efforts to create standard languages. It involves coming to terms with the resources which have accrued during earlier periods of writing (their renunciation, rationalisation or outright acceptance) and adapting the language for its role as a medium of communication in a modern society.

Inasmuch as this reformist orientation may constitute a repudiation of a foreign language model or of a language associated with former political, cultural or linguistic domination it may lead directly to a closure to elements from these languages. It is in this light that we should see the efforts of Swahili, Hausa, Hindi and other languages of the Third World to break with a colonialist past, of Turkish to remove traces of its Ottoman and Islam-centred past, of Hebrew to transform itself from a cult language into a prestigious, polyvalent medium for a reconstituted nation, of Hungarian and Czech to shake off a German-dominated past, or of renaissance French, Italian and English to come to terms with the overwhelming presence of Latin elements in their respective languages at the very time that they were seeking to usurp the latter's social functions.

Playful purism

Even if motivated by non-rational factors, the four forms of purism we have discussed so far are controlled by *bona fide* perceptions and concerns about the native language and are intended to have some improvement of the language as an end result. Not all purism shares this intention; there are instances where the purism is an end in itself, little more than a literary or aesthetic game. Such playful purism is almost invariably the result of individual activity, more likely to irritate, shock or amuse the reader than to convince him of the need to use such idiosyncratic creations.

It is particularly characteristic of the Baroque, where playfulness was a fundamental part of the literary aesthetic. It is hard, for example, to take seriously some of the inventions of Philip von Zesen, cf. *Gesichtsvorsprung* 'nose' (lit.: facial projection), *Jungfernzwinger* 'nunnery' (lit.: virgins' pen or den), or his Czech contemporaries, cf. *vonocit* 'nose' (lit.: smell-feel). Indeed, Dobrovský was right to say that his compatriots Rosa, Pohl, Schimek and Tham had created these and similar words 'oft durch ihren spielenden Witz'[15] (Dobrovský 1799: 67).

While in most cases these idiosyncratic neologisms replace well-established foreign words there are also cases such as the creations of Wolke quoted in Chapter 3 which are designed to deconstruct the semantics of a particular word by simultaneously replacing the lexical item and its referent. Such an orientation is interesting precisely because it lies outside the general pattern of linguistic purification.

Xenophobic purism

Xenophobic purism involves the eradication or replacement of foreign elements, whether their source is specified (*targeted xeno-phobia*) or unspecified (*general xenophobia*). This distinction, which corresponds to Ševčík's xenophobic and x-phobic categories, is

[15] often as a witty game [lit. through their playful wit]

important because it involves totally different attitudes in the speech community. Furthermore, there are other important distinctions (for example, between loanwords and calques) which are essential for understanding the intensity of puristic feeling.

Anti-purism

According to Brozović (1970: 79), anti-purism is a puristic reaction to a manifestation of purism; that is to say it is directed at the results – positive or negative – of puristic intervention. Potentially, therefore, it is of great importance both in the process of evaluating purism and in diminishing its impact. It is most often directed at xenophobic purism but may adopt any of the other orientations, except that it is rarely playful.

Anti-purism should, of course, be carefully distinguished from apuristic attitudes, which proceed without reference to purism and from rational critiques of purism, which, although seeking to undermine its credibility and expose its lack of rationality, do not attempt to undo its effects.

A framework of puristic orientations

Playful purism and anti-purism may be immediately excluded from our framework as not having a single orientation. The primary distinction for the other five puristic orientations is that between the external perspective (xenophobic purism), which is unmarked, and the internal perspectives (all other types), which are marked. It is understandable, therefore, why purism as a whole should be widely identified with xenophobic purism, the archetypal puristic orientation.

The internal perspectives are arranged on two evaluative axes: social and temporal. The ethnographic and élitist orientations are based on the evaluative dimensions of language attitudes (Ryan *et al.* 1982: 8–9), whereas the reformist and archaising orientations are based on the standardisation/vitality determinants of attitudes to variation (Ryan *et al.* 1982: 3–4) (see Figure 4).

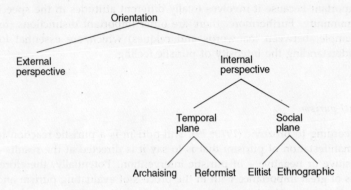

Figure 4: A framework of puristic orientations

Typically, xenophobic purism exists in conjunction with a member of one or both of the pairs of internal perspectives. Each member of these pairs may occur in isolation or in conjunction with one of the members of the other pair. This arrangement may be illustrated in the form of a cube of orientations (Figure 5).

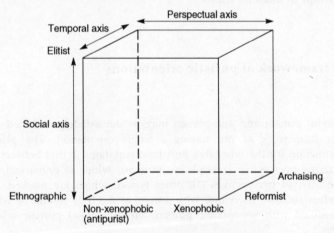

Figure 5: A cube of puristic orientations

Acccording to this scheme, the following 17 puristic orientations are possible:

1. One dimensional: 5 (xenophobic, élitist, ethnographic, reformist, archaising).

82

2. Two dimensional: 8 (xenophobic/élitist, xenophobic/archaising, xenophobic/reformist, xenophobic/archaising, élitist/reformist, élitist/archaising, ethnographic/reformist, ethnographic/archaising.
3. Three dimensional: 4 xenophobic/élitist/reformist, xenophobic/élitist/archaising, xenophobic/ethnographic/reformist, xenophobic/ethnographic/archaising).

In addition, this scheme allows for compromise positions along one or more of the axes.

The taxonomy of puristic orientations presented here covers all the forms of purism described in the literature. Furthermore, this schematic structure offers a typological framework against which a given instance of purism may be accurately described and compared with other instances. We are now ready to look at the processes which these puristic orientations set in motion.

CHAPTER 5

The purification process

Introduction

While it may be proper to view purification as a single unified activity, there is also a great deal to be learned about its nature by examining in turn the discrete events involved in this process. Such a processual approach also helps identify the tasks confronting the would-be purist.

Purism is an attempt to intervene in the development of a language. This *prescriptive intervention* – to use the term introduced by Wexler (1974) at the suggestion of Uriel Weinreich – consists of eight separate, but closely related modes of activity: recognition of need, identification of targets, censorship, eradication, prevention, replacement, reception and evaluation.

Recognition of need

There can be no purism – not even of the *playful* variety – without recognition of the fact that a language is in need of purification. This consciousness of supposed deficiencies is dependent on extralinguistic factors: a speech community can remain oblivious to, or choose to ignore, elements which to others at a different time are deemed undesirable. For example, ignorance of the structures of Slovak following its emergence in the second half of the nineteenth century as an autonomous standard language prevented a puristic reaction to the whole-scale borrowing of abstract words from closely related Czech (Horecký 1967: 42–3). Only with the growth of linguistic knowledge and of anti-Czech nationalism in the 1920s and 1930s did such a reaction set in.

It is not only essential that purists themselves recognise the need for purism, the fact must also be communicated to their compatriots. An important aspect of puristic activity, therefore, is the propagation of ideas about the deficiencies and threats to the well-being of the native language. These Jeremiads and threnodies for the plight of the language if it is not liberated from certain undesirable elements constitute a high proportion of the literature on purism. Despite the different literary traditions and national characteristics with which they are imbued, these apologias have a remarkable stylistic and textual consistency. The following extract from a letter of John Cheke (1514–57) to Thomas Hoby dated 16 July 1557 may serve as a typical example:

> I am of this opinion that our own tung shold be written cleane and pure, vnmixt and vnmangeled with borrowing of other tunges, wherein if we take not heed bi tijm, euer borrowing and neuer payeng, she shall be fain to keep her house as bankrupt, for then doth our tung naturallie and praisiblie vtter her meaning, when ſe bouroweth no counterfeitness of other tunges to attire her self withall, but vseth plainlie her own with such shift, as nature, craft, experiens, and folowing of other excellent doth lead her vnto: and if she want at ani tijm (as being vnperfight she must), yet let her borow with suche bashfulnes, that it mai appeer that, if either the mould of our own tung could serue to fascion a woord of our own, or if the old denisoned wordes could content and ease this neede, we wold not boldly venture of vnknowen wordes. (Quoted in Prein 1909: 29)

An alternative way of highlighting the dangers confronting a language is to indulge in outrageous parody, as in this letter supposedly written by a Lincolnshire clergyman seeking preferment in *The Art of Rhetorique* (London 1553) by Thomas Wilson (1525–1581):

> Ponderyng, expeeding, and revoluting with my self, your ingent affabilitie, and ingenious capacitie, for mundane affaires: I can not but celebrate and extolle your magnificalle dexteritie, aboue all other. for how could you haue adepted soche illustrate prerogative, and domesticall superioritie, if the fecunditie of your ingenie, had not been so fertile, and wonderfull pregnant. Now therefore, beyng accersited, to soche splendent renoune, and dignitie spendidious: I doubt not but you will adiuuate soche poore adnichilate orphanes, as whilome ware condisciples with you, and of antique familaritie in Lincolne shire. Emong whom, I beyng a scholasticall panion, obtestate your sublimitie, to extoll myne infirmitie. There is a sacerdotall dignitie, in my native countrey, contigate to me, where I nowe contemplate: whiche youre worshipfull benignitie could sone impetrate for me, if it would like you, to extende your sedules, and collaude me in theim,

to the right honourable lorde Chauncellour, or rather Archigrammarian of Englande. You knowe my literature, you knowe the pastoral promotion, I obtestate your confidence, and as you knowe my condigne merites, for soche a compendious liuyng. But nowe a relinquishe, to fatigate your intelligence, with any more friuolous verbositie, and therfore, he that rules the climates, be euermore your beautreux, your fortresse, and your bulwarke. Amen. Dated at my Dome, or rather Mansion place in Lincolnshire, the penulte of the moneth Sextile. Anno Millimo, quillimo, trillimo. Per me Johannes Octo. (Quoted in Prein 1909: 28)

Such output is, of course, only one side of the debate. Those opposed to purism may explicitly reject not only the claims that a language is in need of purification but the very notion of purity as an attribute of language. They too use tracts, sometimes but not always calmer and more reasonable in tone, to combat the views of the purists and win over the opinion of those as yet uncommitted.

Identification of targets

It is precisely at the identification stage that decisions are made about what categories of words are deemed to be desirable (Thomas 1988b: 99). As we have seen, the various types of purism identify different sets of targets for their disapproval. Since this identification is so crucial to the form purism takes in a given language it is essential to say something of the premises and linguistic knowledge on which it is based.

Even the task of identifying foreign elements is not as easy as it might at first appear. We cannot always rely on a kind editor putting foreign words in one script and native ones in another as in late nineteenth-century German (Schultz 1888: 38). Even in Basque with no known cognates mistakes are sometimes made in the recognition of loanwords (Rebuschi 1983: 127). This is not only because words which are familiar to the ear are readily accepted as native (as with German loans in Dutch, see de Vooys 1946: 45) but also one of the marks of successful language reform – as advocated, for example by Sir Sayyid Ahmad in the case of Urdu (Zaidi 1983: 420) – is the incorporation of foreign elements in such a way that their presence is virtually undetectable even to the trained eye. How much greater, therefore, might be the temptation for the uninitiated. In Nazi Germany, for example, it was noted of Yiddishisms that even though their low stylistic level would be obvious to the most unlearned speaker their origin would not (von Polenz 1967: 90). On the other hand, paranoia about foreign influence can lead to unfounded suspicion about the origins of a given linguistic element. Indeed, Zubatý went so far as to transform this obsession into one of his two ironies on Czech purism: 'everything which in Czech expression corresponds to German is a Germanism'. His other irony, incidentally, is also worth repeating: 'if anything can be said in Czech in two ways one of them must be wrong' (Mathesius 1933: 81).

It is not surprising, therefore, that not infrequently the words which purists wish to remove as 'foreign' are actually native words. For example, the German purist von Zesen wanted to replace some items of impeccable native pedigree presumably because of their similarity to their Latin cognates: *Nase, Ohr, Auge* (Kirkness 1975: 102). Some Czech purists of the late eighteenth century not only took exception to the Czech cognates of these very same words (Bílý 1904: 68) – surely no coincidence – but even went to the trouble of coining *mořská řetkev* 'horseradish', a blatant calque of G *Meerrettich* on the mistaken assumption that the native word *křen* was a loan from G *Chren*, when in fact the German (dialectal) word is a loan from Czech (Thomas 1978b).

There are also instances of the reverse: the acceptance as native of a word of undoubted foreign origin. For example, Schottelius, a German purist of the seventeenth century, thought *Idiot, Elephant, Quartier* to be genuine German words (Kirkness 1975: 40). Similarly, Turkish purists were convinced that *kand* 'village' was a dialectalism (and therefore acceptable), while in fact it is a loan from Iranian (Bazin 1983: 168–9). Some Iranian purists were convinced that many so-called Arabic words had been borrowed by Arabic from Iranian at an earlier stage (Jazayery 1983: 254–5). This is somewhat reminiscent of the Sun Language theory propagated by Turkish purists which held that all languages are ultimately derived from Turkish thus providing a convenient justification for the large numbers of western loanwords in modern reformed Turkish (Heyd 1954).

On a more sophisticated level, identification of suitable targets for purism does not end with a successful etymology. *Á propos* of loanwords in Bulgarian, for example, Moskov (1976: 58–9) proposes a number of questions to be asked, even after the source has been determined:

1. Is there an exact Bulgarian equivalent?
2. Is it phonologically and morphologically adapted?
3. Is it usable in various styles?

4. Is it widespread?
5. When was it loaned?
6. Is it found in other European languages?

The answers to these questions are crucial in deciding which, if any, foreign words are to be removed.

For some purists, identification is to be determined by the intuition of the individual. Thus while Aasen identified the words to be eradicated from Nynorsk as foreign on the basis of their outer form and whether they conformed to native phonological and morphological patterns (Gerdener 1986: 39, 155), the *Samnorsk* movement introduced as a decisive new principle for deciding on a word's acceptability not etymology but 'die Frage, ob es als norw. empfunden wird oder nicht'[16] (Gerdener 1986: 159). Hellewik, for example, maintained that the language feeling of the individual must be the deciding factor; for him Anglo-Saxonisms constituted a greater danger than old German loanwords which had long been integrated into Norwegian: better, for example, *bestanddel*, a calque of G *Bestandteil* current in the other Scandinavian languages, than the loanword *komponent* (Gerdener 1986: 164). However, such subjectivity can quickly lead to anarchy.

While identification is an obvious prerequisite for the other modes of the purification process, it can happen that purism – and not just of the *playful* variety – does not proceed beyond this stage. This is because of purism's symbolic or rhetorical function: 'the existence of unwanted material in a language may be bewailed without any action being taken or advocated; the very act of declaring words non-native may be "cathartic" in itself' (Thomas 1988b: 99).

Censorship

The husband whom we observed earlier drawing his wife's attention to her use of loanwords when speaking East Sutherland Gaelic (Dorian 1981: 101) was indulging in a form of *censorship*. Editors with their blue pencil carry out similar functions on behalf of, but not necessarily with the complicity of, the author of a text. None of this

[16] the question whether it is perceived as Norwegian or not

editorial censorship, however, quite matches in its infringement on human freedom the case of the President of Czechoslovakia and quondam dissident playwright Václav Havel, who according to an article in *The Independent* (25 February 1989) was allowed to write to his wife Olga from prison in 1979 provided his letters met a number of formal conditions. Among these was the stipulation that they should contain no foreign expressions!

The character Sologdin in Solzhenitsyn's novel *First Circle*, who has privately abjured the use of foreign words and makes a note of each time he transgresses, is practising *self-censorship*. A graphic illustration of self-censoring purism is provided in the autobiography of Anthony Burgess (1986: 198–9), an author with a deep sensitivity for linguistic problems. While at Manchester University in 1939 he met a student named Ian McColl:

> McColl was so soaked in Anglo-Saxon that it was a natural instinct for him to avoid Latinisms and Hellenisms even in colloquial speech. He was quite prepared, like the poet Barnes, to call an omnibus a folkwain or a telephone a fartalker. He knew German but hated the Nazis, who, after all, were only disinfecting their language of exoticims in McColl's own manner.

Burgess quotes from a poem of McColl's in which he uses the phrase *multitudinously puked*. This 'blatant Latinism', writes Burgess, 'he excused since it was being vomited up or out'. Using similar imagery but on a somewhat more elevated poetic plane, Ben Jonson in his *Poetaster* (1600) makes a plea for self-censoring purism when he has 'Horace' (i.e. Jonson himself) tell 'Caesar' that he has an emetic to help 'Crispinus' (i.e. John Marston (1575–1634)) deliver himself of a whole host of Latinate words, whereupon 'Virgil' gives the following advice to the writer:

> You must not hunt for wild out-landish Termes,
> To stuffe out a peculiar Dialect;
> But let your Matter runne before your Words:
> And if, at any time, you chaunce to meete
> Some Gallo-Belgick Phrase, you shall not straight
> Racke your poor Verse to giue it entertainment,
> But let it passe: and doe not thinke your selfe
> Much damnified, if you doe leave it out,
> When not your Vnderstanding nor the Sense
> Could well receiue it. This fair Abstinence,
> In time, will render you more sound and Clear.

In all these cases, whether self-inflicted or not, the censorship is undertaken consciously. However, it seems likely that unconscious (self-)-censorship purism is a much more widespread phenomenon and may well be the most prevalent form encountered. In languages like German, Czech, Croatian and Slovene, with their large numbers of synonymous pairs consisting of a foreign word and a natively formed one the individual may unconsciously proscribe the use of the foreign word. A rather different instance of unconscious self-censorship is to be found in Tamil, where speakers indulge in widespread code-switching to English in order to keep their Tamil utterances pure (Zvelebil 1983: 435. Such code-switching, which is also used during moments of excitement and embarrassment and for the discussion of topics subject to taboo in the native language, is a feature of all stylistic registers of the written and spoken language (Zvelebil 1983: 436). This process must by its very nature remain unproven, but its outcomes, e.g. a text or speech act which excludes certain items more than the statistical norm, may be open to investigation.

Compared with the spontaneity of speech, writing involves a greater degree of premeditation. It is only to be expected, therefore, that censorship is a mode of activity most closely identified with formal written discourse. This explains why written texts are relatively free of foreign words compared with the spoken vernacular, cf. the virtual absence of Italianisms in the language of the Dalmatian poets and dramatists of the seventeenth and eighteenth centuries, a time when the spoken language was probably inundated with Italian words (Deanović 1936; Hyrkkänen 1973: 609–15). Indeed, censorship purism constitutes one of the most important features separating linguistic codes in situations of diglossia.

Inasmuch as censorship purism is concerned only with *performance*, it has no direct effect on the inventory of the language itself. Rather its impact is to be seen in the discouragement of certain linguistic items which may result from their absence in an influential journal, the works of a much respected writer, or an authoritative grammar or dictionary. There is plenty of evidence to suggest, however, that it would be unwise to exaggerate the power of dissuasion, implicit in a word's absence from such sources.

Conducted in isolation from the other modes of puristic activity, censorship is essentially negative. It proscribes some linguistic item without suggesting a suitable alternative. More than any other mode of purism, it curbs the expressive freedom of the language concerned. This is the case in Nynorsk, for example, where the prohibition against certain suffixes ultimately of German origin is essentially unhelpful to the predicament of the native speaker searching for the means to express himself: 'Die heute verbreitete Abwehrhaltung, die diesen Einfluss zu ignorieren versucht, müsste dabei allerdings durch eine konstruktivere Haltung ersetzt werden'[17] (Gerdener 1986: 305).

Eradication

The activity most often associated with purism is the removal of undesirable elements, be they well-established items or those threatening to inundate the language. Strictly speaking, the image of *eradication* is somewhat misleading: although a word can certainly be considered no longer a part of the standard language, it can never be actually destroyed; it may lie dormant waiting like fat-cells in the body to resume its former activity. In the words of Mary Douglas: 'That which is negated is not thereby removed' (Douglas 1966: 163). Many foreign words 'eradicated' during the European language renewals of the nineteenth century, for example, were reinstated later in a milder puristic climate.

The successful purging of established words clearly requires greater effort than stemming the tide of new words. For this reason, and because many purists would happily confer rights of citizenship on well-adapted and customary loanwords, the removal of old words of foreign origin is symptomatic of a much more extreme attitude. Hence, the distinction between the two targets of eradication is a useful measure of the intensity as well as the pragmatism of the purism involved.

Purism does not always entail eradication of undesirable words. It may be content to limit their stylistic range, to promote a native synonym without insisting on the removal of the targeted word, or simply to preach restraint in their use. However, such purism may be characterised as very mild.

Prevention

Prevention is the act of safeguarding a language from elements yet to gain admittance. This activity is quite rare and limited to

---

[17] The currently widespread defensive posture which attempts to ignore this influence would have to be replaced to be sure by a more constructive attitude.

those language situations where a language academy or its equivalent – often in collaboration with scientific institutions, patent offices and inventors – attempts to provide an appropriate name for a newly discovered or created object before the general public has the chance of naming it spontaneously. One thinks, for example, of the care taken by the Hebrew Language Academy to provide Hebrew appellations for items of technology or of the elaborate precautions taken by the *Allgemeiner Deutscher Sprachverein* to think up words with native morphemes for 'telephone', 'radio' and 'television' (*Fernsprecher*, *Rundfunk* and *Fernsehen* respectively) before the general public became aware of their existence. In the long term their efforts were only partially successful: while *Fernsehen* has established itself in Austria, Switzerland and the former Federal Republic of Germany, *Television* is used in the former German Democratic Republic; *Fernsprecher* and *Rundfunk* have official blessing but in everyday usage *Telefon* and *Radio* appear to predominate.

The importance of the prevention mode is stressed by Gerdener (1986: 20), who defines purism as 'das Bestreben, die eigene Sprache von fremden Einflüssen *freizuhalten* bzw. zu befreien'[18] (my italics). This is accomplished by trying 'für neue Begriffe einheimische Wörter zu finden oder zu bilden, um die Uebernahme eines fremden Wortes zu verhindern'.[19] If this is true for Nynorsk, Gerdener's area of interest, it is even more so for Icelandic, where individual linguists with the cooperation of the media and the Society of Engineers have been highly successful in this enterprise (Groenke 1983: 150). According to a report in *The Independent* of 25 February 1989 (p. 15):

> Computer scientists at the University of Iceland have developed a program capable of recognising neologisms, and helping the operator to coin them according to the complex grammar of the Icelandic language. The program could in theory be used to invent new words in other minority languages [sic!] such as Welsh.

Even so, the internationalism of modern science and technology, the ease of electronic data transfer and the communications revolution mean that only a very determined, well-organised, tightly integrated insular society like that of Iceland can have much chance

[18] 'the attempt to keep the native language free or to liberate it from foreign influences',

[19] 'to find or form domestic words for new concepts in order to prevent the taking over of a foreign word'.

of preventing the introduction of internationally accepted terminology.

Replacement

The provision of an acceptable alternative to the elements identified as undesirable is an essential component of all active purism. Many purists provide long lists of suggested replacements for unacceptable items. Here by way of an example are some words suggested by William Barnes to replace Graeco-Latinisms in English:

> *starkin* (a calque of G *Sternchen*) for *asterisk*, *downcast* (a poetic word) for *abject*, *gainsay* (an archaism) for *contradict*, *withstand* (an old, established word) for *resist*, *mainland* (an old word with a somewhat different meaning) for *continent*, *gleecraft* (an archaism) for *music*, *lawcraft* (a neologism) for *jurisprudence*, *talecraft* (an archaism) for *arithmetic*, *wortlore* (like *wortcunning* a pseudo-archaism) for *botany*, *starcraft* (an archaism) for *astronomy*, *fireghost* (a neologism) for *electricity*, *faith-heat* (a neologism) for *enthusiasm*, *outcullings* (a neologism, cf. G *Auszüge*) for *excerpts*, *wordstore/wordbook* (a calque of Du *woordenboek* or G *Wörterbuch*) for *glossary*, *midding* (a neologism) for *mediocre*, *forspeech/forerede* (both archaisms) for *preface*, *statespell* (a neologism) for *embassy* (Jacobs 1952: 37).

Not infrequently, purists suggest whole categories of possible replacements. Thus, the Czech language renewer Josef Jungmann, drawing on the ideas of Joachim von Campe, suggests the following as acceptable replacements (Auty 1972: 44):

1. The revival of archaic Czech words.
2. Dialectalisms.
3. Words from modern writers.
4. Borrowings from other Slavonic languages.
5. The formation of new words from native elements.
6. Calques.

William Barnes lists ten possible sources (Jacobs 1952: 39):

1. The revival of obsolete words: *inwit* for *conscience*.
2. The invigoration of obsolescent words: *chapman* for *merchant*.
3. The popularisation of socially or geographically restricted words: *outskirts* for *environs*.
4. Calquing: *greatmindedness* for *magnanimity*.

5. The creation of new words according to Anglo-Saxon word-building patterns: *glee-mote* for *concert*.
6. The use of Anglo-Saxon affixes: *fair-hood* for *beauty*.
7. Composing nouns from phrasal units: *out-cullings* for *excerpts*.
8. The popularisation of a native synonym against a loanword: *freedom* for *liberty*.
9. Increasing native words by adding to parts of speech: *inly* for *internal*.
10. Inventing neologisms: *faith-heat* for *enthusiasm*.

In most cases, the replacement mode is simultaneous with identification and eradication: closure to one source of enrichment presupposes opening to another. It may happen, however, as we saw above, that purists are content to suggest a replacement without insisting on the eradication of the undesirable element. In such cases, one presumes, they are happy in the knowledge that an acceptable alternative exists: the remedy has been provided; it is left to the good sense of the speech community to take appropriate action.

As we saw in the previous chapter, the choices from among the available replacements provide a guide to the typology of the puristic orientation. For this reason, any description of purism needs to concern itself as much with the replacements suggested as with the elements they are destined to replace. Any studies which give a breakdown of the sources of replacement favoured by individuals or groups are therefore especially valuable. Jacobs (1952: 71–2), for example, provides an estimate of Barnes' replacements:

1. Direct revivals of Old or Middle English words: 7 percent.
2. Neologisms: 43 percent.
3. Dialectalisms: 14 percent.
4. Words advanced or resuscitated: 30 percent.
5. Words with new meanings: 6 percent.

Figures are available for another famous purist – Philip von Zesen (Blume 1967: 175–80):

1. Word-building calques: 36 percent, of which:
   (a) *Lehnübersetzungen*: 53 percent, of which:
      (i) from Greek and Latin: 22 percent
      (ii) from Dutch: 78 percent
   (b) *Lehnübertragungen*: 47 percent
2. Semantic calques: 35 percent
3. Native neologisms: 29 percent

One of the ironies of purism is that the replacements suggested may themselves be subject to puristic criticism. For example, an anonymous Serbian purist wrote in *Javor* in 1863 that it would be better to use a foreign word than many of the puristically inspired and in his view badly formed neologisms emanating from Croatian Zagreb (Herrity 1978: 208).

Reception

The replacements proposed by individual purists may elicit praise, acceptance, ridicule or outright condemnation. Indeed, to a great extent the reception by the speech community determines the impact of the active modes of purism: 'Darüber, ob puristische Bemühungen Erfolg haben, entscheidet vor allem die Einstellung der Sprecher gegenüber den vorgeschlagenen Wörtern'[20] (Gerdener 1986: 21). For example, public support for the reform programme of the Persian language academy (*Farhangestān*), created in 1934 by personal decree of Reza Shah Pahlavi and reinstituted after the war by his son, was minimal, only a small élite being interested in language purification (Jazayery 1983: 265). In Turkey, too, there was opposition – in part a conservative religious backlash – to the artificiality and impoverishment resulting from the efforts of the Turkish Linguistic Society to banish Persian and Arabic words (Heyd 1954: 44). There is, however, fortunately no parallel, at least as far as I am aware, to the way the moderate and pragmatic reforms of the Persian purist Kasravi were received: he was assassinated by Moslem fundamentalists (Jazayery 1983: 258).

However, our concern should be not so much for the fate of the purist himself – though this admittedly somewhat extreme case does illustrate the heat of passion which puristic polemics can engender – but for the extent to which his attempts are accepted, resisted, ridiculed, rejected or simply ignored by his compatriots. It is not uncommon for words to be resisted or ridiculed at first appearance only to gain full acceptance later. While von Zesen's contemporaries, for example, reacted with amusement rather than imitation to many of his suggested neologisms, his successors proceeded to adopt many of them without trouble (Blume 1967: 195–6). Many of the new coinages in Danish in the 1740s were modelled on German calques of

[20] Whether puristic efforts are successful is decided above all by the attitude of the speakers towards the suggested words

Romance words: *beundre* 'to admire' (cf. G *bewundern*), *virksom* 'active, effective' (cf. G *wirksam*), *fordom* 'prejudice' (cf. G *Vorurteil*), *lidenskab* 'passion' (cf. G *Leidenschaft*). 'Though at first ridiculed by some writers a surprising number of such neologisms were soon generally accepted instead of, or as current synonyms of, their foreign equivalents' (Karker 1983: 286).

The belated acceptance of items proposed by purists is to be explained not only by the resistance to innovation, so characteristic of speech communities, but also by the undoubted lag which exists between public opinion on the one hand and the actual state of a language and linguistic theory on the other (Tejnor *et al*. 1982: 301). Conversely, public opinion may continue to be supportive of purism long after it has ceased to be justified by functional criteria.

Purists may play an active role in promoting the acceptance of their suggested replacements. A stratagem employed almost universally by purists is to put the word to be replaced in brackets. This serves as an aid to recognition and memory. Others highlight neologisms with asterisks. Juraj Palkovič, a disciple of Josef Dobrovský, in order not to spoil the purity of the Czech language, decided to use an even more elaborate marking scheme for neologisms: 'Wörter, selbst jene die von mir herrühren u. in meinen Schriften vorkommen . . . mit + u. mit ? (ohne übrigens über ihren Werth od. Unwerth abzusprechen), u. meines Erachtens schlechten, mit ++, mit +++ bezeichnet'[21] (Palkovič 1820: ix). The Norwegian purist Aasen promoted domestic words by giving them a proper description in his dictionaries, while loanwords were simply listed without comment – a manoeuvre sure to be noticed by anyone using the dictionaries (Gerdener 1986: 37–8). The Bulgarian purist Aprilov suggested that teachers hang up lists of foreign words and their Bulgarian equivalents in the classroom for their pupils to study (Moskov 1958: 18).

It is not uncommon for purists to promote their cause by public campaigns. In the nineteenth century, for example, the Hungarian Academy offered prizes for essays on the the requisite measures for the correction of Hungarian (Sauvageot 1971: 291–3). In the 1930s newspapers were active in the popularisation of native sporting and technical terms by organising competitions. The degree of public interest can be gauged by the fact that the newspaper *Nemzeti sport* received some 4,000 letters containing over 12,000 suggestions for replacements of loanwords; 150 were accepted by the editorial boards

---

[21] Words – even those originating with me or attested in my writings [are] marked with + or with ? (irrespective of their worth), while those which in my opinion are bad are marked with ++ and +++

and some of them are now freely used by the younger generation to the exclusion of their native equivalents (Fodor 1983a: 64–5). Recent efforts have been less successful: in 1975 the Hungarian Chamber of Commerce advertised a competition to replace *know-how*, *marketing*, *public relations*, but to no avail (Fodor 1983a: 67). In Poland, too, there was a competition before the Second World War to replace *skyscraper*; the prize was awarded for *drapacz chmur* (a calque of G *Wolkenkratzer*). After the war there was an opinion poll to find a substitute for *weekend*, but none of the suggestions found favour. More successful was the attempt by the magazine *Życie praktyczne* to replace the German loanword *szlafrok*: the winner was *podomka* (from *dom* 'house') (Cienkowski 1983: 345). In South Africa support for the movement to purify Afrikaans of Anglicisms was mobilised with the cooperation of the universities, the South African Academy and the press with the result that *weekend* was replaced by *naweek* and *bar* by *kroeg* (Botha 1983: 235).

Potentially, the most influential factor in the reception of puristic activity is the registration of the elements deemed desirable in dictionaries, grammars and guides to good usage. This is the purpose of John Evelyn (1620–1706) in proposing to Wyche, the chairman of the committee for improving the English language, the publication in an appendix to a forthcoming grammar of 'a Lexicon or collection of all the pure English words by themselves; then those which are derivative from others' as well as 'a full catalogue of exotic words, such as are daily minted by our Logodaedali' (Flasdieck 1928: 31–2). In many cases, of course, the purists were the recognised arbiters of good usage and have themselves compiled important standardising dictionaries and grammars: Josef Jungmann for Czech, Bogoslav Šulek for Croatian, Joachim von Campe for German, Ivar Aasen for Nynorsk.

In the case of Portuguese, from the early nineteenth century puristic activity has led to the publication of glossaries and critical essays advocating the replacement of foreign words and constructions. Some of these replacements have become fixtures: *pedibola* (a calque) for *futebol*, *verificação* for *controle* (Malaca Casteiliero 1983: 408). In Icelandic, too, dictionaries played a large part in furthering puristic ends (Groenke 1983: 146). In Nynorsk, the situation is more complicated: despite being registered in the dictionaries (including the influential *Norsk Ordbog*) Bokmål words of Danish origin are not regarded as 'vollständig akzeptable Wörter im guten, schriftlichen Nn.'[22] (Gerdener 1986: 140; for a comprehensive picture of the impact

---

[22] totally acceptable words in good written Nynorsk

of purism on Norwegian dictionaries, word-lists and handbooks see 133–54).

Conversely, the cause of purism can also be ill-served by dictionaries. For example, the Croatian–German dictionary of Broz and Iveković (1901) refused to register many of the puristically inspired neologisms of the middle third of the nineteenth century (Thomas 1988a: 143–4). In this, they were supported by several handbooks and grammars (for example, Maretić 1899, 1924). These words were, thus, consigned to a state of limbo. As a result, while some words continued in usage despite dictionary disapproval many others did not survive. According to Jacobs (1952: 72–4), the Oxford English Dictionary has consistently ignored the words proposed by the English nineteenth-century purist William Barnes with the result that very few of them have gained acceptance in everyday English usage. By Jacobs' calculations only 77 items (i.e. 1 percent of Barnes' proposals) have been registered. The culprit, he suspects, was F. J. Furnivall (1825–1910), editor of OED. Be that as it may, it is surely the case that many of Barnes' suggestions would have been unacceptable in the climate of late Victorian England, quite apart from the fact that OED was an historical dictionary not a prescriptive guide to contemporary usage.

Of all the modes of purism, reception is surely the most varied. This is not only because of the number of possible reactions to the stimulus of purification but also because it is susceptible to the complexities of a whole range of *sui generis* language situations. To describe the reception of puristic endeavours, therefore, is to become involved in problems of language policy, language planning and language cultivation. Yet, it is this very interaction between the purist and the speech community he seeks to serve which provides the colour and vitality to any account of purism.

Evaluation

The next stage involves an assessment of the previous modes – separately or as a whole – by the persons active in them or by others. If the evaluation is positive, the intervention may be pronounced successful, and the process is more or less complete. However, since the risk of further infiltration cannot be ruled out, continued vigilance may be recommended. If for any reason the evaluation is negative, however, the question must be re-opened. In cases where the initial need for purism is called into question the whole process may be aborted. Where the evaluation leads to a new identification of targets or possible allowable replacements, purism will continue but with a fresh orientation. In some cases, there may be no evaluation. This may mean either that the previous activity has simply been accepted without demur or that it has been quietly forgotten. It may also happen that the evaluation takes place only after a long time-lag.

Summary

The process of purification can be divided, then, into eight discrete but closely linked modes of activity. While it is usual for all of them to be constituent elements in any purist movement, it may happen that some stages are absent. The first two modes constitute the absolute minimum.

The order in which the modes of activity have been presented represents the logical sequence, but on occasion there may be some regression. The purification process like language intervention in general (Radovanović, forthcoming) is essentially cyclical in nature. On completion of the cycle, the intervention begins again at the point required by the evaluation, or else ceases. This is presented schematically in Figure 6.

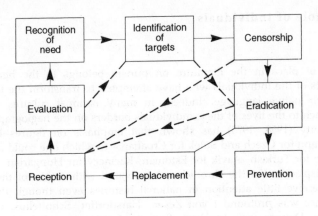

Figure 6: A flow chart of purification processes

CHAPTER 6

The social organisation of puristic intervention

Introduction

All forms of purism except the self-censoring variety presuppose some attempt to influence the usage of others. In Chapter 5 we examined the processes whereby prescriptive intervention is carried out and some of the methods employed to facilitate acceptance by the public at large of its results. This chapter examines the role of individuals, élites and institutions in promoting these reforms.

The role of individuals

Pride of place in the literature on purism belongs to the heroic exploits of the individuals who have attempted to transform the face of their native language. Indeed, in many national cultures the approach to the lives of these individuals borders on the hagiographical. Auty (1958, 1973) has shown that emphasis on figures like Jungmann for Czech and Šulek for Croatian – to which one could add Gökalp for Turkish, Aavik for Estonian, Kacinczy for Hungarian – is not misplaced. Yet the chronicles also abound with names of those who receive little attention in national histories even though their influence was profound : von Zesen, Harsdörffer, Schottelius, von Campe, Dunger, von Stephan, Sarrazin for German; Babukić for Croatian; Hallgrimsson for Icelandic; Benyák, Faludi, Pintér, Nagy for Hungarian; Hooft, Sterin, Kok for Dutch; Stiernhielm, Columbus, von

Dalin, Tegnér for Swedish; Eilschow, Fleischer, Sneedorff for Danish; Yakhinson, Max Weinreich for Yiddish. Others have been chiefly remembered – sometimes unfairly – as objects of vilification or ridicule: Barnes for English; Bogorov for Bulgarian; Kurelac for Croatian; Shishkov for Russian; Rosa, Pohl, Haller for Czech. However, a mere roll-call of saints and sinners is unsatisfactory. We need to know more about their social, professional and age profiles, their linguistic knowledge and their general frame of mind.

The disfavour with which many professional linguists have regarded purism has meant that the purist ranks have been filled largely by amateur enthusiasts. For example, Behagel, Dunger and Kluge were the only prominent linguists who actively supported the *Allgemeiner Deutscher Sprachverein* (hereafter: ADSV); most were fundamentally opposed to it. Many of the committee members were amateurs, and its presidents included museum directors, engineers, army officers and construction consultants (Dunger 1910: 4). Not surprisingly, these amateur enthusiasts had different levels of understanding of the way that norms operate in standard languages but for the most part were guided by linguistic intuition. Such intuition is based more on how would-be codifiers think they speak – or should speak – than on how they in fact speak (Bartsch 1987: 91): it is adjusted towards the usage of 'great authors' and selected representatives of the speech community.

Almost invariably, purism among non-linguists tends to be more extreme. Consequently, the growing professionalisation of puristic circles resulting from the validation of purism within the various theories of language cultivation has had a decidedly moderating effect. This can be corroborated by examining a complete run of one of the many puristically inspired journals.

If professional linguists have been rather under-represented in the puristic pantheon, writers and educators have certainly made up for this deficiency. Indeed, the charge has often been made that purism is the domain of less gifted writers, especially those of a pedantic bent. A typical unflattering portrait is given by Goethe: 'geistlose Menschen. . . welche auf die Sprachreinigung mit zu grossem Eifer dringen: denn da sie den Wert eines Ausdrucks nicht zu schätzen wissen, so finden sie gar leicht ein Surrogat, welches Ihnen eben so bedeutend scheint'[23] (quoted in Kirkness 1975: 271). While it is true that many second-rate or insignificant writers have espoused the

---

[23] dull people who insist on language purism with too much zeal, for, as they do not know how to assess the value of an expression, they have no trouble finding a surrogate which seems to them to be equivalent in every way

cause of purism, it cannot be denied that proponents of language purification have also borne such illustrious names as Daniel Defoe, John Dryden, John Evelyn, Joseph Addison, Noah Webster, Jonathan Swift and Ben Jonson – to name only representatives of a literary tradition not normally associated with a concern about foreign words.

At the same time, it is important to remember that the most vociferous – and certainly the most effective – opposition to purism has also been conducted by writers. This opposition is prompted not only by doubts about the efficacity or necessity of purism but also by a deep concern about the unwarranted restrictions it puts on the freedom of individual expression. There is no more eloquent testimony to the creative writer's instinctive distaste for purism than this poem by Goethe and entitled 'Die Sprachreiniger':

> Gott dank! dass uns so wohl geschah:
> Der Tyrann sitzt auf Helena!
> Doch liess sich nur der eine bannen,
> Wir haben jetzo hundert Tyrannen;
> Die schmieden, uns gar unbequem,
> Ein neues Kontinental-system.
> Teutschland soll rein sich isolieren,
> Einen Pestkordon um die Grenze führen,
> Dass nicht einschleiche fort und dort
> Kopf, Körper und Schwanz von fremdem Wort.[24]

(Goethe 1988: 741)

As a postscript, Goethe has added: 'Wir sollen auf unseren Lorbeern ruhn,/Nichts weiter denken, als wir tun.'[25]

It is in literary circles, then, that the puristic debate has been at its most intense. This is not surprising when we recall the importance of aesthetic considerations in the formation of puristic and anti-puristic attitudes. Furthermore, as we shall see in the next chapter, purism is intimately connected with stylistic variation within standard languages.

---

[24] Thanks be to God that the tyrant sits on St Helena! Yet no sooner has one tyrant been banished than now we have a hundred. They are forging – to our great discomfort – a new continental system. Germany shall be isolated uncorrupted, shall draw a plague barrier around the border so that neither the head, the body nor the tail of any foreign word should sneak in at any time.

[25] We are to rest on our laurels, think nothing more than we do.

It is important to bear in mind the various modes of the purification process in which individuals have been involved and the opportunities they have had to influence the usage of others. Some, like Mustafa Kemal Atatürk of Turkey, Reza Shah Pahlavi of Persia and Friedrich Wilhelm IV and Kaiser Wilhelm II of Prussia, were little more than political instigators – though, admittedly Friedrich Wilhelm has been accredited with the replacement of *Kapitän* by *Hauptmann* (Kirkness 1975: 363). Such was the dictatorial authority of the Shah that purism was foisted on a largely unwilling populace. The opponents of purism kept silent as long as he was in power, and large sectors of the terminological vocabulary were reformed. However, his abdication in 1941 led to a rapid reversal of the earlier puristic policy (Jazavery 1983: 252). Prominent writers might also have the authority to propose language reform without being involved in the *minutiae* of purification. Even so, their espousal of the puristic cause is no guarantee of success. For example, the characteristically radical puristic proposals made by Dean Swift had little practical effect in the British Isles; only in America were they taken up by the anti-British purist John Adams, second President of the United States (Flasdieck 1928: 86–7).

A more active role in the purification process, however, was often played by those occupying key administrative positions such as Otto Sarrazin, the Prussian Minister for Transportation, who saw to it that German equivalents for railway terminology were found and propagated. Among the words – all of them now fully part of the everyday vocabulary – for which Sarrazin was responsible are: *Abteil* 'compartment' (for *Coupe*), *Bahnsteig* 'platform' (for *Perron*), *Fahrgast* 'passenger' (for *Passagier*) (Kirkness 1975: 367). Another keen purifier in the field of communications was the Prussian Postmaster Heinrich von Stephan, who in 1874 and 1875 was responsible for coining such words as *Fahrschein* 'ticket' (for *Passagierblatt*), *postlagernd* (for *Poste restante*), *Postkarte* 'postcard' (for *Correspondenz-Karte*), *Umschlag* 'envelope' (for *Couvert*). The success of these coinings is attributable – at least in part – to the energy and decisiveness shown by von Stephan's officials (Kirkness 1975: 363).

More often, however, the image of the purist is that of the scholar working away quietly in his study surrounded by massive dictionaries attempting – sometimes in vain – to find an equivalent in his native tongue for a word in a foreign text which he needs to translate. Such a man was the Czech reformer Josef Jungmann, whose first important literary activity was his translation of Milton's *Paradise Lost*, which already demonstrates his ability to coin new words (Jedlička 1948). In 1820 Jungmann produced a small book entitled

Slovesnost, in which he provided a moderate puristic framework for the further lexical enrichment of Czech. The crowning achievement of his life, the publication in 1835 of the first modern dictionary of Czech, was made possible by the cooperation of a small group of friends, experts in a number of key disciplines, who supplied him with the terminology so essential to the fledgeling standard language.

The role of groups and societies

The assistance Sarrazin obtained from his minions and Jungmann from his friends serves to remind us that language reform is more likely to be effective when it involves collective action than when conducted by individuals acting independently. Indeed, language reformers of all persuasions have long since recognised the advantages accruing from association with like-minded individuals. Such association takes many forms, but underlying all of them is a recognition of the importance of élites as organising and galvanising forces. It also involves suppression of individualism, as can be seen in the case of the Illyrian Movement which was responsible for the major reform of Croatian in the nineteenth century:

> When we come to look at the human beings who espoused Illyrianism, we are struck by their remarkable unity of purpose and communality of outlook, presumably because they were able to suppress some of their individualism in a common stance in which they all believed so fervently. A similarity of social background, a common Romantic frame of mind, the sense of belonging to the generation entirely educated in a Habsburg Empire slowly recovering from the Napoleonic Wars were the fuel which needed only Gaj's charisma to set it alight. It was of enormous importance for the lexical reform of Cr[oatian] that this surge of energy be channelled into a cooperative effort rather than be dissipated in individualistic wordmaking. (Thomas 1988a: 158)

In neighbouring Hungary, too, language reforms were carried out not by central organisation but by collective private intitiative (Sauvageot 1971: 263).

It would be naive, however, to suggest that individuals are always able or even willing to suppress their own views. Most groups have witnessed some degree of internal polemic between moderates and extremists, pragmatists and idealists, populists and élitists, reformers and conservatives, particularists and cosmopolitans. These clashes may remain unresolved or end in victory for one of the parties. More usually, however, they end in some form of *modus vivendi*, often encapsulated in a short statement of objectives and principles as in the case of the Hebrew Pure Language Society and its successors, where changes in orientation and in the ordering of objectives resulted in a series of different statements of intent (Saulson 1977).

A feature of the organisation of language reform among the Slav peoples in the nineteenth century was the emergence – first in Serbia then copied elsewhere – of philologically orientated patriotic groups known as *Matice* (lit. 'queen-bees', for details, see Herrity 1973). The idea behind this apicultural image was that the language – together with other aspects of the national culture – would be sustained and nurtured from the centre and, if necessary – as was the case with the Czech *Matice* in the 1830s (Jelínek 1971: 24) – in a spirit of purism.

Elsewhere groups sprang up which were exclusively concerned with language reform. In 1779 in Copenhagen, for example, a group of expatriate Icelanders was formed for the purpose of reforming their native language and developing language consciousness in their homeland. Three paragraphs of its constitution dealt explicitly with the means needed to purify the language of foreign words and expressions (Groenke 1983: 145).

Perhaps the most illustrious examples of such activity are the Turkish and Hebrew language societies (Heyd 1954; Saulson 1977). According to its stated objectives, the Council of the Pure Language Society (*Safah Berurah*)

> shall search the treasures of all Hebrew literature, extracting therefrom all Hebrew words which possess a Hebrew form; and it shall publish these words so that they be known to everybody. Likewise the Council shall examine and create new words, contacting the best grammarians and authors in our language to reach agreement on them. (Saulson 1977: 26)

Even so, it is worth remembering that however much planning of Hebrew by committee there may have been 'there was still room for non-official activity, based on the linguistic sense of certain speakers and guided by their intuition' (Morag 1959: 263).

As élite organisations these groups and societies faced the challenge of propagating their ideals and imposing their reforms on ever widening spheres of the population. This was achieved above all through their own publications such as *Zeitschrift des Allgemeinen Deutschen Sprachvereins* for German, *Naše Reč* for Czech, *Poradnik Językowy* for Polish. In addition to providing a forum for the discussion of possible new words and common language 'mistakes', such journals have served to advertise the need for caution in safeguarding the national linguistic heritage and for renewed efforts in carrying through puristic reform.

It was inevitable that purism with its nationalist orientation and its symbolisation of national identity should be a central concern of such groups and societies. Indeed, in the popular imagination they were often totally identified with purism and puristically orientated language cultivation. Such was the fate of *Der allgemeine deutsche Sprachverein* – perhaps one of the most illustrious and active language societies in Europe. Its slogan 'Gedenke auch wenn du die deutsche Sprache sprichst, dass du ein Deutscher bist'[26] was generally interpreted to mean that things as various as menus, dance cards, railway timetables, soccer rulebooks, card games and military orders should reflect the national spirit of Wilhelmine Germany by containing only German words. The ADSV promoted its activities through local branch societies, and maintained and encouraged links with commerce, sporting associations, local and national newspapers and government ministries. Together they published books and pamphlets listing only German equivalents. The fruit of the collaboration between its Dresden Branch and the local victuallers' association, for example, was a book of German culinary terms designed to promote 'ein vaterländisches Gefühl' by seeing to it 'dass die Benennungen der Speisen auf den Küchenzetteln, sowie es ausführbar sei, deutsch seien, und mit deutschen Buchstaben geschrieben werden sollten'[27] (Kamb-Spiess 1962: 381). Establishments using the new German menu were rewarded with free publicity in the pages of the *Zeitschrift* of the ADSV (Dunger 1910: 27). Similarly, competitions were organised and prizes offered to find German equivalents for foreign words despite some opposition within the ADSV to some of the sillier competitions like the one in Berlin in 1898 which produced the following unwieldy winning entries in the search for circus terms: *Hochturnkünstler* (for *Gymnastiker*), *Derbspielkünstler* (for *Knock-about*), *Ueberraschungskunststück* (for *Trick*) and *Werf-Fangkünstler* (for *Jongleur*) (Dunger 1910: 21–3). In Düsseldorf a cigar factory offered a prize for the winner of a competition to find a replacement for *Zigarre*. Over 200 different responses were received; the prize was offered for *Rauchrolle* (lit.

[26] Bear in mind even when you speak the German language that you are a German

[27] a patriotic feeling . . . that the names of dishes on the menus should, as far as possible, be German and written in German letters

'smoke-roll'), but in the end the word was not used by the company and did not catch on (Dunger 1910: 21–5). Still, however minimal the practical outcomes may have been, these competitions reveal the level of public interest in purism (Dunger 1910: 25). The ADSV also tried furthering its aims by having jars available in clubs and hostelries in which to collect fines levied from patrons caught using foreign words (Dunger 1910: 19–21). The result of all these activities in the decade and a half on either side of 1900 was a heightened awareness particularly among the middle classes of the dangers facing German as it sought to shake off its 'enslavement' to French fashion. The ADSV prided itself on its moderation: 'Uebereifrige Fremdwortjäger haben keinen Platz in unserm Verein'[28] (Dunger 1910: 6). It also liked to see itself as classless and non-partisan – if it appeared to be particularly harsh in its criticism of the Social Democrats this had nothing to do with their politic *Weltanschauung* but with the prodigal use of foreign words in their speeches. Indeed, the ADSV imagined itself to be nothing less than the embodiment of the aspirations of the entire German people (Dunger 1910: 7). Undoubtedly, von Polenz (1983: 388) is accurate in recognising that this self-image was illusory and that the puristic attitudes of the period were in actuality a 'pseudodemokratisches Mittelstandsritual'.[29] Nevertheless, it is surely incontrovertible that the ideals of language purification were distributed far and wide throughout all levels of literate German society.

Standing apart from these polite but often fairly ruthless manifestations of middle class concern for language are the genuine mass movements against undesirable features of a language. In the 1930s, for example, there was a strike by the print unions in Warsaw against innovations in Yiddish publications, and in April 1970 there was organised a successful picket of the offices of two New York Yiddish dailies because of their refusal to move away from an anachronistic Germanising spelling (Schaechter 1983: 197). But such groundswells from below are the exception rather than the rule.

One of the few attempts made by a language society to explore popular opinion about language problems was the questionnaire devised and distributed in 1950 by the Turkish Language Society (*Türk Dil Kurumu*) (Heyd 1954: 85ff.). The responses revealed, for example, that etymological spellings of foreign words were generally preferred to phonetic ones.

[28] over-zealous hunters after foreign words have no place in our club
[29] a pseudo-democratic bourgeois ritual

The role of language academies

Of all the élitist language societies pride of place belongs of course to the academies. Whereas a number of the puristically motivated language societies have assumed *de facto* responsibility for language cultivation, the decisions of the academies have often had the force of law. In other cases it is not easy – except in nomenclature – to distinguish language academies from their more humble brethren.

Since academies are so closely associated with the notion of purism, a brief word on their history may not be out of place. The first academy to deal expressly and exclusively with language matters was the *Accademia della Crusca*, founded in Florence in 1572 (Devereux 1968). Its orientation was essentially conservative, favouring a return to the Tuscan language as cultivated in the fourteenth century over the innovations of contemporary renaissance poets like Torquato Tasso. The membership of the *Accademia* was largely patrician and literary. One of its first tasks – as with so many academies to follow – was to produce a large-scale prescriptive dictionary of Italian, the first fascicles of which appeared in 1612. Again, like so many of its successors and despite later additions (the last in 1922), this dictionary remains to this day uncompleted (Hall 1974: 179).

During the course of the seventeenth century a number of *Sprachgesellschaften* (language societies) were formed throughout Germany on the model of the *Accademia della Crusca* (Otto 1972; Bircher 1971). The first and most important of them was the *Fruchtbringende Gesellschaft* founded in Weimar in 1617 by Ludwig of Anhalt-Köthen, himself a member of the *Accademia della crusca* (Kirkness 1975: 23). Like their Florentine exemplar, the German *Gesellschaften* were concerned with correct usage and the avoidance of dialectalisms (Kirkness 1975: 23). However, they also sought to counter archaisms and loanwords, whereas it was not until the eighteenth century that the *Accademia* turned to the problem of foreign influence at a time when Italian was faced by an inundation of Gallicisms (Hall 1942: 22). The foundation of further *Sprachgesellschaften* in other German cities in 1633, 1641 and 1656 – itself a reflection of the fragmentation of German literary life in the Baroque period – tended to hinder rather than help the cause. Moreover, individuals like Schottelius (1612–76), Harsdörffer (1607–58) and von Zesen (1619–89), themselves members of one or other of the *Gesellschaften*, had much greater impact on lexical development. By the end of the century the *Sprachgesellschaften*, as constituted, had outlived their usefulness. Indeed, such prominent individuals as Leibniz were sceptical of their continued existence – he was no less disparaging about the aims of the Italian and French academies – and advocated a less radical and impractical approach to finding native equivalents (Kirkness 1975: 47).

The next academy to be founded – the French – has dwarfed all others in fame and prestige. Indeed, no other institution in human history has been so closely identified by laymen with linguistic purism. Instituted in 1635 by Cardinal Richelieu with royal approval, it not only enjoyed widespread veneration but was invested with *de jure* power. The *Académie Française* with its 40 *fauteuils* has played an almost continuous part in French literary life up to the present day (Robertson 1910; Bellamy 1939). Moreover, the suspicion that if the *Académie* had not existed, French society would have needed to create it is confirmed by the fact that when the *Académie* was disbanded following the Revolution various societies with similar prescriptive aims sprang up to replace it before its final reconstitution by Napoleon in 1803 (Quemada 1983: 101). Its membership was originally drawn mostly from the aristocracy, the military and the higher clergy but in its reincarnation the *bourgeoisie* inevitably came to greater prominence. It is perhaps surprising for an institution which symbolises the literary establishment that less than 50 percent of its membership should have been writers; but even more surprising for an institution aiming to set the course for the French language is the fact that only two members have been philologists – and one of these, as we shall see, was expelled (Hall 1974: 180). It is also not without significance that the first *académicienne* was not elected until 1981.

The outlook of the *Académie Française* grew out of the purism of Malherbe (1555–1628), whose main concern was to proscribe obsolete, dialectal and newly coined words as well as those of foreign (particularly Latin) origin (Hall 1974: 174). Collectively, the puristic attitudes of the *Académie* may be characterised as élitist and archaising. As so often with these kinds of purism the aim is to restrict linguistic expression within limits set by the usage of model writers. This it set out to do with the publication of a dictionary, but its leisurely way of conducting its affairs – meandering after-lunch discussions of individual words – meant that the dictionary in question proceeded at such a snail's pace that it had to be rescued by the one member with lexicographical expertise and whose entrepreneurship was rewarded with expulsion from the *Académie*. Indeed, the concrete achievements of the *Académie* are rather hard to chronicle. Very few French words can be attributed to the *Académie*;

one well-known exception is *taximètre* as the name for a cab with a meter (Hall 1974: 199–200). Nor has the *Académie* been able to restore the flagging prestige of French at home and abroad. This task was taken over by the *Alliance Française*, founded in 1883 as part of the national self-searching which followed the Franco-Prussian War (Gordon 1978: 37). More importantly, the *Académie* has been powerless – and what is more, is seen to be powerless – to stem the invasion of the French language by Anglicisms. Into the breach have stepped a plethora of groups formed with the express aim of countering the evils which beset modern French: *Office de la langue française* (1937), *Office du vocabulaire français* (1957), *Association pour la défense de la langue française* (1959), *Biennales de la langue française* (1965), *Commissions de terminologie* (1970) (Quemada 1983).

However minimal its actual role in regulating French, the *Académie Française* has been held up as a model for other nations. In 1714, for example, Philip V founded the *Real Academia de la lengua*, which soon produced a six-volume prescriptive dictionary and a standard grammar of Castilian (Kohn 1944: 488). In Sweden, Queen Christina had offered to establish an academy for the cultivation of Swedish on the model of the *Académie Française* as early as 1652 (Karker 1983: 286). This was not realised, however, until 1786.

Even England did not escape the shadow thrown by the *Académie Française*. About 1700 concern was voiced in certain quarters about the state of the language:

> An Englishman has his mouth full of borrow'd phrases. . . he is allways borrowing other men's languages. . .I cannot but think the using and introducing foreign terms of art or foreign words is an intolerable grievance. (Daniel Defoe in *Review* 30, No. 10, 1708)

This led some individuals to question whether the time was ripe to establish some form of language institute:

> I have often wished, that as in our constitution there are several persons whose business is to watch over our laws, our liberties and commerce, certain men might be set apart as superintendents of our language, to hinder any words of foreign coin, from passing among us; and in particular to prohibit any French phrases from becoming current in this kingdom, when those of our own are altogether as valuable. (Joseph Addison in *Spectator*, 8 September 1711)

Sentiments like these led a group of prominent literary figures to petition the Crown to set up an academy like the French one. In 1712 it looked as if these efforts were to bear fruit with Oxford, Bolingbroke, Swift, Prior, Pope and Congreve as the first academicians (Flasdieck 1928: 75). Eventually, though, for reasons that are not altogether clear, the scheme came to naught.

In the nineteenth and twentieth centuries those communities where a national standard language was only just emerging as a potent force followed suit: Hungarian (1825), Romanian (1879), for Arabic in Syria (1919) and Egypt (1932), for Iranian (1935) for Hebrew (1953) (Hagège 1983: 43; Jazayery 1983: 252; Eastman 1983: 209, 215). In 1918 an academy with a policy of moderate purism was founded for Basque but it was not given legal status until 1972 (Rebuschi 1983: 128). In Africa and Asia, too, language academies began to flourish. In some instances the academicians found themselves outflanked by those who advocated more radical reform. Recently, for example, the Hausa Language Board was criticised by the young intelligentsia of Nigeria for concentrating on orthographic matters while ignoring the need to enrich the language by creating native neologisms (Jungraithmayr 1983: 276).

It has become fashionable to lampoon language academies for their stuffiness, their smugness and their otherworldliness. A more serious charge, however, is that they are ineffectual in stemming the natural tide of language change. This criticism goes back at least to Samuel Johnson, who writes in the Preface to his Dictionary (1755) of the lexicographer's hope that he 'can embalm his language, and secure it from corruption and decay':

> With this hope, however, academies have been instituted, to guard the avenues of their languages, to retain fugitives, and repulse intruders; but their vigilance and activity have hitherto been vain; sounds are too volatile and subtle for legal restraints; to enchain syllables, and to lash the wind, are equally undertakings of pride, unwilling to measure its desires by its strength. The French language has visibly changed under the inspection of the academy. . . .

Even if the practical effectiveness of language academies to intervene in language development is called into question, we cannot ignore their possible symbolic significance:

> The role of language academies is as much symbolic as it is practical. Academies. . .serve as the markers of linguistic taste, as courts of appeal where people may turn with language questions. The goal of keeping language pure is, for all practical purposes, unattainable. Whether an academy's prescriptions are followed, though, is irrelevant to the goals of a purification plan. It is more important that the Academy exists as a body to prescribe. (Eastman 1983: 213)

One way in which academies may be said to differ from language societies is the very fact of their institution from above. Even their membership is ordained from above or else is the result of internal election. Consequently, it is marked by privilege and does not necessarily reflect fitness for the task. Furthermore, such bastions of privilege are, by their very nature, prone to lose contact not just with the population at large but even with the intelligentsia from which they have sprung. Since Bartsch (1987: 92) has clearly demonstrated that language norms are based on the intuition of the intelligentsia, any proposal from a language academy - or a language society or an individual for that matter – which deviates from this intuition is automatically a mere prescription and as such risks repudiation (Bartsch 1987: 177–8). One of the primary aims of all purism, however, is to instigate language reform precisely by engineering changes in the attitudes as well as the intuition (set of internalised norms) of the intelligentsia of a speech community.

The speech community

Language reform rarely, if ever, begins as a grass-roots, mass movement. It is most often instigated by an individual or group of like-minded individuals, who may see wisdom in forming them-selves into some institution in order both to consolidate their position and to organise the propagation of their common viewpoint in the wider community. As we saw in the last chapter, it is in the reception mode that the wider community – the intellectual élite – first becomes involved in the purification process. It has the prerogative of accepting or rejecting the premises on which the puristic orientation is based and employing or choosing not to employ the linguistic elements which purists have advocated on the basis of these orientations.

Rejection of the puristic alternative implies a wide divergence between the linguistic perception of the purist and the intelligentsia as a whole. Such, for example, was the situation in England in the second half of the nineteenth century, where Barnes' reforms were regarded as harmless but impractical and irrelevant. The intelligentsia closed ranks and made sure that Barnes' innovations did not gain admittance to the new prestigious Oxford Dictionary. In Russia in the early nineteenth century there was a similar rejection by Pushkin and his contemporaries of the idiosyncratic, puristically motivated neologisms of Admiral Shishkov. This set the seal for the subsequent development of the Russian lexicon with its highly accommodative treatment of foreign elements.

Conversely, acceptance of the puristic alternative is a sign of a common linguistic perception, resulting from:

(1) the fact that the puristic orientation has evolved from the overall value systems operating within the intellectual élite; for example, Croatian nineteenth-century purism was a direct response to a pan-Slavonic, cultural nationalism operating in a central European, Austro-Slav but generally cosmopolitan intellectual climate (Thomas 1988a: 157).

(2) the fact that the intellectual élite recognises the wisdom of the approach advocated by the purists as the best possible solution to the dilemmas facing the language; for example, the intelligentsia in much of Norway came to realise along with Aasen that for Nynorsk to survive as an autonomous language it had to eradicate certain features common with Bokmål while at the same time rejecting the neologistic excesses of Icelandic (Gerdener 1986).

Apart from outright acceptance and rejection there are two other possibilities: acceptance by only a section of the intelligentsia or mere acquiescence. In either case, changed circumstances such as changes in internal political structures, changes in the composition of the élite, changes in the overall value system of the community may result in a backlash against a particular puristic orientation or open repudiation of a solution to which the intelligentsia had formerly merely paid lip-service. The varying fortunes of puristic orientations in Turkish, Persian, Ukrainian and Belorussian provide ample evidence of the way a society's attitudes to purism may change radically in a short space of time.

We have already seen that the language norms of a community are set by its intellectual élite. It is, therefore, a short step from élite acceptance of puristic intervention to accommodation on the part of the entire speech community to these new puristically inspired norms. The speed with which this step is carried out depends, of course, on a number of social variables such as communicative structures, literacy, group solidarity and the cohesiveness of the community.

Conclusions

Typically, purism begins as an attitude to language reform on the part of individuals or groups of individuals within a community. The professional profile of these individuals is highly varied, but almost invariably they belong to the highest strata of the intellectual élite. In favourable circumstances, these attitudes together with the behaviour they engender spread through the intellectual élite in ever widening circles until they encompass the whole speech community.

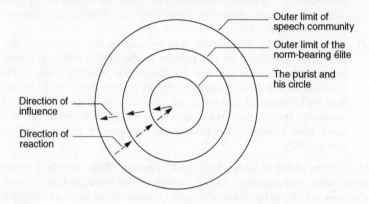

Figure 7: The spread of purism in society

As the circle widens, the passive modes of the purification process tend to be more prominent. A major exception to this is the activity – often conservative in orientation and pedantic in implementation – of teachers and civil servants. Czech and German purism at the end of the nineteenth century provide good examples of such active purism.

The existence of societies, institutions and academies may help to consolidate these efforts and may also provide them with the necessary legitimation. However, if created from above without reference to the value-system of the speech community, these societies serve a symbolic function only: their presence is no guarantee of actual language purification.

THOMAS, G.

Linguistic Purism

LONDON: LONGMAN, 1991

0582037425

CHAPTER 7

The language situation

Introduction

In theory, any code of any language may at any time be the locus of puristic intervention. However, there are certain language situations with which manifestations of purism are particularly associated. For our purposes, these language situations may be treated under three rubrics: language standardisation, language contact and language variation.

Language standardisation

It is probable that some degree of unconscious self-censoring purism is universal and that any attempt at writing involves some form of conscious self-censorship (though not necessarily puristically motivated). All other manifestations of purism, however, depend on the recognition that some variety of a language is to be subject to norms investing it with the prestige necessary for carrying out the social functions of a standard language. Brozović (1970: 49) recognises that every standard language undergoes some form of purism – even if it is not so named – and that purism (in the narrower sense of xenophobic purism) constitutes one of the fifteen criteria of standardness.

This close calibration between purism and standardisation is no coincidence. A standard language is a code in which the separating, solidarity and prestige functions of language are optimally operative, and purism, as we have seen, is one of the possible rational responses to these three functional criteria. Furthermore, each of the puristic orientations – separately or in combination – provides a basis for selecting the corpus of the idiom to be standardised.

Stages of standardisation

The standardisation of languages is a complex process involving several possible stages, which we may identify as: (1) minimal standardisation, (2) pre-standardisation, (3) standardisation proper and (4) post-standardisation. Since each of them presents quite different opportunities and challenges for puristic intervention, it is useful to review their impact separately.

MINIMAL STANDARDISATION

This stage, involving the rise of written dialects often based on a spoken koine, is characterised by an openness to enrichment from all sources. Although closure in the form of self-censorship may be a feature of certain literary genres, examples of the active modes of purism are quite exceptional.

One such example is the puristic activity in Prague in the late fourteenth–early fifteenth century, the high-point of Czech medieval national consciousness. The Emperor Charles IV encouraged the production of a number of dictionaries, which attempted to coin Czech equivalents for widely used German and Latin loanwords. These native coinings not only calqued foreign models but even resorted to back-formations of a highly inventive but ultimately idiosyncratic variety (Lisický 1919: 475–80). This largely ineffectual puristic activity was followed a generation later by more practical steps. The preacher and university professor Jan Hus, saddened by the Germanised Czech of his parishioners, attempted to coin easily decipherable native words: *radnice* 'town-hall' from *rada* 'council, counsel' – ironically considered by some a German loanword – and the suffix -*nice* 'place where something happens or is stored' for *ratuša*, a loan from MHG *rathûs*.

An avoidance of loanwords together with a preference for calques is also a salient feature of those languages created to translate

Christian scripture and liturgical texts. Thus Old High German and Old English resorted to the widespread use of semantic and word-building calques of Latin religious terminology: OE *hālig gāst* for Lat *sanctus spiritus*, OHG *alamatīc* for Lat *omnipotens* (Betz 1936; Vočadlo 1926: 352–3). Similarly, Old Church Slavonic derived much of its new religious vocabulary from calquing Greek: *prĕobražénie* 'transfiguaration' for Gr *metamorphosis*, *blagoslovĕnie* for *eulogia* (Schumann 1958). Yet there is no indication that this avoidance of foreign elements has any purpose beyond a recognition that, in the circumstances, rendering Latin or Greek words by native morphemes is the best solution to the need for a set of new and readily comprehensible terms. Accordingly, this neologising is to be ascribed not to puristic attitudes – a point made clear in reference to Old Icelandic by Groenke (1983: 142) – but to the process of *Sprachanschluss* (Becker 1948a). Nevertheless, it is worth remembering that calquing in the early stages of a written vernacular may be held out to future generations as a model worthy of emulation as Barnes did for English. In the case of Icelandic, the fact that Old West Nordic differed in this respect from Old East Nordic, was of paramount importance in sowing the seeds of later extremist, xenophobic purism.

PRE-STANDARDISATION

This stage sees some move towards a standardised idiom based on a single dialect, a compromise of dialects or a koine. Active forms of purism are well represented in many languages at this stage: Swedish, Danish, Icelandic, German, Dutch, Czech, Finnish and Hungarian. Because at this stage it operates primarily on the written language, purism often has the effect of distancing written from spoken usage: popular chap-books reflecting spoken usage often contain large numbers of foreign words which have been replaced in more elevated literature by native equivalents.

This purism is almost invariably xenophobic in nature and moderate to extreme in its intensity. The purists tend to act individually or in small, loosely organised groups. As a result, the puristic activity displays a high degree of idiosyncrasy which vitiates against its long-term impact. Nevertheless, in certain circumstances purism at this stage can have a profound effect on the eventual shape of the standard language.

Undoubtedly, the best example of purism at this stage is the attempt to replace Latin and French items with newly coined German words during the seventeenth century. Many of these replacements have been retained in standard German: *beobachten* 'to observe' (*observieren*), *Briefwechsel* 'correspondence' (*Korrespondenz*), *Zeitschrift* 'periodical' (*chronographicon*), *Wörterbuch* 'dictionary' (*lexikon*), *Abstand* 'distance' (*Distanz*), *Anschrift* 'address' (*Adresse*), *Augenblick* 'moment' (*Moment*), *Entwurf* 'project' (*Projekt*), *Leidenschaft* 'passion' (*Passion*), *Mundart* 'dialect' (*Dialekt*), *Tagebuch* 'diary' (*Journal*) (Kirkness 1975: 32, 40, 41).

STANDARDISATION PROPER

At this crucial stage, which sees the institution of a single prestigious autonomous standard, the puristic orientation is often inextricably linked to the values lying behind the creation of that standard. Not only may the achievements of this purism find a permanent place in its corpus but such puristic attitudes may remain a norm concept in the consciousness of the native speaker, as is evidently the case for Croatian, Hungarian, Icelandic and Estonian among others. However, purists may have an attitude which sharply conflicts with these value-orientations, in which case their efforts will often be marginalised and their impact on the standard language minimalised as happened to anti-Latin purism in sixteenth-century England and anti-Russian purism in nineteenth-century Bulgaria. The same holds true for anti-purists operating in a milieu receptive to a puristic orientation.

Some standard languages, such as English, French, Mandarin Chinese and Kiswahili, have developed after a long evolutionary process without major re-orientations, changes in dialectal base or discontinuities of tradition. That is to say, there is no visible barrier or hiatus between the pre-standard and standard stages of development. In standard languages of this kind, there is little likelihood of widespread puristic activity as a result of standardisation. This is precisely because the formation of the standard language is the result of unconscious, non-interventionist activity.

Many modern standard languages, including Italian, Turkish, Hungarian, Ukrainian and Czech, are the product of a major reform, revival or re-orientation of a language with an already extensive written corpus. Still others have been created *de novo* where previously no (or a minimal) literary tradition existed: Macedonian, Modern Hebrew, Afrikaans. Both of these types of standardisation lend themselves readily to purism because:

(1) the intervention is premeditated.

(2) it is almost inevitably guided by one of the same value-orientations inherent in one or other of the types of purism.

Furthermore, there is greater likelihood of implementation of puristic activity in such cases since it has been noted that languages which have undergone renewal or creation *de novo* provide wider scope for successful attempts at codification (Daneš 1982: 107). Indeed, in these circumstances the dominance of the non-rational set of value orientations underlying puristic attitudes has been recognised by Daneš (1987: 218) as 'quite natural and also to a high degree functionally justified'.

At the same time, the conscious revival, reform or re-orientation of a standard language is undertaken only because of a perception of some shortcoming in the present state of affairs. This shortcoming is seen as preventing the new standard from occupying a position of prestige in the community. Since the purpose of creating a new standard is to displace an already established one, it follows that the new standard must be maximally differentiated from the old. As we have seen, purism – especially xenophobic purism – serves to symbolise this differentiation, particularly where the two codes are closely related (Nynorsk and Bokmål, Belorussian and Russian, Slovak and Czech, Estonian and Finnish for example) or where one of them is either structurally modelled on, or lexico-semantically indebted to, the other as in the case of Czech and German, Dutch and German, Hungarian and German, Finnish and Swedish.

Equally important to the prestige of an embryonic standard language is the need for lexical enrichment. The would-be language reformer is faced with the dilemma of borrowing or searching for adequate elements from internal resources (Vočadlo 1926: 352–3; Hagège 1983: 41–3). The non-puristic, rational response to this dilemma is that of Nehru:

> I would personally like to encourage Hindustani to adapt and assimilate many words from English. . . .This is necessary, as we lack modern terms, it is better to have well-known words rather than to evolve new and difficult words from Sanskrit or Persian or Arabic. (Nehru 1953: 456).

But for many this response is unacceptable because the process of enriching a language from its own 'most authentic sources' fulfils the purposes 'of external separation and internal consolidation' (Fishman 1973: 67). The standardisation of Modern Hebrew is a case in point:

> It is easy to understand why, at the early stages of the Revival, the official

linguistic attitude towards borrowing from European languages was utterly negative. At those stages, when spoken Hebrew had to struggle for existence, it was imperative to find *Hebrew* tools of speech for the needs of everyday life. A large scale non-Semitic borrowing could not have been accepted as a solution of the vocabulary problem; creating a *langue mixte*, it would have undermined the whole process of Revival. (Morag 1959: 260)

Nevertheless, most renewal purists have recognised the merits of the rationalist position on lexical enrichment and have attempted to come to terms with it. This has resulted in the compromises characteristic of many enrichment programmes of renewal purism. A typical example is provided by Kasravi's principles for the reform of Persian (Jazayery 1983: 253):

1. Common Arabic words should be retained where no Persian equivalent existed.
2. Except in the sciences, words should not be invented, popular usage was to be followed.
3. New words should be formed from the resources of Persian.
4. There need not be a one-to-one correlation between Persian and foreign languages.
5. Synonyms should be avoided.

Similar compromises were encouraged by Turkish reformers (Heyd 1954: 88–91):

1. Preference for Turkish words over their Arabic or Persian synonyms.
2. The collection of words from the vernacular.
3. The revival of obsolete Ottoman Turkish words.
4. The use of words from non-Ottoman Turkish texts.
5. The development of new meanings for existing Turkish words.
6. The addition of an abstract meaning for a word used hitherto in Turkish in a concrete sense only.
7. The calquing of Arabic words.
8. Phonetic Turkisation of foreign words.
9. Word-formation.
10. Neologisms echoing the sound of a foreign word.

While each of these programmes presents different means for coping with the dilemma, they both recognise that the continued use of some foreign words is inevitable. Their intent is to minimise the threat posed by the presence of undesirable lexical elements, not to eradicate it.

It is not surprising, therefore, to discover that purism is so widespread in the standardisation stage of those languages which have been consciously created or remoulded. Together with codification and enrichment it forms an essential part of the process of *Sprachanschluss*, the modelling of a language on a prestigious language of culture so that it can eventually usurp the latter in its social functions (Becker 1948a; Auty 1973: 338).

POST-STANDARDISATION

This stage involves the cultivation and further elaboration of the standard language. Those languages which were reconstituted, reformed or newly created as a premeditated act of intervention tend to face the same dilemma with respect to adopting the new vocabulary needed to match the technical and social changes in the external world. Purism may continue, therefore, to play a role in influencing the selection of new lexical items. However, since the standard language is by now well established, vigilance may be relaxed somewhat. In Hebrew, for example, it has been noted that 'later on, as vocabulary largely composed of Hebrew items was gradually being established, borrowing began to look less perilous' (Morag 1959: 260).

This relaxation reflects not only a recognition that the battle has been won but a subtle re-evaluation of the needs of the standard language. The sheer enormity of the task of providing a language with modern terminology which will satisfy the demands not only of the linguist but also the technical specialist is daunting enough without the added burden that these new terms should be created out of native resources. Many standard languages in which purism has been a feature in the past have been forced like Upper Sorbian to jettison the search for native technical terms and submit to an inundation of internationalisms (Stone 1968: 156). Furthermore, the acceptance of internationalisms in specialist terminology is well grounded in the rational value-orientations for language intervention proposed by Daneš. Moreover, the presence of internationalisms is often tolerated by mild and moderate purist movements. Nevertheless, inasmuch as the most international term may be associated with a specific dominant culture, it may be subject to puristic objections. Hence the debate about internationalisms of Anglo-American origin in French.

The fact that internationalisms are more or less confined to the field of specialist terminology would seem to diminish the threat they pose to the core of the language. However, it should be noted that one of the major trends in modern standard languages is towards *determinologisation*, that is the use of technical terms in everyday discourse without their specialist signification. Thus the way is open for the infiltration of the core of the standard language by hordes of international terms. In these circumstances, the despair and frustration felt by speakers about the fate of their native language may well find expression in outbursts of irrational puristic sentiment and activity, even where previously purism has been dormant or of little consequence.

Language contact

The most obvious result of contact between two linguistic codes is the transfer of certain elements from one to the other (Weinreich 1953). According to Whinnom (1971: 92–7) this transfer of material from one code to another is controlled by four barriers:

1. The ecological (whether or not the languages are in contact).
2. The ethological (whether or not there is some emotional impediment).
3. The mechanical (whether or not there are insuperable structural differences between the languages)
4. The conceptual (whether or not the conceptual world of one speech community is rejected by the other).

While the ecological barrier may prevent contact between specific languages, there is no evidence that any linguistic code exists in splendid isolation from contact with another code. This is precisely why virtually all linguists would agree with Hagège (1983: 43) that the loanword should be rightfully regarded not as 'l'aventure fortuite qui déstabilise mais une des conditions mêmes de la vie des langues'.[30] This is a fact of life which all purists have to come to terms with. Although they may seek to rationalise their objections to certain elements on structural or conceptual grounds, theirs is primarily an emotional response to the threat of hybridisation. The intensity of

[30] a chance destablising occurrence but one of the very conditions of the life of languages

these emotions depends on the level of language consciousness in a given community, the nature of the alien elements themselves and the attitudes towards the speech community from which they have been transferred. In this section, however, we shall investigate the role of another variable – the type of language contact involved.

When two or more communities speaking different languages come into contact and wish to communicate linguistically, a number of outcomes are possible:

1. A contact language (or pidgin) may develop incorporating lexical elements of the languages involved but employing a highly divergent morphology and syntax.
2. Members of one or both of the communities may become bilingual and begin to incorporate some elements of the newly acquired language in their native vernacular.

We shall investigate in turn the impact which each of these forms of hybridisation has on purism.

Pidginisation

The first outcome is most unlikely to lead directly to purism. This is because such *Mischsprachen* are hardly ideal candidates for purification. If, however, this contact language should be creolised (that is to say, become the native language of a community) and if this creole (*basilect*) is in contact with a standard language (*acrolect*) with which it shares the majority of its lexical repertoire, a form of diglossia will develop. In this diglossic situation, it is highly probable that a strongly proscriptivist attitude will develop in the speech community towards elements which the basilect does not share with the acrolect, as with the stigmatisation of elements of *Black English* in standard North American English usage (Romaine 1988: 164–72). If a *post-creole continuum* (with gradated *mesolects* covering the distance between basilect and acrolect) has developed in the community as it has, for example in Guyana (Bickerton 1980: 109; Romaine 1988: 158–9), then this censoring purism may be regarded as *élitist*. If the creole is regarded in the speech community as a distinct code as in Haiti, then the purism may be described as *xenophobic*. If the creole itself should be elevated to the status of a standard language, however, it may also become the locus of puristic sentiment. For example, in Papua New Guinea, where the English-based pidgin Tok Pisin has gained such recognition, fears have been voiced that 'tok pisin bilong taun' (or urban variety) is being so infiltrated by English words as to become divorced from the true language 'tok pisin bilong bus' (or rural variety). This distancing poses a threat both to the solidarity and the prestige of the language (Romaine 1988: 124). The response is a form of purism with a xenophobic and ethnographic orientation.

Bilingualism

The second outcome – bilingualism – has much greater potential for the development of purism. This is primarily because some degree of bilingualism – however minimal – is a necessary prerequisite for any exchange of items between languages. Almost invariably, bilingualism reflects a socio-political imbalance in the relationship between the communities involved, that is to say, one language dominates the other. This is manifest, for example, in the tendency for bilingualism to be restricted to speakers of the dominated language and for there to be a greater flow of linguistic material from the dominant language to the dominated than the other way round. Bearing in mind both the rational and non-rational motivations for purism discussed in Chapter 3, it will surely come as no surprise that purism may be a feature of the dominated but rarely if ever of the dominant language. If we take Swedish–Finnish bilingualism in southern Finland, for example, the competition between these two languages for speakers and social functions threatens Finnish but not Swedish, which is of course firmly entrenched in Sweden. On the whole, bilingualism is confined to the Finnish community. Any interference – except perhaps locally – is limited to the unilateral influence of Swedish on Finnish. Thus, while it would be highly surprising not to find widespread puristic reaction to Swedish elements in Finnish, we would not expect anti-Finnish purism in Swedish. Consequently, when we do encounter purism in a dominating language towards elements from a dominated language, as for example, in the attempts during the Third Reich to purge German of Yiddishisms (von Polenz 1967: 90), it is safe to assume that we are dealing with a reaction, which is, to say the least, abnormal and excessive.

Mention of the German–Yiddish relationship in the same breath as that between Swedish and Finnish serves to remind us that languages in contact may be typologically similar or dissimilar and genetically close or distant. We have already examined the extent to which structural typology has a bearing on purism. It remains to say something about genetic relations.

We might expect material from closely related languages to be assimilated without provoking a puristic backlash. Indeed, in many instances closely related languages are scrutinised for the potential help they can provide. Turkish purists, for example, sought replacements for Arabic and Persian elements in other Turkic languages. Similarly, German purists of the seventeenth century looked towards contemporary Dutch for salvation from the inundation of German by French and Latin elements. As we have seen, this source of enrichment is explored most avidly during periods of cultural pan-nationalism. Almost all the Slavonic standard languages, for example, were enriched in this way in the nineteenth century despite their closure to most other sources (Thomas 1985, 1988a, 1988b, 1989a). However, there are also cases, where purism directed at a closely related language is more intense than any other. In order to understand this, we must look at the typology of contacts between closely related languages in more detail.

A good example of contact between closely related standards is provided by the Slavonic languages. According to Brozović (1970: 70–2), contact between them can be divided into two basic types:

1. Contact between languages in different polities, involving the introduction of cultural and civilisational influences from the 'larger' to the 'smaller' language.
2. Contact between languages in the same political unit, involving three different types of influence:
   (a) normal cultural and civilisational influences;
   (b) hegemony of one language over all others;
   (c) influences in a political unit in which a non-related language is dominant.

Of these types and subtypes of contact, 2(c) in which all of the related languages face a common threat from a non-related language is the least likely to provoke a puristic reaction. For example, in the Habsburg Empire, increasingly dominated by German, the Slavonic standard languages (Slovene, Croatian, Slovak and partially Ukrainian) were fully prepared to accept influences from, and indeed to model themselves on, Czech in their efforts to free themselves from the infiltration of German elements. Subtype 2(a) and type 1 occupy a middle ground: the languages do not threaten each other, and influences from one to another may or may not be acceptable. A particularly good illustration of these situations is provided by the relationship between Serbian and Croatian, which spans phases when the standard codes have been used in different polities (the Habsburg and Ottoman Empires) and in a single state (Yugoslavia) and which is characterised by intermittent periods of convergence and puristic repulsion. Subtype 2(b) represents the case in which puristic reaction is likely to be most intense. This is not only because this situation is most conducive to the introduction of linguistic elements from one language to another but also because the speech community of the dominated language is profoundly aware of the threat posed to its autonomy by the dominant status of the related language. Hence Slovak anti-Czech purism in Czech-dominated Czechoslovakia, Slovene and Macedonian purism directed at Serbo-Croatian in Serbo-Croatian-dominated Yugoslavia, anti-Russian purism in both Belorussian and Ukrainian circles in the Russian-dominated Soviet Union (Thomas 1988b). It is not difficult to appreciate the strength of the feelings generated by these situations, when we consider that in all of these cases at one time or another the very question has been raised whether the dominated language should evolve into a fully autonomous standard language or whether it would make more sense for speakers of the dominated language to be serviced by the dominant language alone for those functions normally assigned to a standard language. Once again, then, purism fulfils the separating function by ostracising precisely those linguistic features which would obscure the boundary between the languages concerned.

A further possible complicating factor is that a language may find itself in contact with, and thus be threatened by, two or more languages simultaneously. This may mean that one part of the speech community is alive to the dangers on one side, while others are more aware of incursions from the other direction. In such cases, purists will not agree on the targets for puristic censorship and intervention, and consequently the cause of linguistic solidarity will suffer a setback. The case of Belorussian and Ukrainian – both subject to widespread influence from Polish and Russian – provides an excellent illustration of this problem (Wexler 1974). The more heavily polonised section of the Belorussian and Ukrainian communities was sensitive to the need to remove Polish elements but was either oblivious of, or indifferent to, the dangers posed by Russian, while their more Russified compatriots saw the problem in reverse. There are only two rational solutions to a dilemma of this kind: to try to fight external influences on both fronts or to abandon the cause of xenophobic purism altogether. In most cases, however, the speech community chooses to give preference to elements from that language which appears to offer least threat to its prestige and independence. Here, of course, Brozović's typology of contacts once more comes into play.

It is also useful to distinguish between two modes of bilingualism:

vernacular and literary. The first arises out of contact between neighbouring or co-territorial languages, the second from the formal acquisition of a standard (even dead) language. This distinction is important because each of the modes leads to quite different puristic outcomes.

In the first place this is because the two modes of bilingualism generate different kinds of linguistic material as potential targets of puristic intervention. Vernacular bilingualism introduces mainly common loanwords and some calques designating items of material culture, some changes in phonetic articulation and some common phraseological and syntactical patterns, whereas literary bilingualism tends to generate abstract and higher style loanwords and calques and a more comprehensive remodelling of syntactic patterns. It must be clear that the products of literary bilingualism are the more easily removable. On the other hand, it is the products of vernacular bilingualism which are the more transparent to the untrained eye. Herein lies one of the paradoxes of linguistic purism.

Secondly, while vernacular bilingualism is determined by the pressures of everyday living, the acquisition of a standard language – however motivated – depends on its having prestige. So much so that some bilinguals pepper their speech and writings in their native language with elements of the other language. This is the phenomenon which we see for example, in the widespread gallomania of the German intelligentsia of the seventeenth and eighteenth centuries and of the Russian intelligentsia a century later. In each of these cases, as we might expect, there was puristic reaction to this overindulgence in the use of French. Once more we are reminded that purism is clearly identified with an identity crisis within the intelligentsia.

Thirdly, the two types of bilingualism often engender quite different levels of linguistic transfer. For example, a vernacular like Slovak which, until the nineteenth century, was a functionally restricted, peasant patois had not suffered the same inroads of foreign speech as had Czech, the language of an urban, intellectual élite (Auty 1973: 339). As a result, the puristic reaction in Slovak was noticeably less intense than that in Czech.

Finally, the effects of vernacular bilingualism are haphazard and unsystematic, whereas formal knowledge of a standard language by a majority – or even the totality – of the intelligentsia may lead to a systematic restructuring of the native language: a modelling of the lexico-semantic and syntactic systems on those of another standard language. In many – if not all – instances, this modelling process, so crucial to the development of a new standard language, is kept in check by a form of puristic intervention, which acts to safeguard the autonomy of the native language. This it does by drawing attention to violations done to the native structures by too close an adherence to the foreign model. The clash of these opposing forces – imitation and renunciation of the foreign model – and its eventual resolution is in my view one of the most crucial questions in the evolution of standard languages. Here, then, is yet another example of the importance of linguistic purism in the implementation of the separating function.

Bilingual individuals living in a bilingual community are constantly faced with the question of which language to use, to whom and when. They may even move from one language to another within a sentence. This *code-switching*, as we saw in the case of Tamils, can be used in order to avoid contaminating their native tongue with elements from another language. In other words, the device of code-switching serves to demarcate the linguistic boundaries within the discourse. This may involve the adoption of a non-native articulation and the preservation of the morphological characteristics of the second language as we have seen in Russian (Waight 1980; Thomas 1983). A similar demarcation can be achieved on the printed page by the use of different alphabets (as in the quotation of French expressions in the Latin alphabet within a Russian text in Cyrillic), different scripts or italicisation.

In bilinguals whose command of their native language is limited, however, code-switching serves to underline their inability to express themselves, i.e. they are forced to resort to the language over which they have better command. This is particularly apparent in situations like that of East Sutherland Gaelic where the language is dying (Dorian 1981). As we saw in Chapter 3, this can induce either censoring purism or some attempt to sanction the code-switching by employing a framing device such as an apologetic interjection or gesture.

In many immigrant communities, too, the younger generation often has severely restricted command of the native language with the result that a macaronic mixture of the immigrant and domestic language (or so-called *interlanguage*) is employed. This interlanguage, as can be imagined, carries little prestige and indeed is a source of shame to its users and irritation to members of the community who do have full command of the native language. The reaction to this state of affairs is often voiced in puristic terms. However, since it is not just the performance but the competence of the speakers which is at issue, a call for purism will not remedy a condition, which requires more drastic and holistic treatment. Nevertheless, extreme cases of this kind serve once again to underline the close connection between purism and the operation of the prestige function in language.

Language variation

It is already evident that purism helps to identify what is intrinsic to a language by earmarking the elements which need to be discarded. Each of the internal orientations puts limits on variation within a language: reformist and archaising purism deal with variation along the temporal frame, ethnographic and élitist purism with the spatial and social parameters. There are two aspects of language variation, however, which impinge particularly closely on our subject: diglossia and stylistic register.

Diglossia

We have already discussed the role of purism in ostracising those features which tend to obscure the boundary between closely related languages. This function is carried out with equal if not greater intensity in those instances where there is a need to maintain a distance between distinct varieties within a single diasystem. It matters little whether these varieties have evolved into independent standard languages as in the case of Dutch, Flemish and Afrikaans, Yiddish and German, Hindi and Urdu, Moldavian and Romanian, or whether they are regarded as regional variants of a single standard as in the case of North American and British English, Serbian and Croatian, or Iberian and American Spanish. In both cases the distancing is achieved not only by closure to features of the other language variety but also by the selection of external puristic targets. Thus in the nineteenth century, while Serbian was open to German loans and internationalisms, Croatian tended to prefer calques from German and loans from Czech.

In certain circumstances a transitional variety may develop which acts as a bridge between the two polarised codes. In Bosnia-Hercegovina, for example, a form of Serbo-Croatian is used which incorporates features from both Serbian and Croatian variants (Thomas 1982). This involves neutralisation of the variant-markedness of certain words and morpho-syntactic features. Thus, while *tvornica* and *fabrika* are the respective Croatian and Serbian words for 'factory', in Bosnia-Hercegovina with its mixed population of Serbs, Croats and Muslims (i.e. Moslemised South Slavs) they are used interchangeably, and no inferences may be drawn from their use about the ethno-cultural identity of the speaker. This neutralisation and the consequent rise of transitional varieties is only made possible by the relaxation of puristic attitudes.

All the examples cited above involve what Britto (1986) calls *pseudo-diglossia*, where Population A uses Code I and Population B uses Code II. Diglossia, in the sense Ferguson (1959) originally described, involves the employment of language varieties side-by-side in a complementary set of socio-communicative functions. To take one of Ferguson's defining situations of diglossia, Katharevousa – at least until recently – was used in formal settings and high-style genres (political speeches, scientific writing, addressing superiors, sermons, belles lettres), whereas Dimotiki was confined to informal settings and genres (addressing equals, conversations with family and friends, personal correspondence). The former, whose very name captures its puristic motivation, is perceived as preserving intact the tradition of ancient Greek. However mistaken this perception may be, it is instructive that the apologists for Katharevousa resorted to a form of archaising and élitist purism in their efforts to prevent Dimotiki, the modern Greek koine, from making significant inroads into their cherished standard. In recent years the adherents of Dimotiki, following a populist and reformist orientation, have succeeded in establishing it as an alternative standard with the result that for many people it has taken over some if not all the socio-communicative functions formerly reserved exclusively for Katharevousa. Interestingly, these opposing puristic orientations appear to calibrate neatly with political *Weltanschauung* – hence the no doubt apocryphal but nevertheless instructive commentary that you can tell a man's politics in Greece by the way he conjugates his verbs. Whatever the eventual outcome of Greek diglossia (for a recent appraisal of the situation, see Browning 1982), the fact remains that the boundaries between the two codes can only be broken down by a relaxation of puristic attitudes.

These attitudes operate similarly in diglossic situations where only one variety is standardised, except that for obvious reasons, only the standard code is affected. Relaxation of purism in the standard will lead inevitably to its *democratisation* – either universally or locally depending on the geographical distribution of the diglossia compared with that of the standard language. For example, the suspension of the puristic censorship safeguarding standard German in Switzerland could lead to the incorporation in it of features of *Swytzerdutsch*. It is highly unlikely, however, that standard German elsewhere would suffer any repercussions from this process.

Many diglossic situations are characterised by the rise of one or more intermediate varieties incorporating elements from both of the opposing varieties. In some highly stratified societies even these intermediate varieties may be kept distinct. This is the case in Tamil, for example, where the distinction is maintained primarily but not exclusively by the degree of openness to Sanskrit elements (Britto 1986). More usually the distinctions between the intermediate varieties become blurred giving rise to a post-diglossic stylistic continuum. Whatever the outcome it is clear that puristic proscriptivism slows the process of removing diglossic polarity and may even forestall its final dissolution.

Stylistic register

There is considerable evidence that purism is a feature of higher not lower styles. Many Italian words registered in popular texts and undoubtedly current in Croatian speech in the sixteenth and seventeenth centuries are simply absent from plays and poetry of the same period (Deanović 1936, Hyrkkänen 1973). A similar distinction is made in the modern language: in informal styles it is usual to encounter words such as *mušele* 'mussels', *paradajz* 'tomato', *krigla* 'mug', *šnicl* 'schnitzel' for their higher style puristic replacements *školjke, rajčica, časa, odrezak* (Thomas 1978a). In certain high styles of modern Slovene, particularly imaginative literature, Serbo-Croatianisms are much less prevalent than elsewhere (Urbančič 1972: 81). Such stylistic distinctions are not confined to the written language as we discovered in East Sutherland Gaelic, where 'the number of loanwords in a verbal performance seems to have become a matter of degree of formality'. The more 'relaxed and casual' the performance, the greater will be the number of loanwords. In more formal utterances – 'for example, established narrative routines reproduced for tape-recording' – the reverse is true (Dorian 1981: 101). Similarly, in modern Russian words like *metro* 'underground railway', *pal'to* 'coat' in higher style speech are not inflected – a feature attributable to puristic intervention – but in common speech they are often assimilated into one of the native declension patterns (Thomas 1983). Variation in performance is reflected too in a distinction between written and spoken usage:

The gap between written and spoken norms can be heightened by the closure of the former and the opening of the latter to a given resource, e.g. colloquial Arabic is more receptive to foreign loans than modern written (classical) Arabic which prefers loan translations formed from native components. (Wexler 1971: 333).

Wexler notes similar distinctions in Armenian with respect to Turkish elements and Ukrainian in its attitude to Russianisms.

In some languages foreign words have a somewhat popular character. This is true, for example, of Turkisms in Bulgarian (Grannes 1970: 13–14). This stylistic colouring is likely to be highlighted if these very words are removed from the standard language. In other languages certain foreign words have friendlier, more intimate connotations: in Belgrade the Turkish loanwords *komšija* 'neighbour', *pendžer* 'window', *ćuprija* 'bridge' are felt to be somehow warmer than the stylistically neutral native equivalents *sused*, *prozor*, *most* (Hill 1975: 123).

All of these examples demonstrate a dichotomy between, on the one hand, neutral, conventional, formal, premeditated language behaviour in which purism is an important constituent and relaxed, informal, spontaneous performance characterised by a relaxation of puristic strictures on the other. The effect is not only to distinguish written from spoken usage but to distance the higher styles from the lower. Indeed some purists, like the Sorb Ćišinski (Stone 1968: 155), have been criticised by their compatriots on these very grounds.

All the examples discussed so far pertain to xenophobic and/or élitist purism, where the impetus is precisely on elevating the language above, or distancing it from, an embarrassing vernacular. When we turn to instances of ethnographic purism (with or without a xenophobic component), however, a totally different picture emerges. This is precisely because the motivation of ethnographic purism is to remove those elements which distinguish the standard language from the vernacular. For example, Turkish purism was – at least in part – an attempt to restore the unity of the Turkish vernacular and Osmanli by divesting the latter of its strong Persian and Arabic component. The very highest styles of standard Turkish still contain large amounts of these elements but the more neutral styles have moved closer to the vernacular in eschewing their use as much as possible.

A particularly good example of the effects of ethnographic purism on stylistic levels is the case of Yiddish. Prior to the First World War spoken Yiddish was open to both loanwords and calques from Russian, while the written language found only calques acceptable. At the same time the literary language (so-called *daytshmerish*) was

heavily Germanised while spoken Yiddish tended to avoid enrichment from standard German (Schaechter 1983: 210). Thus, the
situation of Yiddish approximated that which we have described
above for Croatian. However, one of the main goals of later Yiddish
purists was to make the written language closer to the vernacular.
This move necessarily involved a large-scale de-Germanisation of
written Yiddish (Schaechter 1983: 213). The removal of German
elements from the the standard language had the concomitant effect
of bringing the vernacular and the standard closer together.
Ethnographic purism, then, reduces the distance between the spoken
and written forms of the language while at the same time providing
the standard language with fresh targets for xenophobic purism.

Conclusions

All purism is a response either to some form of language contact or to
variation within a language, or a combination of the two. It serves to
sanction some linguistic features introduced by contact and variation
and outlaw others – the external perspective being chiefly, though not
exclusively, concerned with features arising from contact, the internal
perspectives primarily with variation. If xenophobic purism is the
unmarked type of puristic orientation, then language contact of the
bilingual type must be considered the archetypal situation in which
purism occurs.

The variables we have identified in language contact and language
variation also provide a clue to the intensity of puristic sentiment.
Firstly, there is likely to be a more intense reaction to the introduction
of elements from a socio-politically dominant language than from a
neutral or subservient language, especially where both languages are
used within a single political unit. Secondly, contact on both the
literary and the vernacular levels concomitantly constitutes a greater
threat than contact on just one level and is therefore likely to provoke
a more intense puristic reaction. Thirdly, contact with a language
which performs, has performed or threatens to perform standard
language functions for which a speech community wishes to use its
own vernacular will engender an intense puristic response in that
community, irrespective of whether or not the languages are closely
related. Further intensification of the puristic reaction will doubtless
result where two or more standard idioms are in competition within
one diasystem.

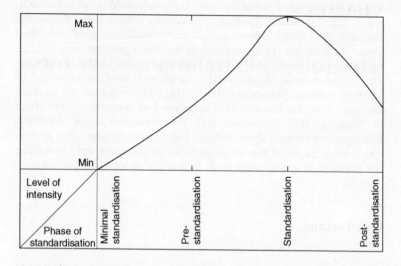

Figure 8: Levels of intensity at phases of standardisation

All puristic intervention can be located somewhere on the standardisation parameter as illustrated in Figure 8. It is likely to be most intense at the standardisation phase and least intense at the minimal standardisation phase with pre- and post-standardisation as intermediate positions. Any deviation from this pattern may be considered a departure from the norm and worthy of special attention. Puristic reactions tend to be most intense in standard languages with non-evolutionary development. This is equally true of languages like Czech which have experienced an interrupted tradition, those like Turkish which have undergone a redefinition of their linguistic base and those like Hebrew which have been created without a prior tradition as a living standard language. The major exception to this model is standard German, where there have been intense eruptions of puristic activity despite the fact that the language has evolved gradually over many centuries. The explanations for this and other examples falling outside this model must be sought in extralinguistic factors, to which we turn in the next chapter.

CHAPTER 8

The role of extralinguistic factors

Introduction

In the last two chapters we have looked at the ways in which the social organisation and the language situation help to shape the concrete form purism takes. In this chapter we complete our examination of the determinants of purism with a survey of the extralinguistic factors: nationalism and literary aesthetics.

Nationalism

Purism has developed in all kinds of economic systems and socio-political contexts, e.g. feudalism, enlightened despotism, tyranny, fascism, colonialism, imperialism, democratic pluralism and even socialism. Although each of them may have some impact on the scope and emphasis of puristic behaviour, they pale into insignificance beside nationalism as a determinant of puristic attitudes. To take just one example: purism in Persian dates from the first stirrings of nationalism in the early nineteenth century. This nationalism was reflected in a rejection of interest in learning Arabic, a growing pride in the culture of ancient Persia and a hostility – or at best indifference – towards Islam. As a result, purism was concerned primarily with divesting the language of its Arabic component and replacing the latter with neologisms or words revived from the ancient literary tradition (Jazayery 1983: 253–6).

Before examining the relationship between nationalism and purism further, it seems appropriate to say a few words about nationalism itself. Like purism, nationalism is notoriously elusive of adequate definition. However, there is surely general agreement that nationalism is a doctrine based on the premise that 'humanity is naturally divided into nations' and that 'each nation has its peculiar character' (Smith 1971: 21). As an ideology, nationalism is concerned with stressing cultural individuality through the accentuation of 'national' *differentiae* and renewing the cultural and social fabric of the nation (Smith 1971: 171). It is an intellectual response to the dilemma facing modern society: to assimilate, to hold fast to traditional values, or to find a higher synthesis of these positions in a re-appraisal – a 'revival' or 'renewal' – of traditional values (Smith 1971: 136–7, 241–4). The relative weighting given to these three positions determines the overall orientation of a nationalist movement. Apart from these substantive criteria, nationalist movements may be further classified according to a set of formal criteria with regard to the intensity of their aims and the extent to which they achieve the aims they have set for themselves (Smith 1971: 211).

Even from this brief description it is clear that nationalism and purism share many core features. Indeed, their closeness prompts the question whether purism is not simply an epiphenomenon of nationalism inasmuch as the desire to rid a language of unwanted foreign elements forms part of a more general wish to divest a culture of alien associations (Thomas 1989a: 6). Nationalism and purism tend to co-occur, co-vary in intensity, and react to influences from the same source. However, it must be remembered that purism and nationalism sometimes occur independently of each other: it is possible to endorse nationalism without recourse to puristic intervention just as the latter may be advocated without reference to nationalistic sentiment.

A more satisfactory approach is to explore the affinities between nationalism and purism and their common source in human nature (Thomas 1989a: 8). The most striking affinity between them is their dualism of outlook and their symbolisation of the dichotomy between the desirable and the undesirable (Thomas 1989a: 9). Both phenomena seek to affirm or discover what is truly native by the exposure, eradication or diminution of precisely those elements which threaten to undermine the prestige, unity or autonomy of native institutions. We can anticipate, therefore, at times of heightened national consciousness a tendency towards maximal differentiation between languages or between varieties of a single language. Alternatively, we can expect those opposed to nationalism to deny the existence, or at least to play down the importance, of these *differentiae*.

Nationalism takes on many ideological forms, and many of these are directly reflected in the typology of puristic orientations. Take, for example, the following correlations between nationalist ideologies and puristic orientations:

1. Populist nationalism with its 'nostalgia and idealisation for the countryside and folk virtues' (Smith 1971: 63) and ethnographic purism.
2. Integrationist nationalism as an antidote to social disintegration (Smith 1971: 225) and élitist purism.
3. Reformist nationalism with its repudiation of a past age of decay and reformist purism.
4. Traditionalist nationalism with its glorification of a past golden age and archaising purism.
5. Independence, irredentist or racialist nationalism with their resistance to foreign domination and xenophobic purism.

An example of the last correlation is the lexical reform for Basque elaborated by Sabino Arana-Goiri (1865–1903), of which Rebuschi (1983: 125) writes: 'Elle se fonde essentiellement sur une attitude puriste, qui n'est pas sans rapports avec l'idéologie xénophobe, voire raciste, du PNV de l'époque.'

In addition, nationalism may involve a recognition of certain values in foreign cultures. Such self-critical, eclectic or outward-looking forms of nationalism are also reflected in the various compromises which are characteristic of the more moderate instances of purism.

A type of nationalist ideology which is particularly important for developing a characteristic, composite puristic orientation is pan-nationalism. The solidarity and reciprocity which are such key features of pan-nationalist movements are clearly reflected in language attitudes. For example, in the framework of a prevailing pan-nationalist ideology a speech community may well be highly receptive to elements from other languages of the same ethnic group. Purism is then directed not at these languages but only at sources outside the larger ethnic group. This form of purism, in which the demarcation of what is 'ours' and therefore acceptable is enlarged, is, as we have seen, characteristic of the Slavonic, Germanic and Finno-Ugric languages as well as the pan-Turkic orientation of Turkish purism. However, recognition of the merits of a related language is not always dependent on pan-nationalism. Some Hebrew purists, for example, were prepared to open their native language to enrichment from other Semitic languages such as Arabic without wishing in any way to promote the cause of 'pan-Semitic' political solidarity! In Romanian too the motivation for making the language as Romance as possible by incorporating loans from Italian, French and Latin was not so much pan-Romance nationalism as a determination to remove Slavonic elements and thereby promote its independence from the surrounding Slavonic languages (Şerban 1983: 224).

Apart from these substantive parallels, there are also some formal similarities between nationalism and purism. They tend to be similarly affected by the stage of economic, industrial and social development. Both are prompted by deep-seated dissatisfactions with the *status quo* and seek solutions which their practitioners at least view as practical and realistic. To be effective both are highly dependent on the growth of a new policy of widespread education. Indeed, the close formal ties between the two ideologies suggest there are grounds for seriously considering the hypothesis that the periodisation of purism may be calibrated with that of nationalism. We shall examine this hypothesis in more detail in Chapter 11.

Perhaps the most striking formal similarity between the two, however, is their social organisation. It has been observed of both movements that they begin as a response to a crisis in the intelligentsia. If we accept Gellner's definition of the intelligentsia as 'a class which is alienated from its own society by the very fact of its education' (Gellner 1964: 169–70), it is easy to understand why both nationalism and purism with their stressing of solidarity, the search for roots and purification of extraneous corrupting influences provide a means for rescuing the intelligentsia from deracination. Furthermore, it has been observed that the introduction of a 'definite, practical collective programme' (Smith 1971: 107) – whether nationalist or purist – engenders a feeling of serenity, a release from the previous ambivalence.

The most fully elaborated framework for describing the dynamics of the social organisation of nationalism is provided by Miroslav Hroch's comparative study of the development of national consciousness among the small nations of Europe (Hroch 1968). He claims (p. 124) that from the sociological perspective the awakening of national consciousness proceeds in three phases:

1. A phase of scholars collecting information about their national culture.
2. A phase involving small groups of patriotic individuals.
3. A mass movement.

The parallels with the distinct phases in the social organisation of purism described in Chapter 6 are striking:

1. The first stages of purism often involve solitary individuals

collecting words out of antiquarian, ethnographic or other scholarly interests.

2. Purism proceeds from the top down rather than from the bottom up. Its effects are seen in ever widening circles of society.
3. Purism, if successful, becomes a value-feature for the whole speech community.

Interestingly, as a single, active principle motivating human activity, purism like nationalism may re-emerge later but when it does so it finds its natural level in the petty bourgeoisie as a sort of *abgesunkenes Kulturgut*.

Finally, many scholars have voiced the opinion that nationalism is an inevitable phase through which any society must proceed on its way towards modernism (Smith 1971: 95). According to this viewpoint, the nationalist ideology and its intensity are determined primarily by the socio-political realities operative at the time that the society is making the transition to the modern world. It is tempting to consider whether purism can be construed in a parallel fashion. If so, the following hypotheses appear to have something to recommend them:

1. Purism is an inevitable phase through which any language must pass on its way to full development as a prestigious, autonomous and polyvalent standard language.
2. The puristic orientation and the intensity of the puristic movement are determined by the aesthetic features which are paramount during the phase of language standardisation.

These hypotheses will be explored further in Chapter 11.

Aesthetics

In Chapter 3 it was established that – the nationalist orientation apart – there is no single set of aesthetic principles governing purism: each type of purism has its own aesthetic basis. It follows, therefore, that '[n]o description of purism is adequate. . .unless it makes proper reference to its foundation in the aesthetics of a particular group of people at a specific time' (Thomas 1988b: 101). The task of this section is to examine these foundations more closely.

Given that the highest form of expression in a standard language is the language of literature and that purism is primarily the concern of the creative writer, it is inevitable that it is in the poetics of literary movements and traditions that we must seek the aesthetic determinants of purism. Each literary age or tradition promotes its own unwritten code of linguistic behaviour based on its own overall poetic aesthetic. Since one of the value-features of this aesthetic may be the desirability or non-desirability of certain linguistic items, there are clearly good grounds for considering the poetics of a particular literary tradition or movement as the determinants of puristic orientation and intensity. We shall explore this notion further by reference first to literary traditions and then to literary movements.

Literary traditions

Literary traditions may follow national, confessional, pan-national, ethnic or linguistic lines. What unites all traditions, however, is their retrospection and aesthetic conservatism. This is particularly true of the poetics of languages like Hebrew, Sanskrit, Latin, Greek and Arabic, which have served as vehicles of the world's great religious cults. Furthermore, in some traditions this conservatism has become a value-feature of the tradition itself and has had a visible impact on puristic attitudes. Many observers have noted, for example, the pervasive conservative element in Arabic literature, which has its roots in the wedding of the traditional nomadic life-style of the desert with Islam. This finds its reflection in archaising and élitist purism, an unwillingness to facilitate the entry of loanwords into the native phonological and morphological systems, a whole-scale invention of new words using Arabic roots as designations of the *realia* of modern technological society, and a perception that local vernacular forms of Arabic are bastardised or debased (Moussa 1955: 41–2; Elgibali 1988: 55–6).

A similar élitist, archaising purism is found in all literary traditions in Islamic societies. This is reflected not only in a reverence for traditional forms of expression and, above all, the immutability of the Koran but in the low prestige of vernacular elements compared with those of Arabic or Persian origin. This is true of languages as typologically and genetically diverse as Osmanli Turkish, Urdu, Malay or Swahili. The poetics operative in these traditions thus favoured Arabic and Persian elements while remaining deeply suspicious of any elements from languages of other confessional traditions.

Traditionalism has also been a feature of the two major western written languages of European antiquity – Greek and Latin. However, neither of them survived as an organic language with native speakers. Moreover, although they exerted considerable influence on the written vernaculars which subsequently emerged as standard languages in western and eastern Europe, the situation in the Christian literary traditions is by no means analogous to that in the Islamic world.

Whenever and however a puristic tradition has developed, the puristic orientation on which it is based becomes a value-feature in the poetics of that particular society. It will remain operative until replaced or amended by the introduction in the community of a new literary poetic.

Literary movements

Literary movements are recognisable precisely because they introduce – consciously or unconsciously – a new set of aesthetic principles on which to base literary production. In order to demonstrate the impact that these changing aesthetic principles may bring to bear on puristic attitudes, we shall examine four major European literary movements: the Renaissance, the Baroque, the Enlightenment and Romanticism. These movements have been chosen not at random but both because they represent the four major cultural paradigms of European modernity and because they held sway at the time when the majority of the European languages were being standardised. Furthermore, since, as we saw in Chapter 7, the standardisation phase is so crucial to the rise of purism, they provide some possible signposts in charting the history of purism – at least from a Eurocentric perspective.

THE RENAISSANCE

Above all, the Renaissance was a movement which sought to renew European culture by repudiating the obscurantism of the Middle Ages and by adapting classical traditions to its own needs. For literature this entailed finding a linguistic form of expression which was both vernacular and in accord with the model provided by Latin. The prestige, solidarity and separating functions required by the vernacular in this situation could only be carried out by a moderate application of purism. Though conditions differed somewhat from language to language, this purism was generally of the élitist and reformist variety. Moreover, the need for Italian, Spanish and French to come to terms with Latin necessarily involved the operation of targeted xenophobic purism. In France this problem continued to surface well into the seventeenth century, indeed it was an important constituent of the *Querelle des Anciens et des Modernes*, initiated by one of the more famous and influential sessions of the *Académie Française* held in 1687.

The languages of northern Europe were generally open to semantic, word-building and syntactic calques of Latin as well as loanwords from Italian, French and Latin. Indeed, some Renaissance figures, such as the Englishmen Carew and Mulcaster, saw the abundance of Latinisms in their native language as one of its chief claims to prestige. Purism merely provided a useful check on the too zealous creation of pseudo-Latinisms and 'ink-horn' terms (Prein 1909: 21–3).

In short, Renaissance purism can be characterised as balanced, moderate and favouring an élitist and reformist attitude to language intervention. Furthermore, it was tempered by the fact that, far from being under threat, the new vernacular languages were encouraged by the intellectual climate of the Renaissance and the Catholic and Protestant Reformations.

THE BAROQUE

The Baroque brought an exuberant, dramatic, grandiose and ornate mode of expression to European culture. In theory, such stylistic freedom would seem to have little to do with the puristic mentality. Nevertheless, at least in some cultures, the very spirit of experimentation and playfulness which characterises the Baroque lent itself rather easily to an unprincipled and non-rational attempt to coin new words to replace ones of foreign origin.

The Baroque also partly favoured a return to medieval obscurantism, which entailed not only a certain archaising trend in linguistic expression but also a diminished respect for the ability of words to express meaning. This aspect of obscurantism gave rise to a predeliction for piling on synonyms in the conviction that this would lead to an ever closer approximation of the essentially ineffable truth. As a result, an important recommendation for a language was that it possess a large number of synonyms. The provision of such synonyms, of course, put an even greater strain on the creative resources of the language in question. Finally, one of the aims of Baroque literature was to instruct and entertain the common people. This involved expanding the repertoire of the language to include lower registers.

Baroque purism may, therefore, be characterised as vigorous, non-rational, idiosyncratic, playful, xenophobic, archaising and ethnographic. Its inherent lack of moderation was further accentuated by the fact that many of the languages which had emerged in the

Renaissance or even earlier were now experiencing a decline both in numbers of speakers (often involving wholesale desertion by their élites) and in the maintenance of a universally acceptable norm. Indeed for some languages their very future seemed to be hanging in the balance.

THE ENLIGHTENMENT

The Enlightenment sought to realise a vision of a perfect world governed in all things by reason, utility and proper regard for the traditional heritage. The goal of purism was to provide an élitist, rationally justifiable critique of a state of language which had yet to attain perfection. Furthermore, the proper regard for tradition assured that there would also be a strong component of archaising purism in the Enlightenment aesthetic. At the same time, the prevailing mood was cosmopolitan in spirit: hence loanwords and other foreign influences – especially those which had become part of the tradition by adoption – were welcome as citizens of a shared world heritage. A central feature of the Enlightenment aesthetic was the principle of analogy: words should be well formed and their etymologies transparent. This had the effect of opening languages up to calques on a large scale, provided that no distortions were made to the syntactic, semantic and word-formational structures of the language concerned.

Enlightenment purism, therefore, may be described as rational, moderate, goal-orientated, élitist, archaising and non-xenophobic. Furthermore, the principle of analogy coupled with the cosmopolitanism of the intellectual climate ensured that purism should be not only severely limited in its scope but required to coexist with the other instruments for perfecting language. Finally, Enlightenment rationalism provided the basis for a thorough and withering critique of previous attempts at language purification, particularly those motivated by the aesthetics of the Baroque. Indeed, the main tenets of the Enlightenment aesthetic continue to dominate the thinking of those critics of extreme, non-rational purism.

ROMANTICISM

To the rationalism and utilitarianism of the Enlightenment, Romanticism preferred idealism, emotionalism and individualism. This preference provided just the right soil for the growth of purism as an ideology for developing the true potential of individual languages.

Furthermore, linguistic nationalism was given for the first time a theoretical underpinning in the cultural relativism of Herder and Humboldt. Therefore, purism – especially of the xenophobic variety – was an indispensable component of the system of values operating in the minds of the progenitors of the many newly emerging standard languages of Europe.

In some quarters, the Rousseauean reverence for the primitive and the natural also had its consequences for language attitudes. It promoted a strong identification both with medieval or oral literature and with rural dialects. Hence there was a tendency towards archaisation and ethnographism in language intervention, though the former was checked to some extent by the reformist zeal which characterised the efforts of the language renewers. The existence of a shared medieval or oral literary tradition might also lead to a strong sense of solidarity with peoples speaking closely related languages. Such solidarity was often translated into an opening to closely related languages as a source of lexical enrichment. For example, a passion for Old Norse literature heightened the awareness of a common heritage among the Scandinavians and led to their cooperation in curbing the growing influence of German on their respective national languages (Karker 1983: 290).

In short, Romantic purism may be characterised as pervasive, idealistic, goal-orientated, often ethnographic, sometimes archaising, reformist, xenophobic but also at times pan-nationalist. Moreover, it flourished in the very intellectual climate which was conducive to the emergence of so many new standard languages. Furthermore, its legacy continued to be strongly felt even in those languages which arose in the afterswell of Romanticism.

Conclusions

The examination of the role of nationalism and of these various systems of literary poetics provides a number of insights into the nature of linguistic purism:

1. Nationalist movements generally act as catalysts for puristic intervention.
2. The dominant puristic orientation of this intervention is primarily determined by the prevailing nationalist ideology.
3. Purism is an inalienable element of an overall cultural paradigm.

4. The emphasis and orientation of a given manifestation of purism is subject to change as a result of the operation of this cultural paradigm.

5. Literary movements and literary traditions provide the parameters for charting this cultural variability, and their inter-action partly determines the nature, the extent, the intensity and the eventual impact of the puristic intervention:

    (a) one may reinforce the other, as in Icelandic where Enlightenment utilitarianism and the spirit of Romanticism both produced puristically inclined neologising in a tradition already predisposed to puristic attitudes (Groenke 1983: 145–6).

    (b) they may compete with the result that the influence of one or the other of them will be nullified or mitigated as in the case of the minimal impact of the Romantic purism of William Barnes on the tradition of English attitudes set during the Renaissance.

In addition, the findings of this chapter offer some other conclusions which are of potential interest for the remaining chapters of this book. For example, the poetics of the Enlightenment and Romanticism continue to influence attitudes to language intervention up to the present day and thus may have an impact on the formation of languages standardised well after these literary movements have ceased to be operative. Indeed, they may be regarded as the progenitors of the rational and non-rational polarities respectively of recent (i.e. 'post-modern') purism. We shall resume this speculation in Chapter 11. It would also seem that the advent of nationalism and the impact of the various literary movements provide us with a potential base on which to construct an absolute and a relative chronology of linguistic purism, a subject which is a major preoccupation of the next chapter.

CHAPTER 9

The diachronic aspect

Introduction

The previous six chapters have provided a theoretical, typological and descriptive framework for a comparative study of purism as a phenomenon occurring in a wide variety of languages. Now it is time to rescue the discussion from the charge of ahistoricism by introducing the diachronic aspect.

A diachronic study of purism necessarily involves an examination of changes and trends in a series of individual languages. Since so much of the literature on purism deals with individual languages – and often from an historical perspective – there is happily no dearth of available secondary material. As one might expect, however, given the different socio-cultural contexts and language situations in which purism has arisen, the comparative picture which emerges from this literature is not only highly complex but also extremely varied. The problem is to do justice to this complexity and variety without becoming mired in the detailed *minutiae* of puristic endeavours in individual languages. To avoid compounding these problems further, it seems advisable in this chapter to dispense for the time being with a discussion of puristic practice. The implementation of purism and the relationship between theory and practice will receive fuller treatment in the next chapter.

Our chief concerns in this chapter are:

(1) To discuss some possible theoretical models and practical approaches to studying purism on a temporal plane.
(2) To document the clash of tradition and change.
(3) To offer explanations for the outcome of the clash.
(4) To provide a reliable chronological framework.

(5) To determine what – if any – patterns emerge in the historical process.

Theoretical models and practical approaches

The need to follow the course of purism in individual languages brings us face to face with a theoretical difficulty: whether it is legitimate to use phrases like 'German purism' as if it were categorically different from, say, 'Hebrew purism'. There can surely be little objection to such usage as long as we are aware that it is merely a convenient shorthand to describe 'the totality of puristic attitudes and behaviour in the German speech community'.

Language purification is best treated not as a single event – or a series of unrelated events – but as an on-going, open-ended process. Indeed, in this respect it may be usefully compared with religious conversion – at least as understood by many modern non-fundamentalist and non-traditionalist theologians. In both spheres we can chart moments of despair – even apostasy – periods of backsliding, shifts in the rationalisations of sins committed in the past, and times of fresh resolve motivated perhaps by changing circumstances, fresh challenges and different sets of ethical principles. The development is not linear but involves constant turns, reversals and abrupt gear-changes.

From the diachronic perspective, then, purism is best viewed not as a sequence of isolated events, but as a non-linear process. The shifts of focus and emphasis involved in this process may be best described as paradigm changes, where a paradigm is understood as 'an entire constellation of beliefs, values, techniques, and so on shared by the members of a given community' (Kuhn 1970: 175). The replacement of one paradigm by another is usually prompted by some perceived failure of the old paradigm and is preceded by a transitional period of uncertainty with the appearance of competing new approaches to the problem. With respect to purism, this involves a debate on how to deal with some threat posed to the integrity and autonomy of the language. The outcome of this debate then provides the basis for a new paradigm, which remains in place until challenged in its turn by some alternative, and so on *ad infinitum*. In other words, the history of purism is a succession of paradigm changes about possible approaches to a language's problems seen from an etymological rather than a functional point of view. The puristic debate may devolve not only on what is the best means for correcting a language's shortcomings but also whether or not purification is an adequate response to them in the first place. Hence, the anti-puristic paradigm also needs to be included in the chronicle of successive paradigm changes.

It is in the nature of paradigm changes that they are first espoused by a small minority (often the younger generation) before gaining wider acceptance. This explains why so often puristic (and anti-puristic) attitudes spread from a single individual or small group of like-minded individuals before being embraced by ever-wider sectors of the community until finally being endorsed as public policy.

In some cases, as with William Barnes' attempts to remove the Graeco-Latinisms from English, the new paradigm is not successful in dislodging the old. It will either disappear altogether or reappear only in more auspicious circumstances. Alternatively, wider acceptance of the new paradigm may be slowed by the resistance of an old guard, often unattuned to the changes of thinking going on around them. Take, for example the situation in Czechoslovakia in the 1920s and 1930s:

> Die ältere, puristische und übertrieben gefühlsmässige Einstellung, die sich gegen alles wandte, was aus fremden Sprachen vor allem auf der lexikalischen Ebene ins Tschechische eindrang, war in der neuen Situation zu einem Anachronismus geworden, der zwar historisch verständlich, vom synchronen Standpunkt aber völlig angerechtfertigt war.[31] (Kraus 1982: 262-3)

While the anti-purists were guided by a new paradigm involving a scientific recognition of the systematicity and functionality of linguistic signs. . .'[D]ie Ansichten der Puristen, die nicht nur in Kreisen von Laien, sondern auch bei Fachleuten bestanden, fanden ihren Ausdruck in zahlreichen Artikeln, die nicht berücksichtigten, dass die Sprachsituation sich verändert hatte'[32] (Kraus 1982: 263). Earlier in Czech history, however, the purists had been the adherents of a new paradigm, when in the early nineteenth century the

[31] The older puristic and exaggeratedly emotional attitude which turned against everything which entered Czech from foreign languages especially on the lexical level had in the new situation become an anachronism, which while historically understandable was from the synchronic point of view however totally unjustified
[32] The views of the purists which existed not only in lay circles but also among professionals found expression in numerous articles which did not take into consideration that the language situation had changed

puristically inspired Jungmann School rejected the scholarly classicism of Josef Dobrovský in favour of an all-out attack on 'fremde Einflüsse, die die Eigenständigkeit der Sprache als eines der wichtigsten Attribute der Nation bedrohten'[33] (Kraus 1982: 262–3). This they achieved with great success despite the rearguard efforts of Dobrovský's conservative pupils Nejedlý and Palkovič (Jedlička 1948: 15). Nevertheless, Dobrovský's critical attitude did have an impact on the younger generation by making them aware of the dangers of extreme purism (Bělič 1953: 199). This is an excellent example of the way that an old paradigm may continue to influence the formulation of its eventual replacement.

In both of these instances, the polemic takes on the form of a generational conflict. Ultimate success of the new paradigm comes only with the demise of the generation supporting the old one. It is also noteworthy that such rearguard actions on behalf of an old paradigm, as well as the slow rate of acceptance of a new one, may result in a considerable temporal overlap of the two paradigms. This is an important point to remember when we come to address problems of relative chronology.

The clash of tradition and change

Thus far we have treated purism as an attitude which either involves criticism of the *status quo* (offensive purism) or sounds alarm bells signalling possible imminent threats to the integrity of a language (defensive purism). In either case, there is a clear implication that the implementation of puristic reform constitutes intervention in the development of a language. Yet their net impact is quite different: offensive purism seeks to force some radical departure from traditional usage, while defensive purism aims to put a brake on undesirable developments. In the one case, purism champions tradition; in the other, change. More often, however, a puristic movement seeks to preserve in some areas while initiating innovation in others. The *Allgemeiner Deutscher Sprachverein*, for instance, at one and the same time wished to remove Gallicisms and Anglicisms already current in German, to introduce and popularise German

---

[33] foreign influences which threatened the independence of the language as one of the most important attributes of the nation

equivalents for the items replaced and to prevent the introduction of new foreign terms. These activities were rightly considered to be inseparable.

As we saw in Chapter 8, a puristic attitude may be a constant element of the literary tradition. Any retreat from purism in a traditionally puristic language like Arabic or Tamil constitutes, therefore, an especially noteworthy paradigm change. Conversely, in a language like English with its long tradition of openness to external influences of all kinds the programme of ethnographic and archaising purism advanced by William Barnes and others in the nineteenth century was regarded by most native speakers as, at best, a well-intentioned, harmless case of pedantic eccentricity. A reversal of the accommodating spirit of the English language would have required a paradigm change motivated by a radically new socio-cultural context or socio-linguistic setting.

Finally, the conflict is not one simply between tradition and change. Even anti-purists would argue that language has to change – indeed may be in need of cultivation – but they would point out that purism does not offer a legitimate criterion for selecting new items. This was precisely the viewpoint of the Prague School in its debate with the editors of the journal *Naše Řeč* in the 1920s and 1930s. Among purists too there is rarely a conflict about the need for change; the crux of any debate is the nature of the shortcomings and the remedies suggested to right them. For example, in Ukrainian circles, some purists feared Russian influences, others Polish; some advocated calques or loans from other Slavonic languages; others favoured native-based neologisms, still others sought enrichment from dialects and earlier stages of the written language; there were also some who preferred a mixed approach to the problem (Wexler 1974).

Explanations of the outcomes

As we have seen, the various paradigm changes in the history of purism in a given language are prompted by a gradual loss of confidence in the old paradigm. Were there no such loss of confidence or were no alternative paradigm available, then no change would take place. For a new paradigm to assert itself, some change in the situational variables is required. Let us briefly consider how some of these factors are reflected in a shift to a new puristic (or anti-puristic) paradigm.

Firstly, it is obvious that changed political, religious or economic circumstances may bring into contact languages formerly cut off from each other. For example, exploration and colonial expansion have opened up established written languages like Swahili, Arabic, Turkish, Hindi, Urdu, Japanese and Chinese to massive influence from English and the other European languages. The spread of world religions, such as Christianity, Islam, Hinduism and Buddhism, has also presented enormous challenges to those who would prefer to keep their native language free from external influences. World trade and commerce too have had an increasingly homogenising effect on the lexical repertoires of langauges operating in the 'Coca-Cola society' – a trend many purists would like to see reversed.

The separation of speakers resulting from movement of population can also have repercussions for purism. An immigrant population cut off from its parent community may experience a loss of the *Sprachgefühl* necessary for maintaining the norms of the standard language. Purists may respond to this situation by criticising the linguistic habits of the immigrants in the hope of bringing them back to the true path. One could cite examples of this kind from virtually any of the immigrant minorities of the United States and Canada, particularly where the immigrant language is being incompletely learned by the younger generation and is becoming heavily infiltrated by competing languages in the community. Alternatively, the desire to divest itself of the colonial tag and achieve cultural independence may lead, as in the case of Noah Webster, to members of the élite wishing to distance their language from the norms practised in the homeland.

However, it is not simply a matter of new instances of language contact but the possibility of fundamental changes in the power relationships between languages already in contact. For example, French and English have been in contact for centuries with French the dominant partner. Now with the partial eclipse of French as a world language and the rise of English as the language of international commerce, technology, diplomacy and tourism the roles have been totally reversed. As a result of this changed state of affairs, there have been impassioned pleas by Étiemble and many others in France for the eradication of *franglais* as the first step to elevate the prestige of *la francophonie mondiale*.

Economic, political and social changes are also instrumental in determining the targets of puristic intervention. In east-central Europe, for example, German was for many centuries the dominant idiom in many spheres of social activity. With the growth of the political power of the Soviet Union over its socialist satellites it has been replaced by Russian. The puristic orientation in the region has shifted accordingly, though the impact of this shift has been somewhat muted perhaps by the undesirability of appearing to criticise the Soviet Union and the dead hand of Marxist–Leninist rhetoric.

National consciousness is also subject to change and fluctuation both in its intensity and formal expression. Purism often serves as an accurate barometer of these fluctuations. For example, whenever, Croatian animosity to the Serbs is on the rise, you may be sure that attempts to distance the Croatian variant of Serbo-Croatian from the Serbian variant will not be far behind. Conversely, periods of mutual tolerance and fruitful cooperation often coincide with calls for diminishing the differences which separate the two codes.

Indeed, in multilingual states like Yugoslavia, national conscious-ness is particularly sensitive to changes in inter-ethnic relations. For example, in South Africa the Afrikaans purist movement, which arose around 1930 and sought above all to replace English words (*lorry* by *vragmotor*, *scooter* by *bromponie*, semantic calques of rugby terms: *goal* by *doel*, *try* by *drie*), was directly related to 'the Afrikaner's struggle for self-preservation and self-realisation in the economic, political and cultural spheres' (Botha 1983: 232–5).

Where such national feeling is harnessed to the machinery of the state, the effects on language attitudes can be daunting. The Shah of Persia, for example, 'brooked no opposition' to his resolve to purify Persian in the years 1935–41 (Jazayery 1983: 252). At his command a language academy was founded, which created 2,400 new words (mostly of a technical nature). This puristic paradigm change was enforced from above and was not accepted by the intellectual élite. In Fascist Italy the situation was rather different:

> Mussolini himself was by no means a purist – personally he had little interest in linguistic questions – but his collaborators tried to re-Italianise the language by proscribing foreign elements and by going back to medieval Italian. Laws were issued which prohibited the use of foreign elements: the newspapers had to institute special columns for linguistic questions; all Italian linguists were invited to collaborate on the purification of the language. (Kramer 1983: 314)

All these efforts came to nothing: the resulting neologisms were rejected as farcical and they died with Fascism. In other words, the enforced paradigm change was embraced only by some opportunists and was seen as an aberration of the period. In Germany, although Goebbels in his instructions to the press never expressly mentioned the subject, the Nazi leadership at first condoned the rekindled interest in purism in the *ADSV* and other sectors of society as an expression of national feeling (von Polenz 1983: 38–9). Many purists took advantage of the situation to create fanciful neologisms in the firm belief that they were serving the interests of the *Führer*. Eventually, Goebbels and Hitler grew impatient of this 'klein-bürgerlich-romantisierende "Deutschtümelei"'[34] (von Polenz 1983: 39) and condemned it outright on several occasions. Here is an instance where purists misinterpreted – perhaps deliberately – the aims of the regime by introducing a radically new paradigm. Like its Italian counterpart, it was generally ridiculed and disappeared with the demise of the political force which had unintentionally fostered it.

One puristic paradigm is also likely to be replaced by another as changes occur in the literary aesthetic. Thus, as German literature passed through the Renaissance, the Baroque, the Enlightenment, Sentimentalism, *Sturm und Drang*, Romanticism, Biedermeier and Modernism, the puristic paradigm changed accordingly with respect to the identification of targets, the choice of replacements, the intensity level and the practicality or idealism of its practitioners. Nevertheless, despite the changes of course dictated by fluctuations in the literary aesthetic, the value-orientations operative at the time of the creation of the standard language may remain as a norm-concept in the consciousness of native speakers.

Nor should it be forgotten, of course, that there are also factors favouring a move away from the puristic paradigm:

1. Internationalism and cosmopolitanism of political outlook.
2. The existence of a long literary tradition ensuring continued prestige of the standard language.
3. The unflinching loyalty of native speakers.
4. Constitutional guarantees for a language's future.
5. The need for inter-language comprehensibility in the technical sphere.
6. *Laissez-faire* and functionalist attitudes to language intervention.

While some of these factors have featured in past stages of standard language development, together they undeniably reflect the liberal, modernist, pragmatic, rational paradigm of inter-ethnic relations. This combination, more than anything else, has led to the retreat from purism which tends to dominate linguistic attitudes in the twentieth century.

The complex interplay of all the above factors determines the degree of likelihood that a paradigm change will take place. Obviously, the likelihood increases if the factors are mutually

[34] petty bourgeois, romanticising 'Germanness'

reinforcing and decreases if they tend to counterbalance one another. Not only is this an important factor for explaining past changes in puristic attitudes but it is also a useful point to consider when future intervention of a puristic kind is being contemplated.

Problems of chronology

If we are to view the development of purism in a given language as a succession of paradigms, each encapsulating a specific attitude of the community to the shortcomings and needs of its language, it remains only to give these paradigms a time reference. A 'succession' implies that one paradigm follows on from its predecessor. If this is so, it should be possible to assign firm dates to this transition. Unfortunately, such is not always the case.

Firstly, as we have observed, the old paradigm may not simply disappear but may overlap – often for a considerable period – with the new. Such overlapping periods are usually marked by the ascendancy of the new paradigm and the decline of the old until such time as the latter has no more adherents. This transitional period may be particularly painful if the debate about the language question becomes fiercely polemical. If during this period, the old paradigm wins fresh converts among the newly emerging élite, then the scene is set for a prolonged and possibly inconclusive struggle for ascendancy between the old and new positions. This period of uncertainty can be very confusing for the community at large, which is being given conflicting signals about what attitudes to adopt, and may have serious long-term consequences for the stability of the standard language. Such was the case when the moderate, reformist purism of the Croatian language renewal gave way in the 1870s to a new, ethnographically orientated paradigm of Serbian origin, which, following Vuk's principles, allowed enrichment only from folk poetry and dialects and was even open to foreign words if they had already been assimilated into the everyday speech of the peasant. This new paradigm was embraced by the majority of Croatian language planners until the 1960s but many – including the one outstanding Croatian writer of the period Miroslav Krleža – were never entirely happy with this solution and remained favourable towards the earlier reformist paradigm (Thomas 1988a: 143–4, 155). This disunity has doubtless been a factor contributing to the ambivalence felt by many modern Croats towards certain elements of their standard idiom.

Secondly, the old paradigm may give way to the new for some time only to be revived – possibly with some modifications – when circumstances and fashion permit. For example, the élitist, archaising purism of the Czech classicist Dobrovský was close to the viewpoint of Renaissance humanism (Havránek 1936: 84). Indeed Dobrovský based his model for the codification of Czech on the language of this period. The Jungmann generation on the other hand adopted much of the puristic paradigm of the Czech Baroque with its focus on removing words of foreign origin and replacing them with newly coined neologisms. It even drew on some of the word-building patterns of the Baroque but eschewed some of its more extreme creations (Jedlička 1948: 12; Jelínek 1971: 22).

Thirdly, two or more conflicting paradigms may continue to coexist, each fighting for supremacy over the other(s). In their jockeying for position, one of them may take the lead for a while only to relinquish it to another. In such circumstances, none of the paradigms can ever be assured ultimate victory. This means that there develops a tension between them pulling the standard language in two or more different directions at once. The result of this tug-of-war may be a stalemate, in which each of the paradigms finds expression. For example, Ukrainian, as we have seen, was subject to all sorts of pressures. While it is possible to identify trends at particular moments in its historical development, none of them has won outright approval. Nevertheless, like the action of wind and water on a sailing craft, the tension set up by these various pressures keeps Ukrainian on a stable course.

Since purism is a reaction to a perceived threat to the well-being of a language, it often serves to check a development which has gone too far in one direction or – to resume the nautical metaphor – to trim the sails on the wind rather than run with it. For example, in Swedish and Danish of the nineteenth century, a reaction against the numerous calques formed on German models – themselves favoured over an earlier French influence – began to set in and fostered a growth of mutual self-help among the Scandinavian languages (Karker 1983: 286–90). It is in terms of checks and balances too that we should understand the anti-Russian purism of the Bulgarian Bogorov. His compatriots had earlier borrowed heavily from Russian as a means of intellectualising and Europeanising the language after years of neglect and Turkish domination. As a result of Bogorov's criticism of the extremes of Russification, Bulgarian writers showed great restraint in their use of Russian in the late nineteenth century and did not propel the language on a wrong course (Moskov 1976: 17–8, 23–6).

Unfortunately, at least from the purist's perspective, the threats a language faces may be considerable and unlikely to disappear: merely trimming them from time to time may not be sufficient. When the temptation simply to accept (and hence to assimilate) undesirable influences is as strong as the resolve to resist them, the struggle is often not only inconclusive but involves a periodic reversion to one course or the other. We have already seen an example of such oscillation in Czech in its attempts over the years to come to terms with an overwhelming German influence: Hussite purism, followed by humanist tolerance, succeeded by baroque purism, giving way to rational Enlightenment acceptance, followed in turn by renewal purism, mid-nineteenth century Biedermeier relaxation, and the negative excesses of the late nineteenth century (Ševčík 1974–5: 51; Jelínek 1971: 25–6).

Another excellent illustration of such oscillation of attitudes over a long period of time is provided by Yiddish and its relationship to German. The first attempts to draw Yiddish closer to German date from the time of the grammarian Buxtorf (1609), who was guided by the premise – as widespread then as it was to be later – that Yiddish was simply corrupt German (Schaechter 1983: 195). Later in the seventeenth century, translations into Yiddish already show the tension between the two poles: to emulate German or to reflect the individuality of Yiddish (Schaechter 1983: 213). In the eighteenth century Yiddish went through a vast expansion of its vocabulary by opening up to European languages, particularly German. However, Jewish scholars of the Enlightenment, for whom German was the symbol of the Europeanisation and secularisation of Jewish life, generally held Yiddish in low esteem and eschewed its use in favour of German (Schaechter 1983: 211). Towards the end of the nineteenth century the tide began to turn: apologists for Yiddish as a written tongue began to appear and the struggle 'against the powerful drive to Germanise Yiddish' was begun (Schaechter 1983: 213). This movement – traditionally associated with Sholem-Aleykhem – sought to distance Yiddish as far as possible from German. Nevertheless, many Jewish nationalist and socialist movements (including Zionism) used *daytshmerish* or *kongresdaytsh* (both heavily Germanised forms of Yiddish) 'albeit more as a matter of social prestige and practical convenience', in which words of German origin like *fórzitsnder* 'chairman' (‹ G *Vorsitzender*), *mítglid* 'member' (‹ G *Mitglied*), *farzámlung* 'meeting' (*Versammlung*) replaced Semitic words (Schaechter 1983: 211). The theatre, the press and the labour movement also helped in this process. Indeed, so close was this Yiddish to German that theatre companies were able to fool the Czarist authorities into believing that their productions were not in Yiddish, which was banned for public use, but in German. Some thought that this Germanised Yiddish would eventually meld into a single supra-dialectal language which would transcend the language's immense dialectal differentiation (Schaechter 1983: 211). Today, this Germanising phase is held in ridicule by all levels of society and there has been a concerted effort to remove some of the superfluous, recent German loanwords while leaving intact the medieval German component, which constitutes 'the very basis of the Yiddish language' (Schaechter 1983: 213). As a result of cultivating features dissimilar to those of German the modern standard language has been brought closer to the spoken language. Nevertheless, the very closeness of German and Yiddish, their common genetic source and the important role that German has played in the cultural life of the Ashkenazim ensure that the problem will never entirely wither away.

The tempo of change

Standard languages do not develop at a constant rate: there are periods when they appear to languish and periods when changes follow one another at an accelerated pace. Generally speaking, a rapid tempo of change coincides with a time of crucial new extralinguistic developments. It is notable that the speed of puristic reform is closely associated with a major reappraisal of the standard language problem. For example, in the years from 1830 to 1842 the face of Croatian was changed totally as a whole new set of principles on which to base the standard language was introduced (Thomas 1988a). The rate of change in Hebrew, following the decision of a few individuals to attempt to adapt the language for the full range of social functions, was if anything even more remarkable.

Such *accelerandi* are marked by two features:

(1) the sheer volume of successive innovations, which depends on the immediacy of the threat and the energy of the speech community in combating it.
(2) the shortness of the time needed for completion of the purificational cycle, which is dependent on factors such as unity of purpose among the reformers, their identification with the aspirations of the wider community, and the practicability of their plan of action.

Patterns of development

Notwithstanding the problems discussed above and periods of limited or poor documentation in some languages, it is by no means impossible to establish a fairly reliable relative chronology of the paradigm changes taking place in a given language. These paradigm changes may then be pegged against the dates of the extralinguistic events with which they are associated in order to provide an absolute chronology. This in turn allows for a periodisation of puristic attitudes and behaviour. From each of these periodisations an overall picture of puristic intervention in a language emerges. The next step is to take each of these diachronic surveys as a basis for a comparison of purism across languages. The difficulties of such a comparison will be discussed in more detail in Chapter 11, but in the meantime it may be useful to examine some of the discernible patterns of development. The first six patterns are presented in increasing order of intensity; the seventh stands outside this scale. The seven patterns are only illustrated here by reference to xenophobic purism but they apply just as well to other types of orientation.

Marginal purism

In this pattern, purism is a marginal or ephemeral occurrence in the development of the standard language. At no stage does it become a value-feature of the entire speech community. On the contrary, the dominant value-feature is openness to sources of enrichment which elsewhere might have provoked a puristic response. Examples: English, Russian, Polish.

Moderate, discontinuous purism

In this pattern, a moderate puristic attitude is discernible over a long period of time in the whole speech community without a continuous tradition of puristic intervention ever developing. Examples: French, Portuguese, Italian, Spanish.

Trimming purism

In this pattern, purism serves as a reactive correction to a potentially dangerous trend in the development of a standard language. It is repeated as often as the speech community identifies the threat as problematic. Examples: Danish, Swedish, Dutch, Slovak.

Evolutionary purism

In this pattern, purism emerges as a value-feature early in the development of a written language, does not undergo radical changes of orientation and reaches its peak during the standardisation process, after which it may be relaxed somewhat as the standard language achieves autonomy, prestige and security of tenure. Examples: Hungarian, Finnish, Estonian, Hebrew, Croatian, Slovene.

Oscillatory purism

This pattern involves repeated pendulum swings between intense purism and more tolerant attitudes. Examples: German, Czech, Yiddish. An oscillatory pattern is also discernible in those languages which find themselves between two language models. Examples: Ukrainian, Belorussian.

Stable, consistent purism

In this pattern, there is no discernible interruption or fluctuation in puristic attitudes either in intensity or orientation. They are a constant value-feature of the speech community. Examples: Arabic, Tamil, Icelandic.

Revolutionary purism

This involves an abrupt and violent change from one of the above patterns to another. The further up or down the scale, the more radical is the shift. Example: Turkish.

Summary

The objection may be made that these patterns do not readily fit certain languages. Some combine features from several patterns. For example, German and Czech, for all their oscillation, otherwise follow the pattern of evolutionary purism; Tamil, though unrelenting in its opposition to Europeanisation but generally open to Sanskritisation, has at times been forced to trim back the Sanskrit element in its vocabulary. In other cases the problem is one of defining the language situation. For example, how is the situation of Norwegian or Greek to be treated: as one community with one language with two different literary traditions, as one community with two standard languages, or as two separate speech communities? The shift from Katharevousa to Dimotiki or from Bokmål to Nynorsk could be seen as revolutionary, or alternatively each idiom could be described separately as displaying a stable pattern.

Despite these objections, it is worth noting that the diachronic development of purism in all the cases described in the available literature lies within these seven patterns. It seems legitimate, therefore, to suppose that the use of these patterns as a framework for examining puristic intervention from a diachronic perspective will not lead to any grave procrusteanisation of the material. The first six patterns reflect six levels of puristic intensity as shown in Figure 9. It may be noted that evolutionary purism – the most widespread and archetypal pattern – is positioned at the break-point in this curve.

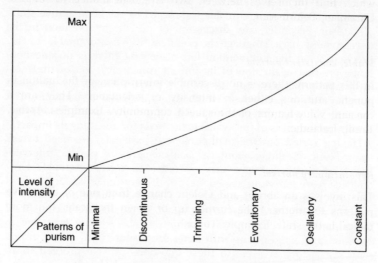

Figure 9: The intensity of patterns of purism

What remains now is to evaluate the impact of the various stages of puristic intervention. We shall then be in a position to re-examine these patterns as a guide to a comparative history of purism.

CHAPTER 10

The effects of purism

Introduction

It is now time to discuss the impact of all this puristic intervention. The evaluation of the effects of purism is crucial for two reasons. Firstly, without it we are unable to proceed to any comparative study of purism. Secondly, any discussion of puristic intervention in the development of a language is pointless if we are unable to say precisely what the intervention has achieved. There is no question, however, that evaluation of its impact constitutes one of the most intractable problems facing the study of purism. Should it be assessed quantitatively or qualitatively? If the former, how is it to be measured? If the latter, on what criteria? Our first task, therefore, must be to review the appropriateness of the available methods for assessing its impact.

Having sorted out the methodological problems, we need to ask some blunt questions about the achievements of puristic intervention. Did purists actually carry out what they had intended? How effective were these puristic endeavours? Were the effects felt only at the time or were they long-lasting? What was more important: the concrete results of purism or a change in linguistic consciousness? Have the effects been positive or detrimental for the language in question and its relations with other languages? Only when armed with satisfactory answers to these questions can we proceed to an overall assessment of purism as an international phenomenon.

Measuring the effects of purism

Some methodological problems

Many of the accounts of puristic intervention founder for want of a properly elaborated model for measuring its effects. Such a model needs to take into account a number of basic theoretical problems.

The first is a fundamental problem in the philosophy of history: how can one determine the extent of an act of intervention when this very intervention obliterates the traces of what would have happened without it? In many cases, of course, this question is unanswerable except to note that without intervention we should expect languages to evolve without abrupt changes of direction. Any departure from normal evolutionary progression may be interpreted, therefore, as the result of some sort of intervention – whether premeditated or not. In others, some other idiom of the same diasystem – to use the convenient term introduced by Brozović (1970: 14) – which has remained unaffected by purism may serve as a control. For example, whereas standard Russian has been influenced by a puristic attitude which assigns loanwords ending in a vowel to a class of their own without markers for case, gender and number, non-standard Russian typically incorporates them into the native declension patterns (Thomas 1983). There are also instances where a standard language exhibits considerable differences from one territorial unit to another. Where one of these territorial variants is subject to puristic intervention while the other is not, a comparison of the two idioms will reveal the differential effect of purism. A good example of this is provided by the regional varieties of standard German: in Austria and Switzerland, the standard language is much less marked by xenophobic purism than it is in Germany. These differences are undoubtedly attributable to the widespread puristic attitudes in Prussia prior to the First World War. On a smaller scale, one can trace the undoubted effects of purism on a single text. For example, Behagel (1917: 157) has compared the first and second editions of Jean Paul's poem *Unsichtbare Loge*. Apart from paraphrases and omissions of foreign words, she documents the following replacements, which stem from the influence of Campe: *kaufmännisch* for *merkantalisch*, *Brennpunkt* for *Fokus*, *Luftschiff* for *Luftballon*, *lehrreich* for *instruktiv*, *Dreiklang* for *Akkord*, *Spottgedichte* for *Satiren*, *Lobgedichte* for *Hymnen*, *Abbild* for *Kopie*.

The second problem is procedural: *how* are the effects of purism to be measured? Since, as we have seen, linguistic purity is a relative notion, it should be possible – at least in theory – to provide for any language a 'purity index' based on the statistical relationship between the 'pure' and 'impure' items in its inventory. A comparison of this purity index before and after the puristic intervention would thus provide a quantitative measure of its effects – at least within the terms set by the purists themselves. However, such a statistical procedure ignores the fact that in a linguistic system some features are central and others peripheral. Clearly, the impact would need to be greater, the nearer the features were to the centre of the system. In the lexical sphere, for example, those items forming part of everyday intellectual discourse assume much greater importance and have a higher profile than, say, items of technical terminology. Moreover, the inclusion in the data base of large numbers of internationalisms common to most languages tends to skew the results of a statistical analysis and even to obscure the extent of the puristic impact altogether. It is imperative, therefore, that a purity index reflects this fact either by a differential adjustment of the weighting given to individual items or by concentrating only on core items. Furthermore, the identification of puristic targets may invest certain items with a symbolic significance above and beyond their centrality or peripherality in the system. Obviously, there is no statistical means for reflecting this state of affairs in an index of purity. Finally, as far as lexical purism is concerned, it must be remembered that the lexicon – unlike the other levels of language – is an open system, and consequently the criteria for defining the corpus are necessarily arbitrary. Moreover, such difficulties are compounded, should the scholar wish to compare one purity index with another. This robs statistical comparisons between languages of much of their validity.

The third problem is a matter of substance: *what* precisely is being affected by purism? The discussion so far has focused on the effects of puristic intervention on a standard language. Yet this begs the question whether we are talking about language in the sense of *langue* – the totality of conventional norms – or in the sense of *parole* – the totality of potential and actual individual usage. Clearly, we are interested in both, but it is important not to confuse them. If the effects of purism on *langue* are being measured, then the contents of a standard grammar or dictionary may serve as the corpus as long as we are aware that this corpus may not always reflect the totality of either the competence or the performance of the speech community. If, on the other hand, we are investigating the effects on *parole*, then we need to consider individual and collective usage. Not only does this introduce the problem of such socio-linguistic variables as stylistic register, subject-matter and social milieu, but it also means that we need to confront the question of word-frequency. Should a word or word-form occurring more than once in our corpus be counted once only or as many times as it appears? If our aim is to measure the impact on usage, then word-frequency must be taken into consideration, otherwise we should fail to register the much greater extra effort required to oust a more frequently used word. Finally, if one of the aims of purism is not simply to intervene in the

163

corpus of a language but to change public attitudes to elements in that language, then quite different measuring devices must be employed.

Before attempting to develop some guidelines for minimising, even if not actually solving, these problems, I should like to illustrate the advantages and disadvantages of various procedures adopted in the past for measuring the effects of purism.

Some case studies using quantitative data

A useful starting point for examining early attempts at quantifying the native and non-native lexical component is Ekwall (1903), who provides a summary of assessments of the Germanic and non-Germanic elements in English. In 1705 George Hickes on the basis of the Lord's Prayer wrote that hardly a tenth of English is of non-Saxon origin. In 1833 Meidinger estimated on the basis of Turner's *History of the Anglo-Saxons* that four fifths of English vocabulary was Germanic. A little later, Rogers credited English with 38,000 words of which 23,000 (60 percent) belong to the Germanic stock, while his contemporary Thommerel, on the basis of Robertson's dictionary, gave figures of 13,000 Germanic and 29,854 Romance out of a total of 43,566. When it comes to individual works, Marsh estimated in 1860 that the Authorised Bible and Shakespeare have 60 percent Germanic vocabulary, while Milton has only 33 percent. Interesting as these figures are, they reveal some alarming discrepancies. Furthermore, they do not provide a basis for developing a thesis about puristic intervention or apuristic tolerance in English.

Dictionaries, of course, are an obvious source of data for the lexical composition of standard languages. According to Zaidi (1983: 399–400), the great Urdu dictionary of 1892 records 54,009 words, of which 22,203 are of Hindi, Punjabi or Purbi origin and a further 17,505 are derivatives from Hindi. The total Indian component constitutes, therefore, 73 percent. There are 13,748 words (26 percent of the total) of Middle Eastern origin, of which 7,584 are from Arabic, 6,041 from Persian, 105 from Turkish. The remaining 1 percent comprises words from European sources (90 percent of them from English). These figures are, of course, invaluable for assessing the various influences which have shaped written Urdu but in themselves tell us nothing of any puristic closure to any of these sources. It is perhaps significant, however, that a comparison with the standard dictionary of Urdu published in 1964 reveals that although the number of words has doubled the proportions remain roughly as before. This suggests that Urdu has successfully resisted the pressures of Europeanisation and that any moves to differentiate Urdu from Hindi have not resulted in any change in the relationship between the Indian and Middle Eastern components. Nevertheless, no very firm conclusions can be drawn about the impact of puristic intervention from these figures. Furthermore, any purity index for Urdu based on them would depend on how the speech community chose to interpret 'native'. Is its linguistic culture seen as Islamic and therefore distinct from Hindi, or alternatively is it Hindustani and therefore de-Persianised?

A similar quantitative analysis has been carried out on the lexicon of standard Romanian (Şerban 1983: 230–6). It reveals that 58.25 percent of the total modern vocabulary comprises new words: 23 percent created by internal means and 77 percent consisting of loanwords. At first these figures do not smack of purism, until one realises that nearly all these loanwords are from other Romance languages (65 percent of them from French alone), which reminds us that the chief motivation of Romanian purism has been to assert its Romance base and thus stress its distance from the neighbouring Slavonic idioms. Şerban's analysis does not stop with dictionaries but includes the vocabulary of modern prose usage, where again French dominates with 40.17 percent of new words, followed by Latin (9.15 percent), Italian (2.30 percent), German (2.03 percent), English (0.79 percent), Russian (0.55 percent) – though the numbers of English words (particularly in the field of sport) have increased rapidly over the past two decades. On the basis of journalism, Şerban estimates the number of words inherited from Latin (the original basic vocabulary) to be 62.46 percent, while the total of all Romance loanwords constitutes 23.99 percent and with Slavonic loans as low as 3.92 percent. Fully 86.45 percent of the lexical elements in modern journalistic prose, therefore, are of Romance origin. Moreover, many Greek, Turkish, Hungarian and Slavonic loanwords registered in Romanian have dropped out of use altogether. The advantages of these figures over those for Urdu are: (1) they allow a comparison of dictionary material with actual usage, and (2) they provide a more complete picture of recent developments. Indeed, if the combined total of words of Romance origin is a reliable purity index then the impact of pan-Romance purism must be adjudged considerable and the intervention highly successful in its own terms. Nevertheless, it should be remembered that Romance languages generally have one great advantage over all others, namely that Latin is one of the foremost elements in the formation of modern international vocabulary. As a result, in the terms set by Romanian purists, the purity index of any modern Romance language stands a good chance of being higher than, say, a German one. One wonders, therefore, how many internationally used pseudo-Latinisms have been counted in Şerban's analysis as if they were of genuine Romance origin.

Several other scholars have tried to estimate the size of the foreign component actively used in a language. Sauvageot (1971: 346) says that Hungarian linguists at the beginning of the century noted with satisfaction that 85 percent of the words in Hungarian texts were of Hungarian origin. He considers this figure somewhat optimistic and takes 70 percent to be a better estimate for that period. The problem is that even if we accept these figures as a purity index we have no way of knowing what the situation was 100 years earlier before the purist movement was underway. In this respect, however, it is interesting to note that Sauvageot reckons that the number of native words would be much lower if recent texts were used. This would appear to indicate a retreat from xenophobic purism in Hungarian in recent years. Another estimate for Hungarian compares the lexical stock of the thirteenth century with that of the present day (Benkő 1972: 202). This comparison reveals that the percentage of foreign words has actually decreased slightly (from 9 to 7 percent) despite the influences of Slavonic, German, Turkish and Latin in Hungarian life, while the number of 'autonomous' words (that is, formed wholly from Hungarian roots) has increased markedly from 51 to 81 percent of the total. This is important for Hungarian, which has according to Benkő (p. 203) only about 1,000 roots – somewhat less than the number of Slavonic loans. However, Benkő (p. 209) also shows that the figures for the method of formation of new words have also undergone drastic changes. Whereas in the thirteenth century only 4 percent of such words were compounds, at the present time 35 percent are formed by compounding. Since it is highly likely that compounding in Hungarian involves calquing of foreign (particularly German) models, this comparison suggests a large increase in foreign influence on Hungarian word-building mechanisms as well as in covert lexical influence from German and Latin. On this basis, we would have to assume an openness to calquing of foreign models on the part of Hungarian language reformers as an answer to the language's enrichment needs. In any case, such information should alert us to the danger of assuming that the percentage of loanwords *per se* gives an adequate index of a language's purity. Benkő (p. 205) also provides a breakdown of the origin of the loanwords in Hungarian: Slavonic 27 percent, Latin 25 percent, German 17 percent, Turkic 16 percent, neo-Latin 5 percent, others 10 percent. For our purposes, it would have been helpful if Benkő had attempted to separate out internationalisms from the Latin, German and neo-Latin components since, as has been continually stressed, puristic reaction to internationalisms is of a different order from the reaction to loanwords from a single identifiable source. However, even allowing for this correction, the percentages of loans from various sources are essentially unhelpful as a guide to the direction of any xenophobic purism, much less to the success or failure of any puristic endeavours undertaken as a result.

The figures produced for the 'Aryan' (Sanskrit or Sanskritised Hindi) component in written Tamil, on the other hand, are somewhat more reliable indicators of the impact of purism. According to A. C. Chettiar, Professor of Tamil at the University of Madras, between 1900 and 1950 the Sanskritised component of Tamil fell from 50 to about 20 percent (Hardgrave 1965: 30). This last figure is confirmed by J. J. Glazov who estimates the number of Sanskrit loans to vary between 18 and 25 percent (Zvelebil 1983: 438–9). Nevertheless, the whole argument for the intensity of the de-Sanskritisation of written Tamil during this century stands or falls on the extent to which Chettiar may have overestimated Aryan words in the first place.

All the calculations discussed above attempt to give figures for a language as a whole. Implicitly or explicitly, they aim to provide a purity index for a language at a given time. To be fair, however, none of them sets out directly to measure the impact of puristic intervention. The few studies which do offer some statistics on the results of intervention are much more limited in their scope and a great deal more cautious in their use of data.

One of the best of these is the comparison by Heyd (1954: 42) of the vocabulary of the 1924 and 1945 versions of Article 26 of the Turkish constitution. Between these dates there had been a systematic move to oust Persian and Arabic words. The text is also well chosen because opposition to Persian and Arabic influence was particularly keen in the political and juridical domain, where widespread secularisation (de-Islamisation) was underway. Crucial too was the opportunity to compare two versions differing only in their lexical stock. Heyd's comparison reveals that, whereas the 1924 version contains 66 words of Arabic and Persian origin and only 7 native Turkish words, the 1945 version has 37 Turkish words and 33 Arabic words. Given its limited scope, it would be dangerous to extrapolate from such a small sample. However, it does illustrate the extent of the revolution which had taken place in Turkish attitudes to Persian and Arabic words and the impact these views had made on public practice. What it does not pretend to do is to quantify the extent of this impact. As a footnote, the 1945 version also contains one French word, a reminder of the generally tolerant attitude on the part of the language reform movement towards European loans especially compared to earlier xenophobic attitudes. But once again, this evidence is only illustrative and has no statistical worth.

A very different approach was taken by Gerdener (1986) in an attempt to measure the impact of purism in Nynorsk. Having isolated a number of affixes ultimately of Low German origin common in Bokmål as the most prominent targets of Nynorsk purism, Gerdener produced a series of graphs demonstrating the varying popularity of these affixes in Nynorsk journalistic usage during the period 1890–1970. Despite variation from newspaper to newspaper and from unsigned editorials to readers' letters, Gerdener shows for the prefix *an-* (p. 194) that it dipped in popularity after 1890, remained at a low level from 1900 to 1930, after which a much more tolerant attitude gradually set in. The popularity graph for words with the prefix *be-* (p. 208) shows a much sharper drop around 1900, followed by a slight resumption of usage after which the prefix is encountered with ever-increasing frequency. The prefix *er-* (p. 240) is not attested at all until 1930, whereafter it once more disappears until its readmittance in the late 1950s, since when opposition to several words containing this prefix (for which there are no Nynorsk equivalents) has been relaxed. Finally, the suffix *-heit* (p. 251), which has been rigorously opposed by Nynorsk purists was found in eight words in 1890, whereas throughout this century it is encountered only in 2 words. There has been no relaxation of this closure even in the generally more tolerant post-war climate. These four graphs reveal a slightly different picture for each of the suffixes. They are united, however, in showing that the impact of purism was at its peak around 1900, that is just after the leading purist Aasen had identified for his compatriots the problems facing Nynorsk in its fight to maintain its autonomy from Bokmål. Gerdener is not content simply to argue for the absence of these affixes as proof of the impact of puristic intervention; he also charts the popularity of the native replacements for them which purists have found, coined or brought to the attention of the speech community at large. This concentration on so-called *anbeheitelse* words (that is, words containing suffixes labelled by purists as non-native to Nynorsk) is an approach worth considering for future explorations of the extent of the impact of puristic attitudes on performance.

Another aspect of the effects of purism was treated in my own work on the impact of the Illyrian Movement on the Croatian lexicon (Thomas 1988a). The study focused on 200 key words coined or consciously revived during the period 1830–42. They comprised 1 loanword, 44 internationalisms, 65 calques (52 of them *Lehnüber-setzungen*), 60 loans from other Slavonic languages, 9 neologisms and 21 words from internal resources (p. 99). These figures led me to conclude that Illyrian purism involved the following characteristics (p. 103):

(1) an almost total closure to loanwords;
(2) a tolerance of internationalisms as marginal alternatives to native words;
(3) a preference for calques and Slavonic loans over other sources of enrichment;
(4) a tolerance for words directly modelled on foreign words;
(5) a preference for adapting rather than uncritically borrowing words from other Slavonic languages;
(6) a disregard for dialectal sources.

In short, Illyrian purism was reformist and moderately xenophobic though not towards Slavonic loans. The subsequent fortunes of the 'native' words created in this puristic climate have fluctuated considerably over the years (pp. 141–7). 19 percent of them having failed to outlive the period when they first arose. Almost all of the remaining 81 percent are attested in the dictionary compiled by Šulek (1860), but in his terminological dictionary (Šulek 1874) some of them have been spurned altogether or are listed after loanwords. The dictionary of Broz and Iveković (1901) – reflecting the new ethnographic paradigm – omits 62 items found in Šulek (1860). Ironically, a contemporary Serbian dictionary, which purports to dislike newly created Croatian words, lists 42 of those omitted from Broz and Iveković (1901). In the dictionary first published in 1967 as a joint venture of the Serbian and Croatian national *Maticas* to reflect usage in both communities, 38 of them have been restored – giving a 56 percent retention rate of the original sample of 'native' words. In sum, these figures illustrate the gradual decline in the impact of this puristically inspired vocabulary on Croatian usage. The latter has been partly displaced by internationalisms and words favoured in the Serbian tradition, reflecting changes in the puristic orientation operative in Croatian society.

An approach of this kind allows a close inspection of the retention rate for a set of carefully selected referents of key notions essential to intellectual discourse and the measurement of the continuing impact of the puristic orientation which their composition reflects. Like Gerdener's approach, it does not attempt to measure the impact of purism on the entire vocabulary but focuses on key items. This is predicated on the conviction that purism is directed primarily at high profile lexical items: as we move to the periphery of the lexicon, the significance of purism diminishes. This, of course, is why purists are so ready to tolerate foreign words in technical terminology while denying them entry in everyday discourse.

There has been no empirical research on the impact of purism on linguistic consciousness. However, some indirect evidence is provided by the survey of Czech public opinion about foreign words conducted by Tejnor *et al.* (1971). This demonstrates that a general aversion to foreign words is not always translated into avoidance of them in practice (pp. 54–5). Furthermore, many people (especially those with less education) tend to under-report their own usage of foreign words (p. 21). Both of these facts suggest that in a speech community noted in the past for puristic intervention a widespread if seemingly moderate puristic consciousness may linger on, particularly in the lower echelons of society. What, of course, does not emerge from this survey is the extent to which this consciousness has changed as a result of puristic activity. Nor are we in a position to make comparisons with the aversion to foreign words in speech communities without such activity. Nevertheless, Tejnor's work is important for revealing the differences between the individual's competence and performance as well as between his actual performance and his assessment of his own performance. This is crucial to an understanding of the differential impact on two modes of puristic activity: active (self-censoring) and passive (identificational) purism.

The use of puristic profiles

We have already determined that the impact of purism should be assessed only on its own terms. The starting point for any assessment, therefore, must be to identify the movement's intent. Narrowing our focus to the lexical level, we may assume that the intent of any puristic intervention is to restrict the numbers of some types of words and to encourage the adoption of others. This means that a general characterisation of a given instance of puristic intervention must necessarily take into account both the classes of words targeted for removal and the classes of words identified as desirable. On the basis of this characterisation we may begin to develop a puristic profile. As bench-marks for such a profile I shall

THE EFFECTS OF PURISM

use the terms *mild, moderate, extreme.* These three words have often suffered in the past from being introduced without explanation of the criteria on which they have been developed but I propose to use them here in a less arbitrary fashion on the basis of six formal criteria.

A crucial aspect of purism – as we saw in Chapter 3 – is the way in which puristic attitudes interact with non-puristic ones. Our first indicator of the intensity of purism, therefore, is the extent to which non-puristic factors are taken into consideration:

1. *Mild purism* gives equal weight to functional and other non-puristic considerations.
2. *Moderate purism* makes some concessions to these factors.
3. *Extreme purism* ignores them.

In Chapter 4 we discovered that there are five basic puristic orientations which, together with an anti-puristic (non-xenophobic) orientation, can be arranged in the form of a cube (see Figure 5). The very centre of this cube, where all the opposing forces are in equilibrium, is totally devoid of purism. Positions close to the centre of the cube represent *mild purism.* The closer we move to the surface of the cube, the less mild the purism becomes. *Moderate purism* generally involves combinations of xenophobic purism with one of the antinomical pairs: (1) xenophobic/archaising, (2) xenophobic/reformist, (3) xenophobic/élitist, (4) xenophobic/ethnographic. The closer we approach the eight corners of the cube the more *extreme* the purism becomes. Since, however, one of the axes contains an anti-puristic pole, the four *most extreme* positions are those combinations of xenophobic purism with the antinomical pairs arranged along the other two axes: (1) xenophobic/reformist/ethnographic, (2) xeno-phobic/reformist/élitist, (3) xenophobic/élitist/archaising, (4) xeno-phobic/ethnographic/archaising.

An important aspect of the puristic profile is the extent to which a purist movement moves through each of the processes in the purificational cycle described in Chapter 5:

1. Purism not proceeding beyond the censorship stage is *mild* in intent.
2. Purism including the replacement stage but not specifying the necessity of eradication and prevention is *moderate.*
3. Purism ensuring that the reforms are accepted by the speech community and evaluating the success of the intervention is *extreme.*

One of the most salient characteristics of purism is that it introduces a criterion for assigning markedness in the language system on the basis of origin. In Chapter 4 I provided a hierarchy of the targets of lexical purism (Figure 3). The first node of the hierarchy divides the lexicon into foreign and non-foreign items. On the basis of the hierarchy of foreign items it is possible to establish a scale of intensity for xenophobic purism: the more marked an item is the more intense is the purism which seeks to remove it:

1. *Mild xenophobic purism* is directed at loanwords.

MILD	Loanwords from a single non-related source:
	    a) unassimilated
	    b) assimilated

MODERATE	1. Loanwords from related languages:
	    a) unassimilated
	    b) assimilated
	
	2. Internationalisms:
	    a) unassimilated
	    b) assimilated

EXTREME	Calques:
	    a) Lehnübersetzungen
	    b) Lehnübertragungen

Figure 10: The targets of xenophobic purism as an index of puristic intensity

2. *Moderate xenophobic purism* is opposed to internationalisms and words from related languages.
3. *Extreme xenophobic purism* is opposed to calques.

Each of these three categories may be subdivided further, as shown in Figure 10.

Inasmuch as the removal of well established words presupposes a greater degree of puristic intensity, it should be assigned to the next, more intense category. For example, whereas the purism directed at a recent loan like *Marketing* in German may be categorised as mild, the attempted removal of G *Zigarre*, a well-established and morphologically fully integrated loanword, is an instance of moderate purism. The hierarchy of non-foreign targets, on the other hand, does not lend itself to the development of a scale since neologisms, archaisms and dialectalisms are the chief targets of one or other of the four internal puristic orientations. However, when we look at the replacements favoured by puristic movements we may include them in a single scale together with foreign targets (Figure 11).

MILD	1. Internationalisms 2. Loanwords from related languages 3. Calques
MODERATE	1. Assimilated loans from related languages 2. Calques conforming to native word-building laws 3. Neologisms 4. Dialectalisms
EXTREME	1. Some Lehnübertragungen 2. Neologisms 3. Dialectalisms 4. Archaisms

Figure 11: Preferred replacements as an index of puristic intensity

This completes the list of criteria for developing a profile of a given instance of purism. If we wish to take account of the diachronic perspective, it remains only to assign a value to the six basic patterns of development:

1. The minimal and discontinuous patterns are *mild*.
2. The trimming and evolutionary patterns are *moderate*
3. The oscillatory and constant patterns are *extreme*.

The three basic profiles of purism may be briefly described as follows:

1. Mild purism is characterised by:
   (a) an equal consideration of non-puristic factors;
   (b) a rough balance among the puristic orientations;
   (c) a lack of thoroughness in pursuit of its goals;
   (d) and (e) (if xenophobic) tolerance of internationalisms, retention of well established loanwords, ready acceptance of calques and loanwords from related languages, hostility or scepticism towards neologisms and dialectalisms;
   (f) a minimal or marginal pattern of development.
2. Moderate purism is characterised by:
   (a) some consideration given to non-puristic factors;
   (b) a distinct preference for one of the puristic orientations;
   (c) non-completion of the purification cycle;
   (d) and (e) (if xenophobic) a rejection of all loanwords felt to be foreign, retention of internationalisms as synonyms to

acceptable native words, acceptance of calques and loan-words from related languages provided they can be assimilated into the morphophonemic system, qualified acceptance of well-formed native neologisms and words taken from dialectal usage;

    (f) a trimming or evolutionary pattern of development.

3. Extreme purism is characterised by:

    (a) the subjugation of all other considerations to puristic ones;

    (b) a xenophobic orientation in combination with one of the antinomical pairs of the other two orientational axes;

    (c) completion of the purification cycle;

    (d) and (e) (if xenophobic) a rejection of all loanwords and internationalisms, scepticism or hostility towards calques (especially *Lehnübersetzungen*) and loans from related languages, encouragement of the use of dialectalisms and archaisms, acceptance of native neologisms;

    (f) an oscillatory or constant pattern of development.

Finally, it may be useful for comparative purposes to assign a numerical value to the levels of intensity demonstrated by these sets of criteria. Using a five-point scale which allows for the registration of borderline cases, a numerical profile would have the format shown in Figure 12.

These figures can then be averaged out to provide an overall index of puristic intensity. A comparison of these indices before and after puristic intervention can provide a measure of its impact independent of any quantitative assessment obtainable by other methods.

Some guidelines for assessing the impact of purism

It must by now be obvious that the purely statistical approach is fraught with difficulties and, used in isolation, might provide a misleading, ambiguous or even meaningless assessment of the impact of purism. However, given the subjectivity to which the study of purism is so prone, it would be unwise to dispense with firm statistical data entirely. The problem, as always, is to use the data with caution and not to force them to appear to convey what in fact they are unable to do. The following guidelines are offered as a way of minimising the risks posed by a quantitative approach and to suggest some other measures which can be adopted:

1. The impact of puristic intervention should only be assessed in terms of its own goals and orientation.

Intensity criterion / Intensity level	a) Weighting of non-puristic factors	b) Configuration of puristic orientation	c) Completion of purification cycle	d) Targets of purism	e) Preferred replacements	f) Pattern of puristic development	Average
MILD	1	1	1	1	1	1	
	2	2	2	2	2	2	
MODERATE	3	3	3	3	3	3	
	4	4	4	4	4	4	
EXTREME	5	5	5	5	5	5	
SCORE							

Figure 12: A numerical index of puristic intensity

2. The starting point for measuring the impact should be the development of a profile of puristic intensity. An index of this intensity may also provide an independent objective qualitative assessment of the impact.
3. The long- and short-term effects should be assessed separately.
4. An assessment should be undertaken not only of the continued use of undesirable items but also of their suggested replacements.
5. High profile items should be given preferential weighting.
6. Assessments should be based, as far as possible, on actual usage rather than on dictionary entries.
7. A balance should be struck between a small manageable corpus and the need to examine the full inventory of a language.
8. The effect on both language usage and language consciousness should be assessed simultaneously.
9. Adequate control mechanisms should be set up to allow proper comparison of the data.

Purism in theory and practice

Any programme for the reform of human behaviour carries the implicit assumption that its champions would welcome its implementation. Indeed, our expectations are that they would not only work for its implementation but also adapt their own behaviour in accordance with that programme. To do otherwise with intent may be labelled – perhaps somewhat uncharitably – as cowardice, dishonesty or hypocrisy, while unintentional inability to practise what you preach may be ascribed to self-delusion. So too with purism. It is important, therefore, to discover the extent to which purists have attempted to implement their own reforms and, what is more, managed to reflect them in their own usage.

First, however, we may safely exclude from treatment here playful purism, which, as we have already seen, is an end in itself. Nevertheless, it is worth noting that even a figure as ludicrous and impractical as Wolke succeeded in providing German with *Fernsprecher*. Admittedly, the meaning of 'telegraph' given it by Wolke was superseded in 1877 by that of 'telephone', but in its new meaning the word has survived to the present day (Kirkness 1975: 363). Indeed, Kirkness (1975: 227) sagely reminds us: 'Gründliche sprachliche Kenntnisse scheinen nicht, wie oft behauptet, eine Voraussetzung für die erfolgreiche Prägung neuer Wörter zu sein.'[35]

As we might expect, the contrast between theory and practice can on occasion be quite stark. Even where a genuine attempt is made to follow through on their own precepts, purists have been forced to throw up their hands in despair at the daunting task which confronts them. The resultant sins of omission are particularly venial in those élites responsible for the cultivation of standard languages in the post-colonial world. In languages like Swahili, for example, the English element is still dominant 'in spite of the deliberate efforts of all those involved in expanding the Swahili lexicon in technical fields or in specified domains like the law, to avoid as much as possible borrowing from the language of the former colonial power' (Polomé 1983: 72).

More culpable perhaps was the practice of the editors of the nineteenth-century Bulgarian journal *Turcija*. Even though advocating the retention of Turkish loanwords and resistance to Russianisms, the journal is in fact full of Russianisms, internationalisms and Grecisms (Moskov 1958: 24). In other instances words slip through for lack of vigilance. This may be true not only of purists but even of anti-purists like Nejedlý, who though ostensibly opposed to the enrichment of his native Czech by means of calques and neologisms – especially if they contravened the language's word-building norms – was himself responsible for coining *povidálka*, a misguided attempt to calque G *Erzählerin* 'narratrix' (Jelínek 1971: 21).

On the other hand, some purists have been only too ready to fulfil their own puristic intentions, often with over-weening zeal. A

---

[35] Basic linguistic knowledge does not appear, as often claimed, to be a prerequisite for the successful coining of new words.

paragon of virtue in this respect was the would-be English language reformer William Barnes:

> Analyzing the defects of the standard speech with reiterated thoroughness, restoring, reviving, supporting obsolete, obsolescent, or neglected Saxon terms, and coining a host of native terminologies, William Barnes hypostasized what his predecessors but devoutly urged. Thereby he became the culmination and climax of centuries of purist reform. (Jacobs 1952: 77)

Moreover, Barnes' own works – especially those of his later years – are written in the same puristic spirit which he preached to others (Parins 1984: 79).

It is clear, then, that purists run the whole gamut from those who attempt to implement their reforms and those who are indifferent to implementation. It is essential that the extent to which the reform programme is put into practice by purists themselves be registered, because this provides an indication of the seriousness or frivolity of their attitudes. Moreover, since it would be unreasonable for a speech community to follow a course of action which reformers themselves are unable or unwilling to embark upon, a readiness to put the puristic ideology into practice would appear to be a necessary precondition for its eventual success.

Concrete achievements

The most visible artifacts of puristic intervention are, of course, the vast numbers of individual words which have been coined as replacements for items deemed undesirable from the point of view of a particular orientation. Their presence has undoubtedly changed the outward appearance of many languages, even where the numbers of items involved are comparatively small. The careful chronicling of the genesis of these words is one of the redeeming features of many studies of purism. To excerpt these lists of the concrete successes and failures here would, however, be otiose. Suffice it to say that sometimes purists invent words which are embraced by the speech community and sometimes their efforts are greeted with deserved mirth or disdain. The ultimate test of success, however, is that a word's artificial origin should no longer be apparent, for only then can it be regarded as a truly native element. In Hungarian, for example, there are many words like *befolyás* 'influence' which few Hungarians nowadays would take for anything but a native word. In fact, it was such a transparent calque of G *Einfluss* that at the time of its creation in the nineteenth century it elicited considerable laughter (Becker 1948a: 74, 91). Similar observations have been made about the acceptability of Czech words artificially created in the early nineteenth century by Josef Jungmann (Dostál 1982: 111).

In Chapter 5 we saw that the replacement mode of purism can engender new, desirable words without the eradication of the old, undesirable ones. This can leave a language with large numbers of synonyms comprising native and non-native words. Such is the case in Persian (Jazayery 1983: 261–2), Hungarian (Sauvageot 1971: 262–3), Croatian (Thomas 1988a: 107–16), Czech (Jedlička 1948) and several others. This synonymy gives scope for subsequent semantic differentiation and for freedom of personal choice. Moreover, as we saw in Chapter 7, it can often lead to stylistic variation where the higher register generally employs the puristically inspired word, the lower register the non-native word. This is true not only for Hungarian (Sauvageot 1971: 262–3), but for the majority of central European languages. It is instructive, for example to compare Croatian with its stylistically differentiated native and non-native synonyms with Serbian, where the non-native word is employed in all stylistic registers.

For many languages, it is still too early to predict what concrete achievements purism will make. Even though words have been coined, their acceptance or rejection lies in the future. For newly revived languages such as Welsh, for example, dominated by a language of international communication, the prospects for the acceptance of a puristically inspired terminology appear bleak:

> In the end, I suspect that attempts of this sort to restore lost registers to the language will be recognized as futile. The question is whether new coinings will pass into general use. It is probable that most Welshmen will continue to say *ambiwlans* and *car parc* and not *cerbyd cleifion* (analagous to German *Krankenwagen*) or *maes cerbydau* (literally: 'field of cars'), two alternatives suggested by Dr Emrys Evans, especially as the majority of terms at present on offer, despite the originality of some, merely reflect English thought processes in Welsh garb. (West 1983: 394)

Long- and short-term effects

Any assessment of the impact of purism must take into consideration not only the immediate but also the longer term repercussions. Just as there are instances as in seventeenth-century Scandinavia where puristic intervention was resisted for a time before taking effect, so also there are cases like the attempts to purify English around 1600 and in the late nineteenth century where the impact did not outlive the puristic movement itself. When it comes to tracing the development of purism in the history of a given standard language, the enduring features should be stressed over the more ephemeral ones.

For the effects to be long-lasting, they must become a stable constituent of the corpus of the language. In Bulgarian, for example, the enormous numbers of Russianisms which invaded the language in the nineteenth century fulfilled a long-term need for whole-scale lexical enrichment from a source which enjoyed high esteem. Therefore, they were quickly accepted and stabilised in common usage. As a result, words of Russian origin play a prominent role in the intellectual and even everyday vocabulary of modern standard Bulgarian. Bogorov's anti-Russian purism, on the other hand, won few adherents – he was regarded as something of a crank – and was able to claim few ultimate successes in promoting acceptable replacements for Russian words: *molba* 'request', *okolnost* 'circumstance' (Moskov 1958: 29). The long-term effect of purism in Bulgarian, then, was its closure to enrichment from Turkish and Greek and its opening to Russian influence (Moskov 1958: 138). Nevertheless, as we saw earlier, the activity of Bogorov and other like-minded individuals had the lasting effect of putting restrictions on the seemingly limitless influx of Russian words.

As one might expect, the effects are especially short-lived when the circumstances conducive to puristic intervention no longer obtain. For example, the highly puristic lexicographical work carried out at the court of Charles IV in Prague at the end of the fourteenth century was discontinued, and as Prague ceased to be the capital of the Empire had little if any impact on succeeding generations. Similarly, Hus' attempts to rid the speech of his parishioners of Germanisms evaporated as ethnic tensions in bilingual Bohemia subsided somewhat as the intellectual climate of the Renaissance inspired a more cosmopolitan frame of mind.

Particularly prone to a swift demise are words coined as a result of an overzealous identification with the nationalistic aims of a Fascist state, for which Italian under Mussolini and German during the Nazi era provide the *loci classici*. Once the state apparatus disappears, so language attitudes – *pari passu* with strict adherence to railway timetables – return to normalcy. Indeed, the products of the previous puristic hysteria are often a source of embarrassment to the succeeding generation and have no hope of remaining in use. A similar fate awaits purism officially sanctioned or indeed imposed under totalitarianism. In Persia, as we have seen, the effects of purism were coterminous with the reign of the Shah, while in the Soviet Union there have been marked fluctuations in the use of foreign words in response to official whim and fancy (Comrie and Stone 1978: 143–6).

The impact on linguistic consciousness

There is no question that beside its practical aims of purging a language of undesirable elements, purism has an important ideological component. Quite apart from its secondary objectives of inspiring feelings of patriotism and inculcating a sense of national identity, purism is primarily designed to make a decisive impact on the development of linguistic consciousness.

Its chief aim is to provide a speech community with the necessary value-orientation for regulating its own linguistic behaviour. Therefore, any assessment of the effects of purism should carefully consider the extent to which language attitudes have been moulded by the puristic ideology. Unfortunately, there has been little attempt to apply quantitative measures to puristic attitudes. Nevertheless, although much of the reporting in this area is, therefore, uncompromisingly impressionistic, it still allows some insight into the impact of the puristic ideology on attitudes in the community in question.

For example, it has been noted that 'after several generations of speakers have been taught to be wary of foreign words, a *moderate purism* has become a value feature in Croatian consciousness' (Kalogjera 1978: 391). The effects of this consciousness are to be seen in word selection where the standard language provides a native and a non-native pair of synonyms: *povijest* not *historija* 'history', *glazba* not *muzika* 'music', *rajčica* not *paradajz* 'tomato' (Thomas 1978a). This consciousness is thrown into greater relief by the contrast not only with standard usage in Serbia but even with non-standard usage in Croatia itself, where a non-puristic consciousness prevails. In Bulgarian, moreover, a heightened social awareness of the need to avoid foreign words in the standard language has been recognised as the most important practical result of purism (Moskov 1958: 138). A similar impact – albeit resulting from a quite different puristic orientation – is apparent in Nynorsk:

Der gegen die Gruppe der *anbeheitelse*-Wörter als Ganzes gerichtete Purismus hat zwar seine Auswirkungen auf das Sprachbewusstsein der Nn.-Verwender gehabt, da alle diese Wörter als Fremdelemente im Nn. angesehen werden.[36] (Gerdener 1986: 301)

As a result, there has been no massive introduction of these words into Nynorsk usage from Bokmål.

Conversely, where puristic intervention did not find a response in the linguistic consciousness of the community, its efforts were ignored and failed to make any lasting impact on usage. In Fascist Italy, for example, 'linguistic purists were regarded as rather whimsical eccentrics, and the publications which warned against the "exoticisms" of Italian did not find any general interest' (Kramer 1983: 314).

In several instances, the puristic ideology did not only attempt to induce self-censorship of linguistic behaviour but also offered a new paradigm for looking at the standard language. This might involve not only acceptance of its reform programme but also a reawakened awareness of the new potentialities of the native language as happened with eighteenth-century Danish (Karker 1983: 286). In some other speech communities, the new awareness went far beyond the original puristic impulse. In South Africa, for example, newly aroused interest in the purity of Afrikaans led to a total re-examination of language policy:

> The purist movement did produce useful insights as a by-product: it showed what Afrikaans could do with regard to spontaneous and conscious enrichment of the vocabulary; thus even today neologisms for new concepts are created with ease and fervour. . . .It proved the value of the retention of contact with Dutch, and that influence was unavoidable in a situation of permanent language contact. Furthermore, it showed that exaggerated purism can have a detrimental effect on language reform. (Botha 1983: 236)

In Turkey the transformation of attitudes to the native language resulting from puristic reform was, if anything, even more radical and extensive. According to Heyd (1954: 110), among the benefits accruing from the reform movement – quite apart from the introduction of new words and technical terms – are that it has 'aroused general interest', 'prompted scholarly research', 'sharpened linguistic feeling', 'done away with outmoded conventialism' and 'induced writers to use simpler and clearer and more exact language'. Advocates of the

---

[36] The purism directed at the group of *anbeheitelse* words as a whole has certainly had an impact on the linguistic consciousness of the users of Nynorsk since all these words are regarded as foreign elements.

intelligibility argument as a motivation for purism would no doubt be gratified to know that some observers have hypothesised about a correlation in some speech communities between a purified corpus and a high level of literacy:

> Es gibt wahrscheinlich einen ursächlichen Zusammenhang zwischen dem einheimisch-volkstümlichen Charakter der finnischen Sprache und dem Umstande, dass die Finnen an Belesenheit alle anderen Völker übertreffen, die Isländer ausgenommen.[37] (Collinder 1965: 69)

These positive ancillary benefits are often included in the statement of aims of puristic reform programmes, and in some cases provide the avowed *raison d'être* of language purification. Dunger (1910: 7), for example, says that German language purification is merely a means for sharpening public sensitivity for the more important task of language cultivation. Indeed, even the most staunch opponents of purism would be prepared to admit that in some cases the cathartic experience has provided the stepping stone to heightened awareness of the need to maintain the status and prestige of the native language. What they would be less prepared to concede is the continued need for purification once this new level of awareness has been attained. According to this view, which is widely held in all those countries influenced by the teachings of the Prague School, puristic reform, having served its purpose of raising linguistic consciousness, should give way to the rational, apuristic cultivation of the native language.

The impact on relations between language varieties

In Chapter 3 we identified the separating function as one of the prime motivating forces of purism. It is pertinent, therefore, to examine whether – and if so to what extent and with what consequences – purism has managed to maintain the necessary distance between linguistic idioms.

There is no question that purism is often directly responsible for the differentiation between two closely related languages and between two codes of the same diasystem. In Nynorsk, for example, it

---

[37] There is probably a causal relationship between the indigenous, folk character of Finnish and the fact that Finns surpass all other peoples except the Icelanders in literacy.

has been claimed that 'Ein Grossteil der lexikalischen Unterschiede zwischen Nn. [Nynorsk] und Bm. [Bokmål] lässt sich durch Auswirkungen des Purismus erklären'[38] (Gerdener 1986: 23). There is plenty of evidence to support similar claims for the relations between Slovene and Serbo-Croatian, Ukrainian and Russian, Afrikaans and Dutch, Yiddish and German, Slovak and Czech, Faroese and Danish, and Croatian and Serbian.

As we saw in Chapter 8, purism is also responsible for maintaining differentiation between codes on the vertical plane. Specifically, élitist and ethnographic orientations play an important role in the preservation of strict diglossia by countering the trend towards democratisation or elevation respectively of the standard language. In addition, purism often, as in the case of Turkish, leads to a widening of the gap between written and spoken usage (Heyd 1954: 47).

However, these undoubted benefits for the prestige and autonomy of the standard language do not come free of charge. As Budovičová (1987: 157) has noted with the relationship between Slovak and Czech in mind, the cost of preserving the purity, genuineness and specificity of a language is its isolation and stagnation. This isolation not only cuts a language off from external influences but also renders it less accessible to non-natives. It has been noted in Icelandic, for example, that 'puristic policy sets up a barrier against easy reading of Icelandic by other Scandinavians' (Haugen 1976: 33). For similar reasons, Czech occupies a roughly analogous position of exclusivity among the Slav languages (Jelínek 1971: 25; Dostál 1982: 111).

One of the ironies of the Czech and Icelandic situations is that their opacity to those speaking closely related languages is the result of resorting to word-building elements which have cognates in those very same languages. In the case of Czech as distinct from that of Icelandic, the supreme irony is that the puristic paradigm under which Jungmann and his circle were operating favoured loanwords from other Slavonic languages – principally Russian and Polish – in a spirit of pan-Slavonic reciprocity. In fact, Czech did borrow extensively from both of these sources (Orłoś 1967; Kiparsky 1933–4; Lilič 1982), but, because of the complicated interrelations of the Slavonic standard vocabularies and the independent developments in each (Thomas 1985), the hoped-for *rapprochement* of their lexical inventories did not materialise. On the other hand, those languages which modelled their lexical reform on the Czech puristic paradigm – Slovene, Croatian, Slovak, Upper Sorbian and partially Ukrainian –

[38] A majority of the lexical differences between Nynorsk and Bokmål can be explained by the effects of purism.

do show considerable parallels in their lexical repertoire but this was principally because they were prepared to adopt Czech words with the necessary sound-substitutions (Thomas 1985: 317–24; Thomas 1988a: 159–62).

It follows from this that the mild to moderate profiles of xenophobic purism, which not only accept but even encourage enrichment from related languages, are less inclined to leave languages isolated than the more extreme profiles. Purism which accommodates internationalisms is still less likely to put up barriers between languages, since it is clear that internationalisms facilitate translation from one language to another and promote international understanding (Keipert 1977b: 308). Interestingly, when this argument was offered to the respondents in the survey of Czech speakers, opinion was equally divided (Tejnor *et al.* 1971: 16). This clearly demonstrates the abiding ambivalence towards internationalisms in a speech community where a somewhat less tolerant puristic paradigm has long been dominant.

Further, it has been suggested that the homogeneity to which purism aspires is also a barrier to its acquisition as a second language. The virtual absence of internationalisms in such languages as Czech, Finnish or Hungarian places an extra burden on the memory of the language learner – a fact which may indeed militate against the use for wider communication of a language strongly affected by purism. Conversely, in the eyes of such late Victorian figures as Kington-Oliphant, Skeat, Watts, Meikeljohn and Earle there was a direct link between the unreformed, hybrid nature of English and its suitability as the language of world domination, a destiny predicted for it by no less a figure than Jakob Grimm (Crowley 1989: 71–5). Indeed, Otto Vočadlo – an Anglicist but also a leading opponent of extreme purism in his native Czech – used this very argument to support his claim that purism brings opacity and cultural isolation (Vočadlo 1926: 354).

The critical appraisal of purism

The final aspect of the effects of purism which needs to be examined is the way in which these effects have been evaluated and submitted to critical analysis. This critical appraisal, as might be expected, tends to dwell on the negative aspects of purism. Nevertheless, inasmuch as it puts the achievements of the purists into proper perspective, this bias is on the whole salutary.

Naturally, some critics remain unpersuaded by the need for purism. Others point out that even on their own terms the purists' efforts have not always been efficacious:

> In the short run purists can do a certain amount of harm, and can bring about results opposite to those they wish to achieve, by interventions in situations concerning which they have little or no first-hand knowledge. (Hall 1974: 199)

Robert Hall, a long-standing opponent of purism (and indeed of all forms of prescriptivism) notes that despite puristic efforts Anglicisms abound in Quebec French (Hall 1974: 209). Even Hungarian purism, generally regarded as thoroughgoing and generally successful, has come in for chastisement:

> En réalité, la réaction puriste a été en grande partie déclenchée par la présence d'un trop grand nombre de termes forgés au petit bonheur et dont beaucoup étaient superflus ou ne remplaçaient pas vraiment les mots étrangers qu'ils etaient destinés à éliminer.[39] (Sauvageot 1971: 342)

Another cause of complaint is the perception that purism sets limits on freedom of expression. This has been noted not only for Czech (Dostál 1982: 111), for example, but even for French:

> . . .chiefly through Malherbe's influence (aided by the servility of later generations) the classical French literary language of the seventeenth and eighteenth centuries was sharply reduced, to the point of impoverishment, in vocabulary and syntax. (Hall 1974: 174)

Furthermore, the reductionism of much puristic activity can lead to a degree of lifelessness in a language. It was on these grounds that Sir Sayyid Ahmad countered the claims of Urdu purists:

> Some people complain that Urdu writers of the present day introduce English words into their writings. But they ought to understand that in a living language there is always a tendency to assimilate or form new and newer words. When a language becomes exclusive or limited in range, it is considered a dead language. (Quoted in Zaidi 1983: 420)

Others claim that purism, far from providing a stepping-stone to a heightened awareness of more general language problems, can induce a form of paralysis. Thus in Slovene society, according to Urbančič

---

[39] In reality the puristic reaction was to some extent activated by the presence of too many unhappily forged terms of which many were superfluous or did not really replace the foreign words which there were supposed to eliminate.

(1972: 80), a preoccupation with the need to counter Serbo-Croatianisation of the national language has taken attention away from more pressing problems in the area of language cultivation.

A more severe case, however, is that of Serbo-Croatian itself. The centrifugal tendencies in the two standard idioms of the language, fuelled by purism, have acted as a block on producing dictionaries and standard grammars (Kalogjera 1978: 394). The most blatant example is the fate of cooperative effort on the part of the Croatian and Serbian *Matice* to produce a joint Serbo-Croatian dictionary in two editions, one in the Cyrillic and the other in the Latin alphabet. The first volumes began to appear in 1967, just at the time when Croatian nationalism was reaching its peak. Criticisms by sections of the Croatian intelligentsia that the dictionary had not only failed to mark the differences between Croatian and Serbian usage but had even mischievously attempted to downplay and distort them finally led the Croatian *Matica* to withdraw from the joint project. The Cyrillic version went ahead, and the full six volumes were published. The Latin version was abandoned after the letter K. As a result of puristically inspired opposition, therefore, the Croats – alone of the major peoples of Europe – are without a dictionary of their modern standard language. The situation in the field of dictionaries of specialist terminology is, if anything, even more dire. Furthermore, every respectable linguist – whether comparativist, socio-linguist, synctactician or dialectologist – has felt it necessary to expound his views on the subject. As a result, attention has been distracted from whole areas of important linguistic research.

Yet not all purists are guilty of the kind of ignorance which Hall is so keen to pin on them. A more nuanced view distinguishes between various types of purism: rational and non-rational approaches, or mild, moderate and extreme profiles. As Dostál (1982: 113) says of Czech purism: 'one has to distinguish wrong-headed purism from a rightful protection of one's language as a representative factor of national identity.' Even defensive puristic regulation, says Ševčík (1974–5: 53), should not be viewed as a negative process but as a protection from destruction of systemic relationships particularly in lexico-semantics and syntax. Botha's comments (1983: 236) on the value of a puristic paradigm, which recognised the importance of retaining the link with Dutch and on the stupidity of the exaggerated form of purism, which treated anything resembling English as an unwanted Anglicism, once again illustrate that it is not purism itself but particular manifestations of it which deserve censorious treatment. Even the guilt by association launched at purist movements which play into the hands of Fascist and other violently nationalistic regibes (Hall 1974: 200) cannot be used to blacken the name of all purism. Each manifestation of purism should be judged not *a priori* but on its own merits – that is, in terms of its overall profile and the particular socio-cultural context and the socio-linguistic situation in which it occurs.

CHAPTER 11

Towards a comparative history of purism

Introduction

The intent of the previous eight chapters has been to provide the necessary parameters for the discussion of any individual case of purism in any language. The first task of this chapter, then, is to summarise the salient points of these chapters and distill them into a synthetic framework. This synthesis will then provide the basis for a model for studying purism as a global phenomenon. Next, a number of hypotheses about purism around the world emerging from this book will be formulated and cursorily examined as the bases for a comparative history. Finally, a short sketch of purism in a European context is offered as an illustration of the way in which a more general history of the problem might proceed.

A synthetic framework

All language intervention is predicated on the assumption that some improvement will accrue. Purism provides a set of principles on which a judgement may be made with respect to which elements are deemed to improve, and which to impair, the corpus of a given language. These principles (the puristic paradigm) are based not on functional (or rational) but on aesthetic (or non-rational) criteria. Some purists also take functional criteria into consideration, in which case their attitudes may be described as a fundamentally rational approach to the problems confronting a language.

The puristic (micro-)paradigm is largely determined by the literary aesthetic (or mesoparadigm) operative within the intellectual élite of a language community at a particular point in time. This aesthetic is formed out of a complex interplay of such factors as tradition, national consciousness and literary poetics (or macroparadigm) as interpreted by individuals or groups of individuals within the élite. This puristic paradigm is subject to modification or replacement as a result of changes in the extralinguistic determinants or in the composition of the élite. Since nationalism is the dominant component of the puristic mind-set, it follows that purism is particularly intense at times of heightened national consciousness. Purism is a response to a dilemma whether to assimilate or reject certain elements marked as somehow 'non-native'. This dilemma is brought into focus by a widespread perception in the speech community that the autonomy, prestige or unity of the native language are threatened in some way. The origin of this threat may be perceived as external or internal, or both combined. External threats are the result of language contact where one language appears set to dominate the other, while internal threats are posed by variation within the language. Purism is directed at those elements associated with the source of the threat. Thus the primary distinction in puristic orientations is based on whether the targets are internal or external. Purism directed at external targets we call xenophobic. Conversely, openness to external elements is non-xenophobic in orientation and is therefore essentially anti-puristic. The internal orientations are bipolar and are sited on two planes: the historical plane (with its archaising and reformist poles) and the social plane (with its élitist and ethnographic poles). Language attitudes equidistant from each of the poles on these three planes are by definition apuristic.

Having recognised the need for purism and having identified the source of defilement, the purist is then faced with problems of implementation: to make others aware of the dangers of using certain elements, to suggest categories of replacements and to encourage their use in the wider language community. This cycle is complete when the situation has been reassessed and decisions made about the need for further purification along the lines suggested by the original paradigm or about the need to introduce a new puristic paradigm. Then the process may begin once more.

Purism may operate at all linguistic levels – usually independently, rarely in concert – but it is evident that its primary target is the lexico-semantic system, which, ironically, is the least fitted on account of its open-ended structure to a total overhaul. Within this system purists may object to any of the following: the words themselves on the basis of their origin, the corruption, debasement or contortion of their 'original' meaning, or the elements or types of combination used to form derivatives and compounds. Furthermore, the targets of lexical purism and the preferences shown in the means chosen for replacing these targets may be placed on scales which provide reliable indicators of levels of intensity.

Purism is concerned with prescribing norms of linguistic conduct. It follows that it is most obviously associated with the phase in the development of written languages when the codificatory norms of the standard language are being established. As a rule, purism is less keenly felt the further one moves in any direction from this phase. Purism deviating from this pattern will be either constant (marginal or consistently intense), will tend to fluctuate in intensity from time to time, or will have undergone a violent change in orientation at some crucial phase in its development.

Finally, purism is an ideology which seeks to imprint a particular set of attitudes (or language consciousness) and a particular code of linguistic behaviour on a contemporary speech-community and on generations to come. Any puristic movement may be judged on the extent to which its reform programme is translated into a new value-system in the community and concrete changes in the repertoire of the language itself.

A comparative-historical model

This short synthesis may stand as a definition of the core features of purism. Furthermore, it provides us with a checklist of characteristics by means of which we can compile a profile of purism in a given language. In order to facilitate comparison from one language to another I have incorporated these characteristics into two standardised questionnaires.

The first questionnaire (Figure 13) seeks to examine the profile of a particular puristic movement. It may be completed for as many different periods in the history of a language as required. A comparison of several such questionnaires may then be used to provide a picture of purism throughout the historical development of a language. Obviously, the more often the exercise is repeated and the narrower the time-frame covered on each occasion, the more accurate and detailed the picture will be. This questionnaire may also

Figure 13: A checklist of characteristics for a single instance of purism

1. To what extent does the purism take non-puristic concerns into consideration in developing its ideology?
   Not at all   To some extent   To a great extent

2. Is the puristic orientation external or internal?
   External   Internal   Both
   If the answer is 'Internal' only, go to Question 9.

3. If 'Both', which orientation is the dominating one?
   External   Both equal   Internal

4. If the threat is wholly or partially external, which of the following describes the source of the threat more closely?
   Non-specific Specific

5. If 'Specific', is more than one language involved?
   No   Yes

6. If 'No', which of the following describes the language most closely?
   From the same diasystem   Related   Unrelated

7. Which of the following best describes the position of the threatening language(s) *vis-à-vis* the language where the purism is located?
   In the same state   In another state

8. Has the threatening language ever served as a language of culture for the speakers of the language where purism is involved?
   Yes   No

9. If the threat is internal, which planes and which poles are involved?
   élitist   ethnographic   :   archaising   reformist

10. Which of the modes of the implementational cycle have been completed in the purism under review?
    Censorship   Eradication   Prevention
    Replacement   Reception   Evaluation

Figure 13 continued

---

11. Is the purism primarily or exclusively directed at the lexical level?
    Yes   No

12. If 'Yes' and the lexical purism is xenophobic, into which of the categories given in Figure 10 do the targets fall?
    Mild   Moderate   Extreme

13. Similarly, into which of the categories given in Figure 11 do the preferred replacements fall?
    Mild   Moderate   Extreme

14. At what phase of the language's development as a standard language did the purism take place?
    Minimal Standardisation   Pre-standardisation
    Standardisation   Post-standardisation

15. What has been the overall effect of the purism on language consciousness?
    Minimal   Marginal   Fair   Considerable

16. Have these effects increased or decreased over time?
    Increased   Decreased

17. What has been the overall effect of the purism on the repertoire of the language?
    Minimal   Marginal   Fair   Considerable

18. Have these effects increased or decreased over time?
    Increased   Decreased

---

be used for horizontal studies across languages. For example, it would enable us to compare the impact of a particular literary poetic on a number of different languages, or the puristic profiles of various languages at the different stages in the process of standardisation. A comparison of two such stages would reveal the existence of trends in the development of purism from one stage to another. Similarly, the comparison of two periods could serve as a useful indicator of general puristic trends in historical time.

The second questionnaire (Figure 14) is concerned with establishing the course of purism over the whole development of a written language. The validity of the answers to this questionnaire will increase in proportion to the extent that they are derived from a series of questionnaires of the type proposed in Figure 13. Not only does the completion of Figure 14 provide an overall puristic profile for the whole historical development of a language but, it enables us to make a standardised comparison of the impact of purism across any number of individual languages. This procedure thus provides a

Figure 14: A checklist of longitudinal features

---

1. Is purism a temporary or intermittent feature of this language?
   Yes   No

2. Does purism follow any of the 6 basic patterns given in Figure 9.
   Yes   No

3. If 'Yes', state which
   Minimal   Discontinuous   Trimming
   Evolutionary Oscillatory   Constant

4. If 'No', has there been a revolutionary change in puristic attitudes?
   Yes   No

5. If 'No', can the purism be described as combining features of two or more of the above patterns?
   Yes   No

6. If 'Yes', state which!

7. If there has been a revolutionary change, which aspect or aspects of purism are reflected?
   Motivation   Orientation   Intensity
   Language level   Target   Implementation
   Effectiveness

8. If there has been a revolutionary change in orientation, is it from a primarily internal to a primarily external orientation, or vice versa?
   Yes   No

Figure 14: continued

---

9. If there has been a change in internal orientation, does it involve a change in dimension or a movement from one pole to another or both?
   Dimension   Pole   Both

10. Did the revolutionary change coincide with some abrupt change in the extra-linguistic situation?

11. Did the level of puristic intensity reach its peak before, during or after the standardisation phase?
    Before   During   After

12. During which phase in the development of the written language did the puristic, apuristic or anti-puristic paradigm which has been retained as the dominant attitudinal feature in the speech-community arise?
    Minimal standardisation   Pre-standardisation
    Standardisation   Post-standardisation

13. Did individuals or groups of individuals have a profound influence on the direction taken by purism in this language?
    Yes   No

---

method for comparing languages of a particular area, from a particular language family, or with a particular structural typology. Furthermore, it could be used to conduct a survey of all the world's languages to provide a comparative history of purism as a worldwide phenomenon.

Clearly, even if all the secondary literature on purism were known to us, such a survey would be beyond the scope of this book. It is sufficient for our purposes to have proposed:

(1) A standardised framework for describing purism, which may then be used by specialists working in one language so that their findings may be cross-tabulated with those working in another.

(2) A model on which a comparative history of purism can be developed.

Some general hypotheses about purism

While it is clearly premature to attempt a comparative history of purism, it would be a pity if the chance were missed to make a few general remarks about purism as a global phenomenon and to suggest, on the basis of the available secondary literature some hypotheses that future research can investigate more systematically.

Hypothesis 1
Purism – at least as defined here – is a universal characteristic of standardised languages

There is no question that all histories or commentaries on standard languages mention some period when purism came into play as a factor in their development, even if eventually the impact of this intervention came to nothing. It is instructive, for example, that almost every article in Hagège and Fodor (1983), which covers the major and many minor languages of the world, specifically mentions purism at some stage. The index gives references to purism in more than 45 languages.

The universality of purism as a feature of standard languages has been duly noted by several scholars (Urbančič 1972: 63; Brozović 1970: 49). Urbančič notes that the complementary universal to xenophobic purism is receptivity to foreign influences. That is to say, all languages are in contact with some other language or languages; all languages accept elements from other languages as a result of this contact; all languages seek to set limits on the introduction of these elements. Similarly, the targets of internally orientated purism are the only ones available to a language as sources of enrichment. It follows, therefore, that any inclination to block off enrichment from them constitutes an act of intolerance. No standard language can be open to all sources of enrichment indiscriminately.

The corollary of this universality hypothesis is that the comparative history of purism consists not in documenting its presence or absence but in tabulating the variation in its motivation, orientation, intensity and impact across the world's languages.

Hypothesis 2
Purism has arisen autochthonously in many parts of the world as a response to specific problems facing individual languages

There is no question that purism has arisen independently as a discrete attitude to language in a large variety of language situations throughout the world. There is no evidence to suggest, for example, that purism is a product of European civilisation which has found its way with colonial expansion into non-European standard languages. Such major languages as Sanskrit, Hebrew and Arabic, for example, were already effectively governed by puristic attitudes before they came into close contact with European languages. This is no less true of other languages from outside the European milieu such as Georgian, Armenian, Turkish and Persian.

In each instance purism depends on specific historical conditions. Thus, puristic attitudes differ widely from language to language (Moskov 1976: 10): in Czech purism is a reaction to German influence; in Hungarian there is opposition to international cultural terminology; in Romanian the source of irritation is Bulgarian elements; and in Turkish the target is the Persian and Arabic component in the vocabulary.

Hypothesis 3
Puristic attitudes operative in one language community may be transferred to another.

The above comments about the autochthonous nature of purism should not be taken to mean that both in Europe and outside there have not at times been instances where the germ of puristic attitudes has not spread from one language to another. Indeed, there is considerable evidence to suggest that purism in one language has served as the model for another in its recognition of need, its selection of targets and replacements and even in its implementation. Let us consider some of this evidence before attempting to identify some patterns in the spread of purism.

We have already seen how many of the various national language academies and societies were founded directly on the model of some foreign institution. Even where academies did not materialise for various reasons as, for example, in eighteenth-century England where the political will was lacking (Flasdieck 1928) or in Bohemia where the fashion for linguistic societies would undoubtedly have borne fruit had it not been for the political and economic decline in the years following the Battle of the White Mountain of 1620 (Lisický 1919: 544), the foreign impulse for their formation was still present. In Iran the founding of a language academy in 1935, which marked the beginning of a strong puristic phase in Persian, was a direct consequence of a visit by the Shah to Turkey, where he was most impressed by the progress being made by the movement to purify Turkish (Jazayery 1983: 252).

In Europe there is a definite pattern to the spread of purism. Thus, Mulertt (1927: 583–4) writes of its genesis in Spanish:

> An und für sich ist der spanische Purismus garnichts Anderes als ein iberoromanischer Zweig der allgemeinen europäischen Bewegung. Der Stammbaum dieser puristischen Strömung ist klar und deutlich genug. Hervorgewachsen ist sie aus jener Periode des italienischen Humanismus, in welcher dieser sich nach anfänglich übermässiger Verherrlichung des klassischen Lateins auf die eigene Volkssprache besann. Man geriet in die Bewunderung des Wertes, der Vielseitigkeit des italienischen Idioms, wobei man die Sprache der Trecentisten als das grosse massgebende Vorbild betrachtete. Der dauernde Niederschlag dieser ältesten puristischen Bestrebungen im neuen Europa ist das Vocabulario der Accademia della Crusca in Florenz, welche, aus einer älteren Schriftstellerakademie hervorgegangen, sich seit 1582 in neuer Form konstituiert hat. 1612 schon wird dieses Wörterbuch verwirklicht, und dieses Jahr ist zu einem wichtigen Datum in der Geschichte der europäischen Sprachreinigungsbestrebungen geworden.[40]

The language most responsible for the spread of puristic attitudes in Europe is, however, German. This is true even of languages where purism has been marginal. For example, the Russian language reformer Karamzin advocated the creation of new words in the fields of philosophy and physics on the model of what had been done in German (Hüttl-Worth 1956: 49). Still more enthusiastic in his admiration for the German way was the Englishman William Barnes writing in *The Gentleman's Magazine* in 1830:

> Where the marching intellect in England seeks new words from other languages, the Germans compound them with the greatest ease and accuracy from their own; and whatever they can do with their language, we can do with ours. . . .There is no need of borrowing, because we can make words to any extent by compounding those we have already. (quoted in Jacobs 1952: 76)

---

[40] In itself Spanish purism is nothing other than a Ibero-Romance branch of the general European movement. The trunk of this puristic stream is clear and evident enough. It has grown out of that period of Italian humanism when the latter after the initially overwhelming glorification of classical Latin turned its attention to its own vernacular. They fell into admiration for the worth and versatility of the Italian idiom wherein the language of the writers of the Trecento was regarded as the authoritative model. The lasting result of these oldest puristic strivings in modern Europe is the Vocabulario of the Accademia della Crusca in Florence, which from an older authors' academy had in 1582 constituted itself in a new form. In 1612 this dictionary had become a reality, and this year became an important date in the history of European puristic endeavours.

Indeed, German has served as a conduit of puristic attitudes for the languages of central and northern Europe. In Czech, for example, the Baroque purist Václav Rosa in his creation of new compounds based himself directly on the puristic precepts already widely adopted in Germany (Jelínek 1971: 20). He even went as far as to avoid the very same loanwords which had caused concern to his German contemporaries (Bílý 1904: 43). Not only was the German example near at hand but the Czechs, like the Germans before them, recognised the decline in their native language and diagnosed impurity as its principal cause (Bílý 1904: 44). However, Jedlička (1948: 8) makes the important point that although Czech purism of the Baroque period was an echo of the European purist movement, it was also a reaction to the Renaissance enthusiasm for foreign elements. A close connection with German purism also marks the next wave of Czech purism at the end of the eighteenth century, of which the most extreme representative was Václav Pohl; once again the model was Zesen (Schamschula 1973: 162: Lisický 1916: 58). Even the anti-puristic phase ushered in by Josef Dobrovský at the end of the eighteenth century and continued by Palkovič and Nejedlý in the early nineteenth was dominated by a German model, Adelung (Svobodová 1955: 31–2; Jona 1970: 323). Finally, in the nineteenth century, when Czech embarked on the course of language reform which was to see the final codification of the standard language, German purism – this time of the Campe School – was an important paragon. In an apologia for the Czech language addressed to his compatriots – written revealingly in German in 1829 – Josef Jungmann, the prime mover of Czech language reform, recognised the similarity of the German and Czech situations and advocated the use of German purism and its sources as a model for Czech (Jungmann 1829: 63–4). This viewpoint is even captured in one of the book's chapter headings: *Die grossartigen Deutschen sind unsere Lehrer in der Sprachreinigung.*[41] Much the same may be said of the Hungarian *njelvújítás* (Czigany 1974: 334). Moreover, as noted by Becker (1948a: 96), one of the ironies of Czech and Hungarian purism was that German puristic models provided a rationale for removing elements of German origin.

The Czech purist movement, in turn, was a model for reform in other Slavonic languages. Not only did it pave the way for the purification of Croatian, Slovene and Upper Sorbian but it also influenced the thinking of the post-1860 generation of purists in Bulgaria, many of whom travelled to Prague, Vienna and Budapest (Moskov 1958: 44). Even puristically minded contemporary Russians like Jugov in his book *Sud'by narodnogo jazyka*[42] published in 1962

[41] The magnanimous Germans are our teachers in language purism
[42] The fate of the national language

have made favourable comparisons between the shortcomings they perceive in their native language and the purified state of Czech (Keipert 1977b: 295).

If we turn to the influence of German purism in northern Europe then a similar picture emerges: a German puristic model being applied to foreign elements often as not of German origin in Danish, Swedish and Dutch (for details, see Rehling 1951: 210; Skautrup 1944–68, Vol. 2: 143–7, 341; de Vooys 1946: 31–44). In Dutch–German relations we encounter an unusual phenomenon: whereas generally speaking German served as a model for Dutch purism, the roles were reversed at a crucial stage in the development of German. The influential German purist Philip von Zesen spent part of his early life in the Netherlands, maintained afterwards warm relations with prominent Dutch literary figures and even wrote poetry in Dutch (Forster 1970: 38). He came to admire the contemporary purist movement in Holland, many of whose members (Coornert, Spiegel, Bredero and Hooft for example) he counted among his close friends. Many of his puristically inspired neologisms were modelled directly on Dutch (Blume 1967: 180–1). This high regard for Dutch was shared by others in the German Baroque purist movement (Blume 1967: 199; Kamb-Spiess 1962: 279).

A further source of puristic inspiration was provided for the newer Scandinavian languages by Icelandic. For example, Aasen, the codifier of Nynorsk in the search for learned vocabulary, 'tried following the Icelandic example of creating new words, but never succeeded in eliminating the Latin-Greek element. Today words like *radio* and *telefon* are as common. . .as in the other mainland Scandinavian languages' (Haugen 1976: 36). However, Gerdener (1986: 22, 40–1) has shown that Nynorsk reformers, although creating words like *ljonkraft* 'electricity' and *tjodskap* 'nationality' in imitation of Icelandic, explicitly rejected the extremes of the Icelandic puristic model on the grounds that it was impractical and that its application would lead to a decoupling from Bokmål as well as a distancing of Nynorsk from the folk language, a move at odds with the ethnographic orientation of Nynorsk purism. Similarly, in written Faroese there has been a 'determined effort. . .to follow the lead of Icelandic and eliminate all possible Danish loans, replacing them with innovations', for example *siglingarfrødi* (Icelandic *siglingafraedi*) 'navigation' for Danish *navigation*, *leidarbraev* 'passport' (Icelandic *leidarbref*) for Danish *pas* (Haugen 1976: 34). However, like Nynorsk, Faroese does not follow Icelandic in rejecting common international words but is more concerned with finding native equivalents (often through calquing) for Danish words (Hagström 1984).

Elsewhere in Scandinavia, we find that the model of Swedish has propelled Finnish into purism, while Finnish in its turn greatly influenced the Noor-Esti movement to Europeanise Estonian while at the same time maintaining the purity of its word-stock (Kurman 1968: 54).

There is clear evidence of a type of purism originating in central Europe. Drawing on the institutional apparatus of the Florentine and French academies and the newly won independence of Dutch from French and Spanish, the puristic movement in Germany sought to change linguistic attitudes in the upper echelons of society. Despite the political fragmentation of Germany it succeeded to such an extent that its aims and achievements could fire similar ideologies in the élites responsible for the cultivation of the newly emerging national standard languages of central, northern and eastern Europe. The success of this new ideology – and the extent to which its precepts were implemented – depended, of course, on the special circumstances of each individual language. Nevertheless, it is incontrovertible that for these languages, a central European type of purism was an inalienable part of the process of *Sprachanschluss*, whereby new standard languages were created on the model of the better established written codes of Europe (Becker 1948a).

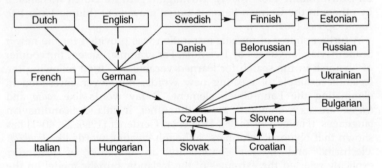

Figure 15: The spread of purism in Europe

Figure 15 attempts to capture the spread of purism in Europe in diagrammatic form.

Hypothesis 4
The most widespread type of purism is that which is directed at external sources.

Society commonly looks outside itself for the scape-goats for the ills which beset it. So too with language: before all else purists are ready to place the blame for a language's lack of prestige on its borrowed component. This is compounded by the fact that national conscious-ness focuses attention on the etymological principle for judging the appropriateness of a given item.

Hypothesis 5
The most widespread form of purism is concerned with elements of the lexico-semantic system

Many accounts of purism are strictly limited to an examination of lexical purism. That lexical purism should so dominate is not surprising. The lexico-semantic system is open-ended and therefore may be added to without difficulty. It is the linguistic level which is most prone to the influence of extralinguistic factors. It is also the most superficial level of language and therefore the most susceptible to restructuring. Hence the lexical system is beset by the greatest dangers and consequently requires the greatest vigilance to ensure that it does not change too rapidly and in a way which is beyond control.

The importance which the vocabulary assumes in maintaining the distinction between codes involved in contact is well illustrated by the detailed case study of the village of Kupwar in Maharashtra, India (Gumperz and Wilson 1971). Here four native languages have been in contact for three or four centuries: Urdu and Marathi (both Indo-European), and Kannada and Telugu (both Dravidian). The high-caste Jains and craftsmen use Kannada, the untouchables Marathi, Moslems Urdu, and rope-makers Telugu. Since some form of communication has to take place across caste and religious barriers bilingualism has developed. This has led to almost total levelling of the syntactic structures in the languages involved. There has also been considerable borrowing to-and-fro of individual words. However, the loss of differences in their surface syntax means that the sole distinction between these linguistic codes is in that part of the native lexicon which has been retained in each of them. Thus the lexicon, the linguistic level most prone to change, may also so symbolise the ethos of a language that it may be the very language component which is most likely to be protected.

Hypothesis 6
Combining Hypotheses 4 and 5, the dominant target of purism is vocabulary of foreign origin.

We have seen with respect to purism that the lexicon is the least marked linguistic level and that external elements are the least marked target of puristic intervention. From the apuristic perspective, loanwords constitute the component of language which carries the greatest level of marking (Ivir 1989). Thus the effect of purism is to reverse this system of markedness. It follows from all this that purism directed at loanwords is archetypal.

Hypothesis 7
The standard languages of the world may be divided into two groups: (1) those basically opposed to enrichment from other languages, (2) those which have generally assimilated foreign elements.

The theory that an individual who is secure in his central identity is unconcerned about peripheral aspects of his personality while an individual who is insecure in his central identity is obsessed by peripheral problems fits very well with the way in which speech communities view their native tongue (Laponce 1987: 48–50). A language which is secure in its written traditions and is not threatened in its status of serving the whole community in all possible functions need not be concerned that it contains some lexical items of foreign origin. Conversely, a language which is insecure in its status and has a fragmented or poor written tradition will pay disproportionate attention to loanwords especially if they emanate from a possible competitor in fulfilling the necessary socio-communicative functions for the community in question. According to this theory, purism is not simply a behavioural reaction to a given set of circumstances but depends on a mentalistic interpretation of these circumstances.

Most investigators have tended to identify two polarised groups. Slavists such as Auty (1973) and Unbegaun (1932), for example, have made a basic distinction between languages preferring calques (Czech, Slovene, Croatian) and those preferring loanwords (Russian, Polish, Serbian). Fodor (1983b: 466) attempts to divide the languages of the world into those 'basically puristic' with respect to loanwords (Afrikaans, German, Croatian, Bulgarian, Persian, Portuguese, Tamil, Czech, Hungarian, Norwegian, Danish, Estonian, Finnish, Georgian, Katharevousa, Hindi, Somali, some of the languages of the Soviet Union) and those ready to adopt loanwords (Ganda, Dimotiki, Hausa, Japanese, Vietnamese, Urdu, Zulu, Xhosa, Wolof). A positive feature of Fodor's list is that it is far from Eurocentric. However, his list makes many obvious omissions and leaves the (no doubt erroneous) impression that xenophobic purism is predominantly a factor of European languages while many of the indigenous languages of India and Africa have not submitted to the same paranoia afflicting European languages. Moreover, it is not clear exactly how Fodor has decided the group to which a language should be assigned. Of course, for reasons discussed in Chapter 9, it is no easy task to quantify purism but it should be possible on the basis of the questionnaires described above (Figures 13 and 14) to arrive at an overall characterisation of the impact of purism in a language which is relatively free of arbitrariness.

The problem with a two-fold classification is that it ignores the considerable variation in puristic intensity found in the world's languages. However, while it is clear that we are not dealing with an all-or-nothing situation in purism, there seem to be grounds for assuming that purism is either dominant or not. Even the intermediate positions, therefore, tend towards one pole or the other. These positions derive from the conflict which may arise in a speech community between the perception of the language itself and perception of the ills besetting it at this particular moment. A community which has pride in its linguistic tradition but recognises the extent of the threat may wish to limit the in-flow of corrupting influences. This is the form of mild purism found in many modern languages subjected to Anglo-American influences. Conversely, a community with a strong sense of pride in its native standard but which, however reluctantly, sees the utility of adopting some elements from the language threatening its autonomy may adopt a somewhat accommodating position with regard to loanwords. This is the moderate purism of many languages of the Third World as they counter the influence of the language of a (former) colonial power. Moderate purism may also involve periodic fluctuations in intensity as the society in question oscillates between a basically hostile and somewhat more conciliatory viewpoint.

On closer inspection, therefore, our binary classification breaks down into a four-point scale of xenophobic purism: the absence of purism and three levels of puristic intensity (mild, moderate and extreme). Interestingly but perhaps not surprisingly, these four positions fit neatly into accommodation theory (Giles and Powesland 1975, Giles and Smith 1979).

Hypothesis 8
Those languages are least prone to xenophobic purism which have enjoyed a long, uninterrupted development as national, written languages going back to the Renaissance or earlier.

Long uninterrupted development ensures the gradual evolution of a standard language, free from the insecurities besetting languages which have had to compete with other tongues or in which several codes have fought for supremacy. Furthermore, the intellectual climate of late medieval humanism and the Renaissance was not conducive to the development of xenophobic purism – despite the savage national rivalries which characterise the beginnings of European colonialism. Linguistic nationalism of this period was more concerned with defining the national heritage, providing the new national language with the necessary prestige and balancing the need to model the new written vernacular on the one outstanding exemplar, Latin, with the necessity of marking out the limits of the latter's influence.

The resultant purism tended to be élitist and archaising but generally accommodating to all but the most superfluous of Latinisms. Of the many European languages which were first written down or first began to flourish as written codes during this period, only four (Spanish, French, Polish and English) have since then consistently flourished as the languages of independent nations. Each of them was established with a strong, centralised norm drawing increasing respect from speakers of all regions – a process completed in France by the beginning of the nineteenth century and yet to be completed in Spain, where there has been dogged and persistent resistance, especially from speakers of Catalan. Furthermore, they have become the vehicle for a voluminous and highly respected body of literature. All xenophobic purism in these languages has been peripheral and short-lived, at least until this century when the emergence of an international culture dominated by English has provoked a general puristic reaction.

Another group of European languages – some of them dating as written codes as far back as the Renaissance or even beyond – have shown periodic symptoms of xenophobic purism without ever being dominated by a puristic paradigm. Despite some of the problems facing them in the past, which gave rise to some form of purism, they have now emerged as stable, prestigious languages with an important body of literature. They include Danish, Swedish, Dutch, Russian, Italian and Portuguese. Any xenophobic purism currently manifest in these languages is similar to that found in French and Spanish.

Hypothesis 9

Those languages are most prone to xenophobic purism which have emancipated themselves from domination by another language of culture during the period of nineteenth- and twentieth-century nationalism.

The combination of the symbolic value of language within the emerging myth of a national culture, the need to protect and assert the prestige and autonomy of a newly codified standard, the fervour of Romanticism, and a new generation of men with the necessary vision, energy and reforming spirit provided the most fruitful soil possible for a deeply rooted, flourishing and long-lived purification of the language's resources. Furthermore, the attitude of such reformers was a positive one – not to impoverish the language by simply removing words of foreign origin but to replace them with words created so that the new standard language could assume parity with the older languages of culture whose social functions it wished to usurp.

The foremost examples of this brand of purism are found in central, northern and eastern Europe: Hungarian, Czech, Slovene, Croatian, Nynorsk, Faroese, Icelandic, Finnish, Estonian, Latvian, Lithuanian, Romanian, Bulgarian, Ukrainian, Belorussian. Within this group there are differences of intensity and in internal orientation. For example, while Estonian, Finnish, Hungarian, Nynorsk, Faroese and Icelandic have favoured neologisms sometimes created *ex nihilo* together with a fair number of calques, the rest have tended to resort primarily to calques and loans from related languages; similarly, while Nynorsk, Faroese, Icelandic, Finnish, Estonian, Hungarian, Belorussian and Ukrainian have combed the dialects as sources of lexical enrichment, the others have done so – if at all – only to a limited extent; those languages which have longish written traditions have occasionally revived old words. The purification process neither began nor ended in these languages simultaneously: for several of them (Belorussian, Icelandic, Faroese, Nynorsk, Estonian) the process was not completed to general satisfaction until well into the twentieth century, while for the others this century has seen a partial relaxation of puristic intervention.

There are two important counterexamples to this hypothesis: Serbian and Dimotiki. Both of these standard languages evolved in the course of the nineteenth century in the spirit of European Romantic nationalism after centuries of Turkish domination. Several common factors in their genesis as standard languages, however, determined that they did not develop in the direction of xenophobic purism. Firstly, in each community the dominant principle was an ethnographic one: the standard language must be based on the language of the people in contradistinction to élitist Slaveno-Serbian and Katharevousa respectively. This ethnographism went so far as to maintain that words used by the people – irrespective of origin – belonged to the repertoire of the standard language. Furthermore, in each case the group favouring the emergence of these new standards was strongly imbued with a spirit of secularism, which sought to shake off the traditions of Orthodox culture. Not only were these languages open to enrichment from European languages but they were also quite tolerant of the many orientalisms – mostly of Arabic and Persian rather than Turkish origin – which permeated the vocabulary of everyday life.

A moderate to extreme purism also characterises three other categories of standard languages:

1. Those which finally emerged as fully fledged standard languages only in this century: Yiddish, Hebrew, Afrikaans, Macedonian, Upper and Lower Sorbian. Their purism shares many of the features found in the new standard codes of the nineteenth century and is thus essentially a continuation of the Romantic paradigm. Although two of these languages – Hebrew and Afrikaans – have evolved exclusively outside Europe, their purism has developed under the influence of European traditions – not surprisingly, when one considers their genesis.

2. Those languages which have been revived in bilingual societies despite constant pressures for monolingualisation: Irish, Welsh, Breton, Catalan, Basque, Friesian. Each of them must not only withstand the flood of words entering from the dominating language in the bilingual community but must also come to terms with the need to keep pace with the exponential increase in technical vocabulary if it is not to become merely a picturesque folkloric patois.

3. Those languages outside Europe with long, honourable written traditions which have had to withstand the onslaught of European languages firstly as a result of colonial expansion then as a consequence of the politico-economic hegemony of Europe over the Third World: Mandarin Chinese, Urdu, Hindi, Tamil, Arabic, Swahili, Malay (to name only the major ones). However, there are also some counterexamples of languages which have not seriously attempted to resist Europeanisation: Turkish, Persian, Japanese.

Hypothesis 10

The modernisation of society leads to two conflicting trends: (1) a retreat from purism, (2) increased opposition to loanwords.

If we understand the modernisation of society to mean economic progress, urbanisation, industrialisation, pluralism, secularisation, cosmopolitanism, democracy and tolerance, then we can anticipate that puristic attitudes will cease to be prevalent in modern society. Indeed, this retreat from purism has been clearly documented in all of the standard languages which emerged during the course of the nineteenth century. Once their future was assured, their prestige and autonomy unassailable, they saw no danger in adopting new loanwords, the more so since the main influx of lexical items introduced elements common to most of the languages of the world. Thus, languages such as Dutch, Danish, German, Czech, Croatian, Finnish and Hungarian have considerably relaxed their puristic closure to external sources of enrichment, especially if these were international in scope. In modern Finnish, for example, 'les mots «internationaux» se mettent à foisonner, evinçant même souvent les calques ou les néologismes par lesquels on les avait remplacés il n'y a pas si longtemps' (Sauvageot 1983: 189). Thus *struktuuri* replaced *rakenne* and words like *tradicio* itself replaced by Agricola in the sixteenth century by *sääty*, which had in turn given way to the dialectalism *perinne*, were reintroduced. In Hungarian too, more and more foreign words are returning: 'ce retour offensif des mots étrangers a, certes, été constate mais il apparaît pas que le public réagisse et les specialistes se bornent à protester' (Sauvageot 1971: 346). In German and Italian, the return to foreign words was halted during the Fascist period but with the normalisation of the post-war years both languages have resumed their former course.

Even more striking perhaps is the readiness of those languages codified only in this century to relinquish the moderate to extreme purism with which they were imbued from the beginning. In Afrikaans, for example, domestic and foreign words are often used side by side. Furthermore, 'nowadays, terminologists are not inclined to create Afrikaans synonyms alongside international terms. This is related to the fact that purism has been shifted to the periphery of the language dispensation' (Botha 1983: 230). In Hebrew, too, the initial plan to exclude 'non-Semitic words, even such as are accepted in all Indo-European languages' was found to be too extreme and unrealistic, so that internationalisms like *psixologia*, *universita*, *radio*, *tayer*, *reaktsia* and *energia* were widespread. As a result, Hebrew is becoming more and more tolerant of non-Hebrew words (Morag 1959: 259–60).

Conversely, modernisation has brought pressures on people of many cultures to conform to a single, homogeneous, international culture dominated by a unified world economic system, based on a universal technology and obsessed by a materialistic, utilitarian philosophy. Not surprisingly, these pressures have evoked a powerful emotional reaction in which traditionalistic, spiritual, anti-rational, anti-colonial and localistic viewpoints have been paramount. These viewpoints are also expressed in a resurgence of purism, particularly in those societies which see their own niche being eroded by the spread of modernism. This reaction may be seen on a number of different levels.

Firstly, the emergence of the nation state has substantially improved the situation of some languages while disadvantaging others. For example, where once languages like Slovak and Slovene were just two of many functionally limited languages of the Habsburg Empire, the creation of Czechoslovakia and Yugoslavia meant that they became the national languages of minorites within the state. As a result, each language underwent – and continues to undergo – a puristic reaction towards elements associated with the dominant languages in these multinational states – Czech and Serbo-Croatian respectively. This will not diminish until the communities speaking these languages are certain that the threat posed to their autonomy has permanently receded.

Secondly, that centralisation which is the hallmark of étatism has in many instances provoked a separatist or independence movement among those peoples who find themselves on the periphery of the state. This too can be reflected in a puristic reaction to encroachment by the language of the central culture. Catalan and Basque in Spain; Breton in France; Welsh, Irish and Scots Gaelic in the British Isles all provide examples of such increase in purism. Perhaps the best examples, however, are provided by the non-Russian speech communities of the Soviet Union, which to a greater or lesser extent are united in their condemnation of the Russification to which their languages have been subjected. The forces presently transforming the face of eastern Europe are likely to unleash a movement to remove some of the more prominent traces of Russian influence from these national idioms and those of the east European satellites.

Thirdly, the communications revolution particularly in the field of electronics has removed what Whinnom (1971) calls the ecological barrier to language contact: modernisation has brought certain languages into direct contact for the first time. Inevitably, this has had profound repercussions for many languages around the world, particularly when seen as a further dimension of western hegemony. The impact of this contact is particularly evident in the Third World, where purism – unlike the earlier European version – is concerned not so much with neighbouring languages but with combating what is seen as European cultural neo-colonialism:

> The tendency to reject European, or more generally 'international' lexical or morphological items even for rather technical scientific or governmental work is increasing through South and Southeast Asia. (Fishman 1973: 81–2)

In those instances where there has been little or no attempt on the part of non-European languages to reject European influence, it is clear that some other aspect of modernisation has triumphed over such considerations.

Lastly, whereas in the past internationalisms were Graeco-Latin in origin and therefore felt to be part of the overall heritage of western civilisation and not associated with a specific living language, they are now strongly identified with Anglo-American culture. Even in well-established world languages, therefore, there has been a pronounced, if somewhat ineffectual, attempt to combat this Anglicisation of the lexicon. Nowhere has the influence of English produced more brouhaha than in France, and for the very obvious reason that English has replaced French as the most widely used international language. The resultant *franglais* – a word first used in *France Soir* on 26 September 1959 – has provided a whole generation of Frenchmen with an easy puristic target. Not only have men such as René Étiemble criticised loanwords like *tennis* – itself ironically a Gallicism in English – but have also pronounced against calques like *souteneurs* for football 'supporters' and pseudo-Anglicisms like *le tennisman, les tennismen* (Étiemble 1964: 58–60, 65). If a language with the stature of French can feel threatened by English, what hope can speakers of less widely distributed world languages hold out for the purity of their native idiom?

An historical sketch of purism

As a conclusion to this chapter I should like to offer a sketch – however tentative – of the history of purism as an attitude to standard languages. Clearly, much work needs to be done to flesh out the whole picture, but it seems to me that an attempt to provide even the flimsiest outline is useful if it can serve as a framework for later research.

Greek philosophers, as is well known, were highly interested in linguistic matters. Plato in his *Kratylos* deals at great length with questions of etymology and its importance for logical argument. At no stage, however, does he translate this etymological obsession into a concern about the make-up of the Greek language. Aristotle, on the other hand, makes a binary distinction between common words (*kyrion*) and foreign or unfamiliar words (*xenikos*). According to him, a pleasant style is created out of a happy mixture of these two types of words (Larkin 1971: 56). In rhetoric and poetry, however, the fundamental principle should be clarity, which is associated with the use of common words (Larkin 1971: 57). Aristotle is not advocating purism but an adherence to the principle of using easily comprehensible items from the centre rather than the periphery of the lexical system. Indeed, these two philosophers seem to reflect a general unconcern about defining the limits of the lexical corpus of the written language. Only the recognition that poetic diction should be elevated gave ground for a somewhat élitist orientation. During the Hellenistic age, however, as the current *koine* and the language of the classical authors were beginning to diverge, the maintenance of correct usage became a major concern (Robins 1967: 16–22).

Written Latin emerged from the shadow of Greek and its lexicon owed much to the Greek model. The widespread calquing of Greek compound words which characterises the vocabulary of classical Latin should not be taken as a reflection of purism but as a more or less conscious desire to lend Latin a prestige equal to that of Greek. The governing principle of Roman poetics is captured in Horace's memorable phrase *aurea mediocritas* (Odes, II, x, 5), which became the watchword for all neo-classical stylistic handbooks. As in Aristotle, this meant in lexical terms a preference for central rather than peripheral items. Writing should also be based on models taken from the canon of acceptable writers. This principle grew in importance with the decline of linguistic and rhetorical standards throughout the disintegrating Roman Empire and provided the basis for an archaising and élitist orientation. The first figure to make an explicit break with this orientation was St Augustine in his *De doctrina christiana*, which avers that classical rhetoric with its dignity of subject-matter has no meaning in the Christian experience. For St Augustine, therefore, 'the definitions and rules of classical grammar, concerning phonology, morphology, barbarisms and solecisms, have no validity but are only habitual observances' (Kaster 1988: 84-5). Moreover, St Augustine perceived that the principle of *integritas locutionis* of the grammarians is nothing but a desire to preserve language from *aliena consuetudo*. In this respect, St Augustine may be reckoned to be the first in an illustrious line of anti-purists in European cultural history.

The early history of the written forms of the European vernaculars is intimately associated with the introduction of Christianity with its attendant terminology. Each of these vernaculars to a greater or lesser extent manufactured calques on the model of Latin and Greek. As we have seen, this calquing was not motivated by puristic concerns. Indeed, throughout the Middle Ages, xenophobic purism was a rarity. Its first stirrings are heard in Prague in the late fourteenth century with the officially sanctioned activity of whole schools of lexicographers to supply Czech with new words to replace the many learned words of Latin and German origin.

Late medieval and early renaissance humanism saw a rapid expansion of the instrumental and poetical functions of many of Europe's written vernaculars and the codification of several of them as stable, prestigious and polyvalent standard idioms. In essence they adopted the classical poetic with its archaising and élitist orientation and were generally well-disposed to borrowings, particularly from Latin and Greek. In those areas, however, where there was considerable influence from an alien culture care was taken to limit the numbers of words admitted in many literary styles.

The situation of those languages which came to be written down as a result of the Protestant commitment to evangelisation in the vernacular, however, was quite different. More stress was laid on their individuality, and as a result a more vigorous attempt was made to provide them with a natively based lexicon. At the same time, élitist purism was muted and indeed in some instances an ethnographic orientation was paramount. With little or no written tradition, these vernaculars were not subject to archaisation but were guided only by contemporary usage.

The seeds of a division of Europe into two types of purism can, therefore, be traced back to the Renaissance:

1. The older written codes with their non-xenophobic, archaising, élitist orientation.
2. The newer written vernaculars with their xenophobic, ethnographic, reformist orientation.

Whatever the orientation, however, it is manifestly clear that renaissance purism was rational (that is to say it was secondary to instrumental language-planning concerns) and was relatively mild in its level of intensity.

The seventeenth and eighteenth centuries saw something of a general decline in the vitality of many of the newly codified written vernaculars of Europe. Mass desertion by national élites to languages of greater prestige and a fashionable larding especially on the part of the semi-literate of the native tongue with words and expressions taken from these prestigious languages contributed significantly to a backlash of non-rational xenophobic purism of moderate to extreme intensity in those languages which found themselves at a disadvantage. In other words, the Baroque in much of central and northern Europe is characterised by a growing polarisation between assimilationists on the one hand and reckless, unprincipled purifiers on the other. For the first time, xenophobic purism became for some writers an autonomous, self-sustaining ideology for planning the corpus of the native language. Unfortunately, a certain *naïveté*, even ignorance, of etymology and word-formational morphology tended to undermine their efforts. Nevertheless, for many languages the Baroque period saw a stemming of the tide of assimilationism and the installation of an intellectual vocabulary composed largely of native morphemes.

At the same time, the better established written languages were absorbed in an increasingly bitter polemic of their own: between a reformist and an archaising orientation. The language academies of Florence and Paris were the loci of this debate in Italy and France respectively. In each case, purism came to be identified with the élitist, archaising orientation in this quarrel between the Ancients and the Moderns. In England, however, opinion on the course of the standard language was not so heavily polemicised. There was a consensus that English was capable of improvement, that its heterogeneous vocabulary was a strength not a weakness, that Latin could serve it well but that the fashionable purloining of Gallicisms should be constantly reined in.

The seeds of the two types of purism have thus matured further:

1. The non-xenophobic, élitist and archaising type has become more polemical and provides the focus for such language cultivation activity as the Italian *Questione della lingua* and rigid French proscriptivism. However, some languages, such as Polish and English, have softened this orientation somewhat and have developed in the direction of a middle-of-the-road consensus.

2. The mildly xenophobic, ethnographic, reformist type of purism has become more extreme and has assumed the central position in the poetics of the non-assimilationist camp of languages such as Dutch, German, Czech, Danish and Swedish. Significantly, some languages, such as Czech (and even German to some extent) have abandoned the first type and joined the ranks of the second.

The growth of enlightened rationalism in the eighteenth century had little if any impact on the first type of purism except perhaps to strengthen the position of the traditional neo-classical model. This is particularly true of late eighteenth-century Italy. The second type of purism was, however, subjected to a thorough critique not only of its aims and methods but of its very *rationale*. Ethnographism and reformism were replaced by a more élitist and archaising orientation, more in tune with neo-classicism. At the same time the cosmopolitan viewpoint of the Enlightenment was fundamentally opposed to the xenophobic obsession with the individuality of the native language. Furthermore, rational neo-classicism rediscovered and elaborated the theory of etymological analogy as the central, organising principle for the formation of new words. There was no longer any virtue in shielding a language from foreign influences – the more so if this meant creating ugly, unwieldy and incomprehensible neologisms.

The overall effect of the Enlightenment was therefore to enforce a *rapprochement* of the two types of purism. Moreover, it produced the first systematic refutation of the whole ethos of xenophobic purism. As we have already seen, this anti-purism has provided the basis for the modern opposition to xenophobic purism. This has led to a mitigation of its extremes and in some cases of its abandonment as a central feature of the national poetic.

Nevertheless, it is ironic that the Enlightenment, so inimical to the notion of linguistic nationalism, should have been the instrument of heightened scholarly interest in many of the slumbering written vernaculars of Europe. This renewed interest was given further impetus by the emergence of the new sentimentalist paradigm with its idealistic view of uncorrupted rural and primitive life and its sensitivity towards the cultural underdog. As a result, the value of promoting these written vernaculars to the status of fully fledged languages of culture began to be recognised in earnest. Since it was axiomatic of this viewpoint that these newly promoted standard languages should be free from overt influences from the older languages of culture, xenophobic purism was an inalienable feature of their development.

While sentimentalism had the effect of countering both the archaisation and the élitism of the first type of purism, its most lasting effects were reserved for the second type. It not only reintroduced a value-system in which xenophobic purism – albeit of a most benign and internationalist temper – could prosper but it also promoted a positive, reformist attitude as the ascendant attitude to language intervention.

Sentimentalism most profoundly affected purism in the already established languages of northern Europe: German, Dutch and the Scandinavian languages. The full force of the revival of the second type of purism was not felt in eastern, central and northern Europe until the advent of full-blown Romanticism. By then, the movement to develop the remaining European vernaculars was in full swing, and in each of them – except Serbian and Dimotiki like Russian before them – xenophobic purism was the governing ideological principle. As we have seen, however, the internal orientations differed markedly from one national tradition to another. Meanwhile, in German, which had provided much of the stimulus and example for these burgeoning new standard languages, xenophobic purism after reaching a high point during the Napoleonic Wars was already beginning to be a peripheral factor in language intervention. Indeed, the prevailing intellectual current was highly sceptical of the excesses perpetrated by the generation following Campe. The mantle of xenophobic purism now passed in turn to Hungarian, Czech, Croatian, Slovene, Romanian, Bulgarian, Finnish, Ukrainian, Belorussian and Estonian. Romantic purism is characterised by greater militancy, cohesiveness and consistency. As each language established its credentials the demand for xenophobic purism diminished somewhat, and the puristic paradigm was overtaken by more moderate and rational attitudes to language intervention. Nevertheless, the change in the balance of power in nineteenth century Europe gave fresh impetus to German linguistic chauvinism and to the insecurities of those languages which saw themselves threatened by the expanded influence of German. Unlike the earlier positive, reformist purism, the new wave of purism which resulted from these political changes was essentially reactionary and archaising in character. This late emanation of purism had the most visible and lasting effects in German, where very few aspects of public life escaped the attentions of the *Allgemeiner Deutscher Sprachverein*, the movement which in all the history of purism has probably enjoyed the broadest public support for its programme of language reform.

For reasons that are readily apparent, modernism has brought about a general retreat from the extremes of both the archaising/élite and the xenophobic types of purism. Even so, on a local scale purism has at times reached new levels of intensity in this century, usually as an epiphenomenon of nationalistic fervour. Even on a global scale, there is widespread evidence of both an élitist and traditionalist reaction to what are perceived as the diminishing standards of functional literacy and the liberalism with which the norms of codified standards have been interpreted as well as a xenophobic response to the extent and speed of the introduction of lexical items arising from the technological revolution and the position of English as the new *lingua franca* of science and commerce. Only the future can tell how the élites of the standard languages of the world will come to terms with these daunting challenges.

CHAPTER 12

Purism and language planning

Introduction

As we have seen, many problems in the study of purism await clarification, and much gathering of primary material is necessary before a definitive analysis can be offered. Nevertheless, it is hoped that, within the limits set by the present state of our knowledge, the task of describing, explicating, assessing and evaluating purism as an ingredient shaping the languages of the world – at least in general terms – is now complete. As a postscript, however, I would like to offer some thoughts on the relationship between purism and language planning in the hope of providing some guidelines to the ways in which the factor of purism may be dealt with in the future.

If we define language planning as a rational, purposeful and organised intervention in language and the social situations in which it operates, it is not difficult to see how purism might be seen as part of this scheme. With the notable exception of playful purism, all instances of purism are goal-orientated: they seek somehow to intervene in the development of the corpus of a language and to promote certain attitudes to language behaviour in a speech community with the ultimate goal of enhancing or safeguarding a language's status or prestige *vis-à-vis* other competing codes. However, there are two words in this definition which ring a false note as far as purism is concerned: 'rational' and 'organised'. To what extent may purism be described as 'rational' or 'organised'? Although each of these questions has been aired previously, they need to be confronted once again in the context of language planning.

If we define language planning as an organised effort to find solutions to societal language problems (Eastman 1983: 29), then once again it is easy to see the appropriateness of viewing purism in such a context. Purists view the removal of undesirable elements as a problem to be solved in order for the language to achieve or maintain its proper status as a prestigious code. The question is, however, whether it is perceived as a single problem or as part of a whole complex of problems requiring solution. We need to consider, then, how purification fits together with the other objectives of language planning. Yet, it may also be argued that purism, far from offering a model for healing a language's ills, is itself a problem in need of a rational solution. If that is so, we must consider ways in which language planners can deal with the effects of puristic intervention on the language usage and attitudes of a speech community.

Only when these four issues have been properly addressed can we return to the relationship between linguistic purism and language planning.

Rational and non-rational purism

In Chapter 3 it was determined that all purism is motivated primarily by what Daneš calls affective and traditionalist attitudes to language. Nevertheless, it is also clear that many purists are prepared to compromise these non-rational attitudes in recognition of the value of Daneš's rational criteria: instrumentality and ethicality. Such compromises, which are no more than an application to language intervention of Parsons' five antinomies of value-orientation, involve:

1. Maintaining personal neutrality towards the elements of the language in question: the desirability of elements should be judged on how they function in the system, not on the basis of personal preferences for elements from one source or another; these elements should be the subject of dispassionate discussion, not emotional commitment.
2. Suppressing idiosyncratic impulses: an objective approach to the problems facing a language is required, in which the speech community's needs have precedence over those of any individual.
3. Recognising the merits of features which unite the language with another code: rather than stressing its specificity, a language should be opened up to enrichment from languages having close genetic, typological or cultural ties with it.
4. Stressing results rather than resorting to rhetoric: the purification

of a language is not an end in itself but is only a means to providing a language with prestige; puristically inspired criticism should not be mean-spirited and negative but constructive and goal-orientated.

5. Integrating purism into an overall interventionary response to a language's functional needs: purism should not be a single-issue ideology but an integral part of language cultivation.

To the extent that purists are prepared to make these compromises, their approach to language intervention may be deemed rational and, consequently, to have a legitimate role to play in language planning.

It must be obvious that the milder the puristic profile, the more likely it is that the puristic paradigm fits with Daneš' conception of rationality in language intervention. Nevertheless, it must be stressed that there is no single paradigm which satisfies the conditions of rational language planning: each speech community must identify a paradigm which reflects the situation and context in which its language is forced to operate.

The organisation of puristic intervention

According to Radovanović (forthcoming), the corpus planning cycle involves ten processes: selection, description, prescription, elaboration, acceptation, implementation, expansion, cultivation, evaluation and reconstruction. Similarly, it was determined in Chapter 5 that purification consists of eight discrete but closely linked modes of activity, also arranged in a cyclical pattern: recognition of need, identification of targets, censorship, eradication, prevention, replacement, reception and evaluation. Although we should not expect purification to parallel corpus planning in every particular, the former may be said to be organised if from its inception it is visualised by its practitioners as an integrated, cyclical process. Hence purism predicated on the need to complete the purificational process in a logical sequence (as presented in Figure 6) satisfies the requirement that planned language intervention not be piece-meal and diffuse but provide a thoroughly integrated approach with the following essential characteristics:

1. A specific set of problems is identified.
2. A policy is formulated to deal with them.
3. Steps are taken to implement that policy.

4. The impact of the implementation of the policy is evaluated.
5. The policy is modified in accordance with this evaluation.
6. Fresh action is taken if deemed necessary.

A further requirement for organised intervention is that it be conducted by an accredited group of professionals. The expertise of professional purists should include not only the necessary theoretical and practical knowledge to pronounce on the desirability of specific linguistic items but also a thorough acquaintance with the basic tenets of socio-linguistics and the theory of standard languages together with a highly developed sensitivity about attitudes to language variation within the community. Even such professionalisation of the puristic cadre is, however, insufficient without some *de jure* – or at the very least *de facto* – recognition of its *vires* in adjudicating linguistic issues. It is essential, therefore, that rational purification – whether or not it calls expert non-linguistic witnesses to advise on matters of terminology – be institutionalised. Where no appropriate institution exists, purists are faced with the additional task of ensuring as part of their language planning activity that such institutionalisation takes place as soon as possible.

Purification and the objectives of language planning

According to Nahir (1977), there are five aspects of language planning: purification, revival, reform, standardisation, modernisation. Furthermore, he says: 'Language Planning agencies may, in the course of time, shift from one function class to another, abandon functions, or adopt new ones, when a change in needs, circumstances, or ideology in a society or speech community takes place' (Nahir 1977: 120). Moreover, there seems to be some justification for the claim made by Eastman (1983: 238–40) that purification, revival and reform give way eventually to standardisation and modernisation. In this book, too, we have seen evidence that once purification is accomplished to a level of general satisfaction, the puristic paradigm is relaxed and attention switches to other needs. Any return to a more extreme level of purism is, therefore, clearly associated with a reactionary frame of mind.

Within the scheme presented above the role of purism depends on the stage which the language has reached in its development. The planning of an unwritten vernacular, the revival of a dead language like Cornish, the reform of a language like Welsh, or the modernisation of an established standard like Estonian provide totally different challenges for puristic intervention. Nevertheless, one thing unites all these situations: purification can never be the single solution to a language's needs. It can only be an aspect of the reform, revival, standardisation or modernisation of a linguistic code. This confirms what was identified above as the fifth characteristic of rational purism: purification cannot be a single-issue ideology.

It follows from this that, as an aspect of language planning purification can only be conducted as part of an integrated approach to the needs and problems of a language. This necessarily means that where purification conflicts with the other objectives of language planning it must undergo some form of compromise. Language cultivation, for example, as Moskov (1976: 6) has pointed out, strives simultaneously to satisfy seven desiderata: euphony, correctness, precision, expressiveness, purity, richness and orthography. The balancing of these seven requirements depends on the mesoparadigm controlling the overall attitude to the standard language in a speech community. Those involved in developing a planned response to the infiltration of undesirable elements should only operate within an agency responsible for language planning as a whole and not as an outside lobby group.

Purism as a language-planning problem

Thus far we have attempted to look at ways in which purism can be made to accommodate the other goals of language planning. Now it is time to reverse this perspective in order to consider how language planners should deal with the problems posed by purism. Let us begin by identifying what some of these problems might be:

1. By favouring etymological over functional criteria in judging the desirability of linguistic items, purism may be a serious impediment to the spontaneous and planned growth of a language in accordance with its socio-communicative needs.

2. By stressing individuality and separateness of a linguistic code, purism may foster a decrease in inter-linguistic comprehension and communication: in situations where language planning is predicated on the need to maintain or promote socio-political or ethno-cultural bonds such differentiation between codes may be particularly inimical to its aims.

3. By preferring nativisation of the lexicon, purism may be seriously detrimental to the drive for modernisation: language planners might legitimately consider that a language cannot afford to stagnate while adequate native equivalents are sought for items of terminology widely distributed in the languages of the world.

If these problems are such a serious obstacle to the implementation of the other objectives of language planning, it would seem reasonable that language planners would seek at least to minimise their impact if not to eradicate them altogether. However, as Daneš (1987: 234) has sagely warned, even if the language planner 'rightly adheres to the scientifically justified functionalist approach' he cannot ignore either the actual 'socio-linguistic situation of the community' or 'public linguistic opinion' if his 'decisions or recommendations' are to have a realistic chance of achieving a successful outcome. In other words, the language situation in which purism has been a prominent factor and the language consciousness which it has engendered must be taken fully into consideration in the formulation of any corpus planning. This inclusion of purism among the planning objectives of a speech community is, therefore, the reciprocal of the moral imperative imposed on the professional purist to integrate his activities within a rationally conceived approach to language intervention.

Since the debate between rational and non-rational purism is often no less acrimonious than that between the purist and the anti-purist in the past, one of the main tasks confronting language planners in speech communities where passions about these issues run high is to explain forcefully and lucidly the principles and objectives of a rational approach to the problem. The objective is to change some widely held perceptions about language in accordance with the five areas of compromise identified with the switch from non-rational to rational purism. However, inasmuch as these perceptions often reflect the overall value system of the community, it would be unwise to be too sanguine about the prospects for a successful outcome.

Purism and language planning: the case of Yugoslavia

Instead of a conclusion, I propose now to illustrate the issues discussed in this chapter by reference to the problem of purism in the cultivation of the three major Slavonic languages of Yugoslavia:

Slovene, Serbo-Croatian and Macedonian. After a brief discussion of the impact of purism on the language situation in Yugoslavia, I shall discuss the merits of the various possible approaches to the problem. Having identified the solution which best fits with the other language-planning objectives of Yugoslavia, I shall offer some suggestions for possible strategies for its implementation (for fuller documentation, see Thomas, forthcoming).

In the course of the nineteenth century there emerged four standard south Slavonic languages: Slovene, Croatian, Serbian and Bulgarian. Slovene and Croatian followed a typical central European pattern of moderate reformist, xenophobic purism. They attempted to create a native vocabulary from their own resources through neologisms and calques. The principal targets of xenophobic purism were German and Latin (and to a lesser extent Hungarian and Italian). On the other hand, both languages were hospitable to the adaptation of words from Czech and Russian. Moreover, they were also ready to engage in a process of mutual enrichment. At first Slovene was the creditor and Croatian the debtor but later on the scales were tipped in the other direction (Thomas 1987). The eventual Slovene debt to Croatian was considerable. In principle the Croatian language renewal was also receptive to enrichment from Serbian but in fact the contribution from this quarter was not large no doubt due to Serbian's own lack of adequate vocabulary in the intellectual sphere. As a matter of course, this Serbian material was passed to Slovene. Once the dangers which threatened the prestige and autonomy of standard Slovene and Croatian had receded, puristic intensity relaxed. Nevertheless, a mild xenophobic purism remains a value feature in the linguistic consciousness of these speech communities. Both Slovene and Croatian have also inherited a certain degree of élitist purism which helps to maintain the strict diglossia characteristic of urban speech (Thomas 1989b: 277–8).

The modern Serbian standard turned from the Church Slavonic–Russian–Serbian amalgam favoured by the Church to an ethnographic, reformist, non-xenophobic orientation. Its intellectual vocabulary was exposed to enrichment not only from German, Latin and to a lesser extent Russian but also from Croatian, with which in any case it shared its dialectal base. Croatian furnished it particularly with calques and loans from Czech. By the end of the century, however, many of these Croatian words were becoming subject to criticism. In this century Serbian has relaxed its ethnographic purism somewhat and has internationalised its vocabulary to an extent exceeded among Slavonic languages only by Russian and Polish. Even the numerous Turkish words in Serbian usage have acquired an informal, even

221

affectionate stylistic colouring. The attitude to Croatianisms, however, has grown, if anything, even less accommodating.

From about 1880, a sharp turn in puristic orientation is discernible in Croatian society: the moderate, reformist, xenophobic orientation was replaced by a Serbian-style ethnographism. As a result, many of the words coined earlier in the century were spurned in favour of a rigid application of ethnographic principles. Some of them disappeared for ever; others reappeared only when a reaction to this Serbification began to be felt during the Second World War and again in the 1960s and 1970s. Furthermore, anti-Serbian feeling gave rise to widespread attempts to eradicate 'Serbisms' and to intensify the differences between the two codes and their traditional attitudes to foreign words. On the other hand, many speakers of Serbo-Croatian would like to play down these differences. This is most notable in the ethnically mixed (Serbian, Moslem and Croatian) Republic of Bosnia-Hercegovina, where language planners, aware of the fact that many of the words which serve to differentiate Serbian and Croatian usage have lost their variant-marking, have seized on the opportunity to publish hand-books in which both sets of lexical items are actively and equally encouraged (Thomas 1982). The potential significance of such an apuristic attitude is readily apparent to language planners in other Serbo-Croatian-speaking republics.

Confronted with a threat to its prestige and autonomy posed by the increasing numbers of Serbo-Croatian items after the formation of Yugoslavia, Slovene embarked upon a course of extreme xenophobic purism. Although directed at more recent borrowings from Serbo-Croatian, this purism suffers from problems of correct identification, which has led at times to a somewhat paranoid suspicion of all non-native words of Slavonic origin. Although this puristic trend has been condemned and effectively slowed by language cultivators in Slovenia, there are signs in the present anti-Serbian climate that certain Slovene intellectuals are having second thoughts about the wisdom of accepting Serbo-Croatianisation of their language's lexical stock.

Macedonian, which first gained recognition as a standard language in 1944, has its origins as a local form of the Bulgarian written tradition. Although sharing with Bulgarian a strong aversion for Turkisms, it is inevitable given the circumstances of its genesis that Macedonian should wish to distance itself as far as possible from Bulgarian. Equally inevitable was its dependence on the vocabulary of Serbo-Croatian. The resultant convergence of the Macedonian and Serbo-Croatian lexical systems has not as yet produced any significant puristic reaction but there are indications that any reduction in the polyvalency of Macedonian in a Serbo-Croatian-dominated Yugoslavia – especially in the current climate of inter-ethnic tension – will generate such a reaction in the future.

It can be seen from this survey that purism is a prominent factor in the relations between these codes and as such needs to be taken seriously by language planning agencies in each of the speech communities as well as in the development of a plan for Yugoslavia as a whole. It seems to me that the following courses of action are available for consideration:

1. *Adopt a laissez-faire policy.*
This is predicated on the recognition that closely related languages are bound to converge somewhat in a multilingual setting. Purism is then a harmless safety-valve in the event that they should come too close. However, such a policy does nothing to remove the widespread perception that any failure to maintain sufficient difference between these closely related codes will lead to only one outcome: the adoption of the Serbian variant of standard Serbo-Croatian – albeit employing the Latin script – as the *lingua communis* – and hence the only polyvalent code – for the whole of Yugoslavia. Any such unitaristic tendency would be linguistic suicide for Croats, Slovenes and Macedonians and would meet with firm resistance especially in the present political climate. A *laissez-faire* policy is therefore not acceptable and may even be politically dangerous.

2. *Adopt an anti-puristic policy.*
This is predicated upon the proposition that the interests of inter-ethnic communication would best be served by the minimalisation of the differences between the various standard codes. The adoption of common terminologies would not only benefit technological progress but would also diminish the costs of coining and perpetuating separate systems of words. However, such a policy fails to recognise that the differences between these codes are imbued with symbolic value. To reduce these differences by force – even supposing it were possible to enforce language usage across republican boundaries which seems unlikely – would be certain to evoke a blacklash of resentment. Furthermore, such a policy would also be ethically questionable since it would be bound to disfavour the Slovenes and Macedonians (and to a lesser extent the Croats).

3. *Encourage linguistic nationalism.*
This is predicated on the notion that purism provides the fullest scope for the development of autonomous native expression as well as safeguarding the prestige of each of the standard languages

concerned. However, such a policy would increase any centrifugal tendencies in the inter-language relations and would seriously jeopardise any chances of achieving that inter-comprehensibility between them which is so essential for the development of inter-ethnic relations within the Yugoslav federation. Furthermore, the nativisation of terminology, which would be an inevitable consequence, would seriously impede technological cooperation between the various communities.

4. *Develop a compromise between extreme purism and extreme unitarism.*
This is predicated upon a recognition that the centripetal and centrifugal tendencies characterising the relationship between these codes can be reconciled only by a rational puristic profile which gives due regard to the other functional requirements of a modern standard language. It is the only one of the available alternatives which would not exacerbate the present political crisis in Yugoslavia and which offers the possibility of a long-term solution.

The implementation of this compromise policy would require a fundamental change in language attitudes in the relevant speech communities from non-rational to rational purism. This change would involve the five sets of value-orientations as described by Daneš. A moderate, puristic profile which would satisfy these conditions would need to have the following characteristics:

1. Openness to internationalisms.
2. Readiness to preserve stable, well-integrated loanwords from whatever source.
3. Acceptance of calquing.
4. Acceptance of loans from other Slavonic languages (including those used in Yugoslavia) provided they do not threaten in any way to undermine the autonomy of the language.
5. Scepticism towards neologisms and dialectalisms as new sources of lexical enrichment.
6. Rejection of the need to revive words which have fallen out of use.
7. Freedom of personal choice in the use of lexical doublets which exist, even if only one of the doublets is shared with one or more of the other standard codes.
8. Tolerance of the freedom of choice of other members of the speech community and a sensitivity to their wishes.

The success of this policy depends on political good-will throughout Yugoslavia and the genuine desire on the part of language planners to perceive the problem from a federal rather than a national perspective. Its implementation requires action on several fronts:

1. *Research*
A thorough empirical investigation should be launched of word use and public attitudes to certain classes of words because no language plan should be undertaken before reliable information is available.

2. *Dissemination*
The results of these investigations should be published even if the facts they reveal are unpalatable. Problems must be confronted and not covered up since ignorance and misinformation do not promote trust and tolerance.

3. *Education*
Programmes in school and in the public media should be introduced to raise public awareness of the desirability of moderate purism since without public support any plan involving a shift in attitudes is bound to founder. An ancillary benefit of raising consciousness about the issue of purism is a heightened awareness in the community of language problems in general.

4. *Cooperation*
A federal advisory commission on terminology should be established, so that the codes concerned can have a coordinated approach to the planning of their terminological needs.

5. *Publication*
Dictionaries and language guides with accurate and up-to-date information on stylistic register and area of use should be published together with single-language and inter-language dictionaries for individual disciplines. Such publications provide easy reference and confirm the norms established through language planning.

These five activities constitute the primary tasks for treating the problem of purism within the context of Yugoslav language planning needs. The successes and shortcomings of these activities need to be constantly monitored and if necessary subjected to modification. Whether or not such a plan will ever be carried out is not the issue here. What is important is that the plan is feasible and answers the demands of the current Yugoslav language situation. Moreover, I hope, in the process of presenting this particular case, to have suggested ways in which a rational approach to language purification can be properly incorporated into a fully developed language plan.

Bibliography

Akulenko, V. V. (1972) *Voprosy internacionalizacii slovarnogo sostava jazyka.* Izdatel'stvo Xar'kovskogo Universiteta, Xar'kov.

Aschenbrenner, K. (1971) *The concepts of value: foundations of value theory.* D. Reidel, Dordrecht.

Auty, R. (1958) The linguistic revival among the Slavs of the Austrian Empire, 1780–1850: the role of individuals in the codification and acceptance of new literary languages. *Modern Language Review* **53**: 392–404.

Auty, R. (1964) Community and divergence in the history of the Slavonic languages. *Slavonic and East European Review* **42**: 257–73.

Auty, R. (1972) Sources and methods of lexical enrichment in the Slavonic language revivals of the early nineteenth century. In Worth, D. S. (ed.) *The Slavic word: proceedings of the international Slavistic colloquium at UCLA September 11–16, 1970.* Mouton, The Hague/Paris, 41–56.

Auty, R. (1973) The role of purism in the development of the Slavonic literary languages. *Slavonic and East European Review* **51**: 335–43.

Auty, R. (1978a) Pannonian parallels and divergences: thoughts on the history of the Croatian and Hungarian literary languages. *Filologija* **8**: 29–35.

Auty, R. (1978b) Literary language and literary dialect in medieval amd early modern Slavonic literatures. *Slavonic and East European Review* **56**: 192–201.

Auty, R. (1979) Language and nationality in east-central Europe 1750–1950. *Oxford Slavonic Papers*, New Series, **12**: 52–83.

Axmanova, O. S. (1966) *Slovar' lingvističeskix terminov.* Sovetskaja Ènciklopedija, Moscow.

Bach, A. (1970) *Geschichte der deutschen Sprache* 9th edn. Quelle & Meyer, Heidelberg.

Bajec, A. (1959–60) O purizmu in puristih. *Jezik in Slovstvo* **5**: 129–34.

Balbir, N. (1983) La modernisation du hindi. In Fodor, I., Hagège, C. (eds) *Language reform: history and future.* Buske, Hamburg, vol. 1, 101–26.

Balibar, R., Laporte, D. (1974) *Le français national: politique et pratiques de la langue nationale sous la Révolution.* Hachette, Paris.

Bartsch, R. (1987) *Norms of language; theoretical and practical aspects.* Longman.

Bazin, L. (1983) La réforme linguistique en Turquie. In Fodor, I., Hagège, C. (eds) *Language reform: history and future*. Buske, Hamburg, vol. 1, 155–77.

Becker, H. (1948a) *Zwei Sprachanschlüsse*. Humboldt-Bücherei, Leipzig.

Becker, H. (1948b) *Der Sprachbund*. Humboldt-Bücherei, Leipzig.

Behagel, E. (1917) Verdeutschungen bei Jean Paul. *Zeitschrift des Allgemeinen Deutschen Sprachvereins* 32.

Bělič, J. (1953) Zákonodárce nové spisovné češtiny: k dvoustému výročí nározeni Josefa Dobrovského. *Naše Řeč* 36: 193–201.

Bělič, J. (1969) Poznámky a postavení německých přejatých slov v dnešní češtině. In Krauss, W. *et al.* (eds) *Slavisch-deutsche Wechselbeziehungen in Sprache, Literatur und Kultur: Festschrift für Hans Holm Bielfeldt*. Akademie-Verlag, Berlin, 7–19.

Bellamy, H. (1939) *L'académie française*. Le crapouillet, Paris.

Benkö, L. (1972) The lexical stock of Hungarian. In Benkö, L., Imre, S. (eds) *The Hungarian language*. Mouton, The Hague/Paris, 171–226.

Bergman, N. G. (1947) *A short history of the Swedish language* Trans. F. P. Magoun Jr, H. Kökeritz. Swedish Institute for Cultural Relations, Stockholm.

Betz, W. (1936) *Der Einfluss des Lateinischen auf den althochdeutschen Sprachschatz*. Germanistische Bibliothek, Abt. 2, Band 40, Heidelberg.

Betz, W. (1944) Die Lehnbildungen und der abendländische Sprachenausgleich. *Beiträge zur Geschichte der deutschen Sprache und Literatur* 67: 275–302.

Bickerton, D. (1980) Decreolisation and the creole continuum. In Valdman, A., Highfield, A. (eds) *The national orientation in Creole studies*. Academic Press, New York, 109–29.

Bílý, F. (1904) *Od kolébky našeho obrození*. J. Otto, Prague.

Bircher, M. (1971) *Die Fruchtbringende Gesellschaft: Quellen und Dokumente in vier Bänden*. Kosel, Munich.

Blackall, E. A. (1959) *The emergence of German as a literary language*. CUP, Cambridge.

Blume, H. (1967) *Die Morphologie von Zesens Wortneubildungen*. Dissertation, Giessen.

Botha, T. J. R. (1983) Afrikaans: origin and lexical evolution. In Fodor, I., Hagège, C. (eds) *Language reform: history and future*. Buske, Hamburg, vol. 1, 213–37.

Bradac, J. J. (1982) A rose by any other name: attitudinal consequences of lexical variation. In Ryan, E. B., Giles, H. (eds) *Attitudes towards language variation*. Edward Arnold, 99–115.

Brang, P., Züllig, M. (eds) (1981) *Kommentierte Bibliographie zur slavischen Soziolinguistik*, 3 vols. Peter Lang, Bern/Frankfurt am Main.

Britto, F. (1986) *Diglossia: a study of the theory with application to Tamil*. Georgetown UP, Washington D.C.

Browning, R. (1982) Greek diglossia yesterday and today. *International Journal of the Sociology of Language* 35: 49–68

Broz, I., Iveković, F. (1901) *Rječnik hrvatskoga jezika*, Karl Albrecht, Zagreb.

Brozovic, D. (1970) *Standardni jezik*. Matica hrvatska, Zagreb.

Budovičová, V. (1987) Literary languages in contact (a sociolinguistic approach to the relation between Slovak and Czech today). In Chloupek, J., Nekvapil, J. (eds) *Reader in Czech sociolinguistics*. J. Benjamins, Amsterdam, 156–75.

Burgess, A. (1986) *Little Wilson and Big God*. Weidenfeld & Nicholson.

Cienkowski, W. (1983) Trends in the development of contemporary Polish vocabulary. In Fodor, I., Hagège, C. (eds) *Language reform: history and future*. Buske, Hamburg, vol. 1, 321–50.

Close, E. (1974) *The development of modern Romanian: linguistic theory in Muntenia 1821–1838*. OUP, Oxford.

Collinder, B. (1965) *Finnisch als Kultursprache*. Ropp, Hamburg-Volksdorf.

Comrie, B., Stone, G. (1978) *The Russian language since the Revolution*. Oxford UP.

Crowley, T. (1989) *The politics of discourse: the standard language question in British cultural debates*. Macmillan.

Czigany, L. G. (1974) Hungarianness: the origin of a pseudo-linguistic concept. *Slavonic and East European Review* **52**: 325–36.

Daneš, F. (1968) Dialektické tendence ve vývoji spisovných jazyků (příspěvek sociolingvistický). In *Československé přednášky pro vi. mezinárodní sjezd slavistů v Praze*. Academia, Prague 119–28.

Daneš, F. (1982) Dialektische Tendenzen in der Entwicklung der Literatursprachen. In *Grundlagen der Sprachkultur: Beiträge der Prager Linguistik zur Sprachtheorie und Sprachpflege* vol. 2. Akademie-Verlag, Berlin, 92–113.

Daneš, F. (1987) Values and attitudes in language standardization. In Chloupek, J., Nekvapil, J. (eds) *Reader in Czech sociolinguistics*. J. Benjamins, Amsterdam, 206–45.

Daňhelka, J. (1969) Husův postoj k slovům německého původu. In Krauss, W. et al. (eds) *Slavisch-deutsche Wechselbeziehungen in Sprache, Literatur und Kultur: Festschrift für Hans Holm Bielfeldt*. Akademie-Verlag, Berlin, 37–41.

Daube, A. (1940) *Der Aufstieg der Muttersprache im deutschen Denken des 15. und 16. Jahrhunderts*. Deutsche Forschungen, vol. 34, Frankfurt am Main.

Deanović, M. (1936) Zašto dubrovački književnici nisu pisali kako su govorili? *Hrvatsko Kolo*, 62–7.

Deme, L. (1972) Standard Hungarian. In Benkö, L., Imre, S. (eds) *The Hungarian Language*. Mouton, The Hague, 255–97.

Deutsch, K. W. (1942) The trend of European nationalism: the language aspect. *The American Political Science Review* **36**: 533–41.

Deutsch, K. W. (1953) *Nationalism and social communication: an inquiry into the foundations of nationality*. Technology Press of Massachusetts Institute of Technology and John Wiley, Cambridge, Mass.

Devereux, R. (1968) The Crusca Academy and its *Vocabulario*. *Italian Quarterly* **44**: 67–86.

Dobrovský, J. (1779) *Böhmische Litteratur auf das Jahr 1779*. Prague.

Dobrovský, J. (1780) *Böhmische und Mährische Litteratur auf das Jahr 1780*. Prague.

Dobrovský, J. (1799) *Die Bildsamkeit der Slawischen Sprache an der Bildung der Substantive und Adjective in der Böhmischen Sprache dargestellt*. Prague.

Dorian, N. (1981) *Language death: the life cycle of a Scottish Gaelic dialect*. U of Pennsylvania P., Philadelphia.

Dostál, A. (1982) Concerning new and old forms of purism in the Czech literary language. *International Journal of Slavic Linguistics and Poetics* **25/26**: 109–14.

Douglas, M. (1966) *Purity and danger: an analysis of concepts of pollution and taboo.* Routledge & K. Paul.

Drake, G. F. (1977) *The role of prescriptivism in American linguistics 1820–1970.* Amsterdam studies in the theory and history of linguistic science, series 3, Studies in the history of linguistics, vol. 13, Amsterdam.

Dunger, H. (1910) *Festschrift zur Funfundzwanzigjahrfeier des Allgemeinen Deutschen Sprachvereins, 10 September 1910: die deutsche Sprachbewegung und der allgemeine deutsche Sprachverein 1885–1910.* Allgemeiner Deutscher Sprachverein, Berlin.

Eastman, C. M. (1983) *Language planning: an introduction.* Chandler & Sharp, San Francisco.

Efremov, L. P. (1960) Kal'kirovanie i ego otličie ot zaimstvovanija. *Izvestie Akademii Nauk Kazaxskoj SSR* **14**: 16–26.

Ekwall, E. (1903) *Shakespere's vocabulary, its etymological elements.* Upsala UP, Upsala.

Elgibali, A. (1988) The language situation in Arabic-speaking nations. In Paulston, C. B. (ed.) *International handbook of bilingualism and bilingual education.* Greenwood Press, New York, 47–61.

Étiemble, R. (1964) *Parlez-vous franglais?.* Gallimard, Paris.

Fasold, R. W. (1984) *The sociolinguistics of society.* Basil Blackwell.

Feldmann, W. (1906) Fremdwörter und Verdeutschungen des achtzehnten Jahrhunderts. *Zeitschrift für deutsche Wortforschung* **7**: 49–99.

Fellman, J. (1973) *The revival of a classical tongue: Eliezer Ben Yehuda and the Modern Hebrew language.* Mouton, The Hague.

Fellman, J. (1974a) The role of Eliezer Ben Yehuda in the revival of the Hebrew language: an assessment. In Fishman, J. A. (ed.) *Advances in language planning.* Mouton, The Hague, 427–55.

Fellman, J. (1974b) The Academy of the Hebrew Language: its history, structure and function. *Linguistics* **120**: 95–104.

Ferguson, C. A. (1959) Diglossia. *Word* **15**: 325–40.

Festinger, L. (1957) *A theory of cognitive dissonance.* Row, Peterson, Evanston, Illinois.

Fichte, J. G. (1808) *Reden an die deutsche Nation.* Berlin.

Fishman, J. A. (1971) The impact of nationalism on language planning. In Rubin, J., Jernudd, B. H. (eds) *Can languages be planned?* UP of Hawaii, Honolulu, 1–20.

Fishman, J. A. (1973) *Language and nationalism: two integrative essays.* Newbury House, Rowley Mass.

Fishman, J. A. (1974) Language planning and language planning research: the state of the art. In Fishman, J. A. (ed.) *Advances in language planning.* Mouton, The Hague, 15–36.

Fishman, J. A. (1983) Prefatory remarks. In Fodor, I., Hagège, C. (eds) *Language reform: history and future.* Buske, Hamburg, vol. 1, 1–9.

Flasdieck, H. M. (1928) *Der Gedanke einer englischen Sprachakademie in*

Vergangenheit und Gegenwart. Jenaer germanistische Forschungen, Vol. 11, Jena.

Fodor, I. (1983a) Hungarian: evolution – stagnation – reform – further development. In Fodor, I., Hagège, C. (eds) *Language reform: history and future*. Buske, Hamburg, vol. 2, 49–84.

Fodor, I. (1983b) Quelques conclusions: comment les "Esqimaux" développent-ils leurs parlers en langues littéraires? In Fodor, I., Hagège, C. (eds) *Language reform: history and future*. Buske, Hamburg, vol. 3 455–81.

Fodor, I., Hagège, C. (eds) (1983) *Language reform: history and future*. Buske, Hamburg, 3 vols.

Forster, L. W. (1970) *The poet's tongues: multilingualism in literature*. Cambridge UP.

Francis, J. F. de (1950) *Nationalism and language reform in China*. Princeton UP, Princeton.

Friedman, V. A. (1975) Macedonian language and nationalism during the nineteenth and early twentieth centuries. *Balkanistica: occasional papers in Southeast European studies* 2: 83–98.

Fryščák, M. (1978) The two official languages of Czechoslovakia. *Folia Slavica* 1: 343–52.

Gellner, E. (1964) *Thought and change*. U of Chicago P, Chicago.

Gellner, E. (1983) *Nations and Nationalism*. Basil Blackwell.

Georgieva, E., Lilov, M. (1983) Die bulgarische Literatursprache und die Sprachreform. In Fodor, I., Hagège, C. (eds) *Language reform: history and future*. Buske, Hamburg, vol. 1 113–35.

Gerdener, W. (1986) *Der Purismus im Nynorsk: Historische Entwicklung und heutiger Sprachgebrauch*. Dissertation, Münster.

Giles, H., Powesland, P. F. (1975) *Speech style and social evaluation*. Academic Press.

Giles, H., Smith, P. M. (1979) Accomodation theory: optimal levels of convergence. In Giles, H., St Clair, R. N. (eds) *Language and social psychology*. Basil Blackwell, 45–65.

Goethe, J. W. von (1988) *Sämtliche Werke*. Abt. 1, Band 2. Deutscher Klassiker Verlag, Frankfurt am Main.

Goosens, J. (1975) Vlaamse purismen. *Tijdschrift voor Nederlands Taal en Letterkunde* 91: 112–32.

Gordon, D. C. (1978) *The French language and national identity 1930–75*. Mouton, The Hague.

Grannes, A. (1970) *Étude sur les turcismes en bulgare*. Universitetsforlaget, Oslo.

Groenke, U. (1972) How 'archaic' is modern Icelandic. In *Studies for Einar Haugen*. Mouton, The Hague/Paris, 253–60.

Groenke, U. (1983) Diachrone Perdurabilität, Sprachpflege und Sprachplanung, der Fall Isländisch. In Fodor, I., Hagège, C. (eds) *Language reform: history and future*. Buske, Hamburg, vol. 2 137–55.

Gross, M. (1971) Einfluss der sozialen Struktur auf den Charakter der Nationalbewegung in den kroatischen Ländern im 19. Jahrhundert. In Schieder, T. *et al.* (eds) *Sozialstruktur und Organisation europäischer Nationalbewegungen*. R. Oldenbourg, Munich/Vienna, 67–92.

Gumperz, J. J., Wilson, R. (1971) Convergence and creolization: a case from the Indo-Aryan/Dravidian border in India. In Hymes, D. (ed.) *Pidginization and creolization of languages.* Cambridge UP.

Gutschmidt, K. (1976) Zum Zusammenhang von kultureller und literatursprachlicher Entwicklung in der Epoche der bulgarischen Wiedergeburt. *Zeitschrift für Slawistik,* **21**: 716–21.

Gvozdanović, J. (1989) Defining markedness. In Mišeska-Tomić O. (ed.) *Markedness in synchrony and diachrony.* Mouton de Gruyter, Berlin/New York, 47–66.

Haeringen, C. B. van (1960) *Netherlandic language research* 2nd edn. E. J. Brill, Leiden.

Hagège, C. (1983) Voies et destins de l'action humaine sur les langues. In Fodor, I., Hagège, C. (eds) *Language reform: history and future.* Buske, Hamburg, vol. 1, 11–68.

Hagström, B. (1984) Language contact in the Faroes. In Ureland, P. S., Clarkson, I. (eds) *Scandinavian language contacts.* Cambridge UP, 171–89.

Hakulinen, L. (1961) *The Structure and development of the Finnish language* trans. J. Atkinson. Indiana UP, Ural Altaic Series, 3, Bloomington, Indiana.

Hall, R. A. (1942) *The Italian questione della lingua: an interpretative essay.* U of North Carolina, Studies in the Romance Languages and Literatures, 4, Chapel Hill, North Carolina.

Hall, R. A. (1974) *External history of the Romance languages.* American Elsevier, New York.

Halleux, P. (1965) Le purisme islandais. *Études Germaniques* **20**: 417–27.

Harbrecht, H. (1912–13) Verzeichnis der von Zesen verdeutschten Lehn- und Fremdwörter. *Zeitschrift für deutsche Wortforschung* **14**: 71–81.

Hardgrave, R. L. (1965) *The Dravidian movement.* Popular Prakashan, Bombay.

Hartmann, R. R. K., Stork, F. C. (1972) *Dictionary of language and linguistics.* John Wiley & Sons, New York/Toronto.

Haugen, E. (1966) *Language conflict and language planning: the case of modern Norwegian.* Harvard UP, Cambridge, Mass.

Haugen, E. (1976) *The Scandinavian languages: an introduction to their history.* Faber & Faber.

Havránek, B. (1936) *Spisovný jazyk český a slovenský.* Československá Vlastivěda, řád 2, Prague.

Hawkins, P. (1979) Greek diglossia and variation theory. *General Linguistics* **19**: 169–87.

Herrity, P. (1973) The role of the Matica and similar societies in the development of the Slavonic literary languages. *Slavonic and East European Review* **51**: 368–86.

Herrity, P. (1978) Puristic attitudes in Serbia in the second half of the nineteenth century. *Slavonic and East European Review* **56**: 202–23.

Heyd, U. (1954) *Language reform in modern Turkey.* Israel Oriental Society, Jerusalem.

Hill, P. (1975) Lexical revolution as an expression of nationalism in the Balkans. *Melbourne Slavonic Studies,* **9/10**: 121–8.

Horálek, K. (1948) La fonction de la structure des fonctions de la langue. *Receuil linguistique de Bratislava* **1**: 39–43.

Horecký, J. (1967) Vzťah spisovnej slovenčiny k spisovnej češtine. In Ružička J. (ed.) *Kultúra spisovnej slovenčiny.* Slovenská Akadémia Vied, Jazykovedny ústav, Bratislava, 41–5.

Horecký, J. (1975) Postoj k cudzím slovam v slovenčine a češtine. *Slavica Pragensia* **18**: 207–10.

Hroch, M. (1968) *Die Vorkampfer der nationalen Bewegung bei den kleinen Völkern Europas: eine vergleichende Analyse zur gesellschaftlichen Schichtung der patriotischen Gruppen.* Universita Karlova, Prague.

Hüttl-Worth, G. (1956) *Die Bereicherung des russischen Wortschatzes im xviii. Jahrhundert.* A. Holzhausen, Vienna.

Hyrkkänen, J. (1973) *Der lexikalische Einfluss des Italienischen auf das Kroatische des 16. Jahrhunderts (Die italienischen Lehnwörter im Sprachgebrauch der dalmatinischen Kroaten im Licht der kroatischen Renaissance-Literatur.* Dissertation, Helsinki.

Ivir, V. (1989) Internationalisms: marked or unmarked. In Mišeska-Tomić, O. (ed.) *Markedness in synchrony and diachrony.* Mouton de Gruyter, Berlin/ New York, 139–49.

Jacobs, W. D. (1952) *William Barnes Linguist.* U of New Mexico Publications in language and literature No. 9, Albuquerque.

Jaffe, H. L. C. (1967) *De stijl* trans R. R. Symonds. Harry N. Abrams, Inc., New York.

Jageman, H. C. G. von (1899) Philology and purism. *Publications of the Modern Language Association* **15**: 74–96.

Jakobson, R. (1932) O dnešním brusíčství českém. In Havránek, B., Weingart, M. (eds) *Spisovná čeština a jazyková kultura.* Melantrich, Prague, 85–112.

Jakopin, F. (1968) O deležu ruskih elementov v razvoju slovenskega knjižnega jezika. *Slavistična Revija* **16**: 65–90.

Jazayery, M. A. (1983) The modernization of the Persian vocabulary and language reform in Iran. In Fodor, I., Hagège, C. (eds) *Language reform: history and future.* Buske, Hamburg, vol. 2, 241–68.

Jedlička, A. (1948) *Josef Jungmann a obrozenská terminologie literárně vědná a linguistická.* Česká Akademie Věd a Umění, Prague.

Jelínek, M. (1971) O českém purismu. *In Přednášky ve xiv běhu Letní školy slovanských studií v roce 1970.* Prague, 18–37.

Jernudd, B. H., Shapiro, M. J. (eds) (1989) *The politics of language purism.* Mouton de Gruyter, Berlin/New York.

Johnson, S. (1755) *A dictionary of the English language.* J. and P. Knapton, T. and J. Longman, C. Hitch and L. Hawes, A. Miller, R. and J. Dodsley.

Jona, E. (1970) Profesor Juraj Palkovič a jeho slovník. *Slovenská Reč* **35**: 321–31.

Jungmann, J. J. (1829) *Beleuchtung der Streitfrage über die böhmische Orthographie.* Fürsterzbischöfliche Buchdruckerei, Prague.

Jungraithmayr, H. (1983) Spontaneous and planned development of Hausa, a West African language. In Fodor, I., Hagège, C. (eds) *Language reform: history and future.* Buske, Hamburg, vol. 2, 269–84.

Kahane, H., Kahane, R. (1988) Language spread and language policy: the prototype of Greek and Latin. In Lowenberg, P. H. (ed.) *Language spread and language policy: issues, implications, and case studies.* Georgetown UP, Washington, D.C., 16–24.

Kalogjera, D. (1978) On Serbo-Croatian prescriptivism. *Folia Slavica* 1: 388–99.

Kamb-Spiess, R. (1962) *Lehnprägungen der deutschen Sprache.* Dissertation, Tübingen.

Karker, A. (1983) Language reforming efforts in Denmark and Sweden. In Fodor, I., Hagège, C. (eds) *Language reform: history and future.* Buske, Hamburg, vol. 2, 285–99.

Kaster, R. A. (1988) *Guardians of language: the grammarian and society in late antiquity.* U of California P, Berkeley.

Katičić, R. (1973–4) O purizmu. *Jezik* 21: 84–90.

Katz, D. (1940) The psychology of nationalism. In Guilford, J. P. *et al.* (eds) *Fields of psychology.* D. Van Nostrand, New York, 163–81.

Kaufmann, E. (1939) Der Fragenkreis ums Fremdwort. *Journal of English and Germanic Philology* 38: 42–63.

Keipert, H. (1977a) *Die Adjektive auf -tel'n": Studien zu einem kirchenslavischen Wortbildungstyp.* vol. 1, O Harrassowitz, Wiesbaden.

Keipert, H. (1977b) Puristische Tendenzen in der russischen Sprachpflege der Gegenwart. *Osteuropa* 28: 285–309.

Kiparsky, V. (1933–4) Über Neologismen im Tschechischen. *Slavia* 10: 700–17.

Kirkness, A. (1975) *Zur Sprachreinigung im Deutschen: eine historische Dokumentation 1789–1871.* Narr, Tübingen.

Kloss, H. (1952) *Die Entwicklung neuer germanischer Kultursprachen von 1800 bis 1950.* Pohl & Co., Munich.

Kohn, H. (1944) *The idea of nationalism: a study in its origins and background.* Macmillan, New York.

Komárek, M. (1953) K problematice cízích slov a purismu v národním jazyce. *Slavia* 22: 215–19.

Kramer, J. (1983) Language planning in Italy. In Fodor, I., Hagège, C. (eds) *Language reform: history and future.* Buske, Hamburg, vol. 2 301–16.

Kraus, J. (1982) Zu soziolinguistischen Aspekten der Sprachkultur in der Tschechoslovakei. In *Grundlagen der Sprachkultur: Beiträge der Prager Linguistik zur Sprachtheorie und Sprachpflege* vol. 2. Akademie-Verlag, Berlin, 256–71.

Krysin, L. P. (1963) Kul'tura reči i jazykovoj purizm. *Russkij jazyk v škole* 24/3: 26–32.

Kuhn, O. (1970) *The structure of scientific revolutions* 2nd edn. U of Chicago P, Chicago, Illinois.

Kurman, G. (1968) *The development of written Estonian.* Indiana UP, Bloomington, Indiana.

Laponce, J. A. (1987) *Languages and their territories* trans. A Martin-Sperry. U. of Toronto P., Toronto/Buffalo/London.

Larkin, M. T. (1971) *Language in the philosophy of Aristotle.* Mouton, The Hague/Paris.

Lencek, R. (1989) The role of sociolinguistics in the evolution of Slavic linguistic nationalism. *Canadaian Review of Studies in Nationalism* **16**: 99–115.

Lilič, G. A. (1982) *Rol' russkogo jazyka v razvitii slovarnogo sostava češskogo literaturnogo jazyka (konec 18. – načalo 19. veka).* Izdatel'stvo Leningradskogo gosudarstvennogo universiteta, Leningrad.

Lisický, A. (1916) Zřeštěna češina Jana Václava Póla a Josef Dobrovský. *Osvěta* **46**: 57–67, 121–9.

Lisický, A. (1919) Z dějin zápasu o české slovo. *Osvěta* **49**: 473–83, 537–48.

Lisický, A. (1920) Jan Václav Pól v zápase o české slovo. *Osvěta* **5039**–46, 214–22, 285–93, 343–52, 415–23, 459–67.

Lockwood, W. B. (1964) *An informal history of the German language with chapters on Dutch and Afrikaans, Frisian and Yiddish.* Cambridge UP.

Lötzsch, R. (1968) Einige Auswirkungen des Purismus auf die grammatische Normierung slawischer Schriftsprachen. In Fasske, H., Lötzsch, R. (eds) *Beiträge zur sorbischen Sprachwissenschaft.* Domowina-Verlag, Bautzen, 21–36.

Magner, T. F. (1967) Language and nationalism in Yugoslavia. *Canadian Slavic Studies* **1**: 333–47.

Malaca Casteleiro, J. (1983) Réforme et modernisation de la langue portugaise. In Fodor, I., Hagège, C. (eds) *Language reform: history and future.* Buske, Hamburg, vol. 2, 393–418.

Maretić, T. (1899) *Gramatika i stilistika hrvatskoga ili srpskoga književnog jezika.* L Hartman, Zagreb.

Maretić, T. (1924) *Hrvatski ili srpski savjetnik za sve koji žele dobro govoriti i pisati književnim jezikom našim.* L. Hartman, Zagreb.

Masson, M. (1983) La renaissance de l'hébreu. In Fodor, I., Hagège, C. (eds) *Language reform: history and future.* Buske, Hamburg, vol. 2, 449–478.

Mathesius, V. (1932) O požadavku stability v spisovném jazyce. In Havránek, B., Weingart, M. (eds) *Spisovná čeština a jazyková kultura.* Melantrich, Prague, 14–31.

Mathesius, V. (1933) Probleme der čechischen Sprachkultur. *Slavische Rundschau* **5**: 69–85.

Mathesius, V. (1947) *Čeština a obecný jazykozpyt, soubor statí.* Melantrich, Prague.

Meillet, P. J. A. (1918) *Les langues dans l'Europe nouvelle.* Payot, Paris.

Minogue, K. (1967) *Nationalism.* B. T. Batsford, New York.

Mistrík, J. (1973) K procesu internationalizácie slovenčiny. *Jazykovedný časopis* **24** : 40–44.

Morag, S. (1959) Planned and unplanned development in Modern Hebrew. *Lingua* **8**: 247–63.

Moskov, M. D. (1958) *Borbata protiv čuždite dumi v bălgarskija ezik.* Bălgarska Akademija na Naukite, Institut za Bălgarski ezik, Sofija.

Moskov, M. D. (1976) *Za čist bălgarski ezik.* Narodna Prosveta, Sofija.

Moussa, S. (1955) Arab language problems. *Middle Eastern Affairs* **6**: 41–4.

Mønnesland, S. (1971) Synonymy and literary standard in Serbo- Croat. *Scandoslavica* **17**: 217–34.

Mukařovský, J. (1940) Estetika jazyka. *Slovo a Slovesnost* **6**: 1–27.

Mukařovský, J. (1977) *The word and verbal art: selected essays* trans. J. Burbank, P. Steiner. Yale UP, New Haven.

Mulertt, W. (1927) Aus der Geschichte der spanischen Sprachreinigungsbestrebungen. In *Estudios eruditos: in memoriam Adolfo Bonilla y San Martin* Vol. 1, Madrid, 583-603.

Nahir, M. (1977) The five aspects of language planning. *Language problems and language planning* 1: 107–24.

Nehru, J. (1953) *An autobiography.* Bodley Head.

Němec, I. (1968) *Vývojové postupy české slovní zásoby.* Academia, Prague.

Němec, I. (1970) Nova slova Hušova a J. A. Womenshého. *Slovo a Slovesnost* 31: 313–24.

Niedzielski, H. (1979) Language consciousness and language policy in Poland. *Word* 30: 134–59.

Nielsen, N. A. (1949) Dansk sprogrensning i 1700-tallet. *Arkiv för nordisk filologi* 64: 246–78.

Orłoś, T. Z. (1967) *Zapożyczenia polskie w słowniku Jungmanna.* Polska Akademia Nauk, Cracow.

Otto, K. F. (1972) *Die Sprachgesellschaften des 17. Jahrhunderts.* J. B. Metzlersche Verlagsbuchhandlung, Stuttgart.

Palkovič, J, (1819–21) *Böhmisch-deutsch-lateinisches Wörterbuch mit Beifügung der den Slowaken und Mähren eigenen Ausdrücke und Redensarten.*Bratislava.

Parins, J. W. (1984) *William Barnes.* Twayne, Boston, Mass.

Parsons, T. (1951) *The social system.* Free Press, Glencoe, Illinois.

Perelmuter, J. (1974) Russian substandard usage and the attitude of Soviet lexicography. *Canadian Slavonic Papers* 16: 436–47.

Polenz, P. von (1967) Sprachpurismus und Nazionalsozializmus: die Fremdwort-Frage gestern und heute. In Wiese, B. von, Heuss, R. (eds) *Nationalismus in Germanistik und Dichtung.* Erich Schmidt, Berlin, 79–112.

Polenz, P. von (1983) Sprachnormung und Ansätze zur Sprachreform im Deutschen. In Fodor, I., Hagège, C. (eds) *Language reform: history and future.* Buske, Hamburg, vol. 2, 23–52.

Polomé, E. C. (1983) Standardization of Swahili and the modernization of the Swahili vocabulary. In Fodor, I., Hagège, C. (eds) *Language reform: history and future.* Buske, Hamburg, vol. 3, 53–77.

Prein, W. (1909) *Puristische Strömungen im 16. Jahrhundert. Ein Beitrag zur englischen Sprachgeschichte.* Baehr, Eickel i. W.

Quemada, B. (1983) Les réformes du français. In Fodor, I., Hagège, C. (eds) *Language reform: history and future.* Buske, Hamburg, vol. 3. 79–117.

Radovanović, M. (forthcoming) Standard Serbo-Croatian and the theory of language planning. In *Language planning in Yugoslavia.* Macmillan.

Raede, J. W. (1967) De-Germanization of the Upper Lusatian language. *Slavic and East European Journal* 11: 185–90.

Raffaelli, S. (1983) *Le parole proibite: purismo di Stato e regolamentazione della pubblicità in Italia 1812–1945.* Mulino, Bologna.

Ray, P. S. (1961) The value of a language. *Lingua* 10: 220–33.

Ray, P. S. (1963) *Language standardization.* Mouton, The Hague.

Rebuschi, G. (1983) Réforme et planification en basque: une expérience en cours. In Fodor, I., Hagège, C (eds) *Language reform: history and future.* Buske, Hamburg, vol. 3, 119–38.

Rehling, E. (1951) *Det danske sprog* 3rd edn. J H Schultz, Copenhagen.

Remenyi, J. (1951) Ferenc Kacinczy, Hungarian critic and neologist. *Slavonic and East European Review* **29**: 233–43.

Robertson, D. M. (1910) *A history of the French Academy 1635 (1634) – 1910.* T. F. Unwin.

Robins, R. H. (1967) *A short history of linguistics.* Indiana UP, Bloomington.

Romaine, S. (1988) *Pidgin and creole languages.* Longman.

Rosario, G. del (1967) Consistency, not purity, is the important factor in language development. *Philippine Education Forum,* June, 1–11.

Rosario, G. del (1968) A modernization-standardization plan for the Austronesian-derived national languages of Southeast Asia. *Asian Studies* **6**: 1–18.

Ross, A. S. C. (1938) Artificial words in present-day Estonian. *Transactions of the Philological Society* 64–72.

Rothstein, R. A. (1976) *Kultura języka* in twentieth-century Poland and her neighbors. In Magner, T. F. (ed.) *Slavic linguistics and language teaching.* Slavica Publishers, Columbus, Ohio, 58–81.

Ryan, E. B., Giles, H., Sebastian, R. J. (1982) An integrative perspective for the study of attitudes towards language variation. In Ryan, E. B., Giles, H. (eds) *Attitudes towards language variation.* Edward Arnold, 1–19.

Salzmann, Z. (1989) Foreign influences on Czech as a measure of Czech nationalism and internationalism. *Canadian Review of Studies in Nationalism* **16**: 63–77.

Saulson, S. B. (1979) *Institutionalized language planning: documents and analysis of the review of Hebrew.* Mouton, The Hague.

Sauvageot, A. (1971) *L'édification de la langue hongroise.* Éditions Klinksieck, Paris.

Sauvageot, A. (1973) *L'élaboration de la langue finnoise.* Libraire C. Klinksieck, Paris.

Sauvageot, A. (1983) Le finnois de Finlande (Suomi). In Fodor, I., Hagège, C. (eds) *Language reform: history and future.* Buske, Hamburg, vol. 3, 173–90.

Schaechter, M. (1983) Yiddish language modernization and lexical elaboration. In Fodor, I., Hagège, C. (eds) *Language reform: history and future.* Buske, Hamburg, vol. 3, 191–218.

Schäfer, J. (1973) *Shakespeares Stil: germanisches und romanisches Vokabular.* Athanäum, Frankfurt am Main.

Schamschula, W. (1973) *Die Anfänge der tschechischen Erneuerung und das deutsche Geistesleben 1740–1800.* Wilhelm Fink, Munich.

Schultz, H. M. (1888) *Die Bestrebungen der Sprachgesellschaften des xvii. Jahrhunderts für Reinigung der deutschen Sprache.* Vandenhoeck & Ruprecht, Göttingen.

Schumann, K. (1958) *Die griechischen Lehnbildungen und Lehnbedeutungen im Altbulgarischen.* O. Harassowitz, Wiesbaden.

Seidel, E., Seidel-Slotty, I. (1961) *Sprachwandel im Dritten Reich: eine kritische*

Untersuchung faschistischer Einflüsse. Verlag Sprache und Literatur, Halle-Saale.

Şerban, F. (1983) Modernisation de la langue roumaine. In Fodor, I., Hagège, C. (eds) *Language reform: history and future*. Buske, Hamburg, vol. 3, 219–38.

Ševčík, D. (1974–5) Český jazykový purismus z hlediska funkční teorie spisovného jazyka. *Sborník prací Filosofické fakulty Brněnské university, Řady jazykovědné* **22/23**: 49–58.

Shevelov, G. Y. (1977) Language planning and unplanning in the Ukrainian SSR. In Thomas, G. (ed.) *The languages and literatures of the non-Russian peoples of the Soviet Union*. McMaster University, Hamilton, Ontario, 237–67.

Simonyi, Z. (1907) *Die ungarische Sprache: Geschichte und Charakteristik*. K. J. Trübner, Strassburg.

Skautrup, P. (1944–68) *Det danske sprogs historie*, 4 vols, Gyldendalske boghandel, Copenhagen.

Smith, A. D. (1971) *Theories of nationalism*. Duckworth.

Stone, G. C. (1968) Der Purismus in der Entwicklung des Wortschatzes der obersorbischen Schriftsprache. In Fasske, H., Lötzsch, R. (eds) *Beiträge zur sorbischen Sprachwissenschaft*. Domowina-Verlag, Bautzen, 152–7.

Šulek, B. (1860) *Němačko-hrvatski rěčnik*. Zupan, Zagreb.

Šulek, B. (1874) *Hrvatsko-njemačko-talijanski rječnik znanstvenoga nazivlja*. Zagreb.

Svobodová, Z. (1955) *Dobrovský a německá filologie*. Rozpravy ČSAV, Prague.

Tachau, F. (1964) Language and politics: Turkish language reform. *The Review of Politics* **26**: 191–204.

Tauli, V. (1968) *Introduction to a theory of language planning*. Almquist and Wiksells, Upsala.

Tauli, V. (1983) The Estonian language reform. In Fodor, I., Hagège, C. (eds) *Language reform: history and future*. Buske, Hamburg, vol. 3, 309–30.

Tejnor, A. *et al.* (1971) Cízí slova v českém jazyce. Ústav pro výzkum verejného mínění, Prague.

Tejnor, A. *et al.* (1982) Sociolinguistische Untersuchungen zur Sprachkultur. In *Grundlagen der Sprachkultur: Beiträge der Prager Linguistik zur Sprachtheorie und Sprachpflege* Vol. 2. Akademie-Verlag, Berlin, 272–302.

Thomas, G. (1975) The calque – an international trend in the lexical development of the literary languages of eighteenth-century Europe. *Germano-Slavica* **6**: 21–41.

Thomas, G. (1978a) The origin and nature of lexical purism in the Croatian variant of Serbo-Croatian. *Canadian Slavonic Papers* **20**: 405–420.

Thomas, G. (1978b) The role of calques in the early Czech language revival. *Slavonic and East European Review* **56**: 481–506.

Thomas, G. (1982) The role of the lexical variants in the present-day language situation in Bosnia-Hercegovina. *Language Problems and Language Planning* **6**: 29–44.

Thomas, G. (1983) A comparison of the morphological adaptation of loanwords ending in a vowel in contemporary Czech, Russian, and Serbo-Croatian. *Canadian Slavonic Papers* **25**: 180–205.

Thomas, G. (1985) Problems in the study of migratory loanwords in the Slavic languages. *Canadian Slavonic Papers* **27**: 307–25.

Thomas, G. (1987) The Slavization of the Slovene and Croatian lexicons: problems in their interrelationship in the nineteenth century. *Slovene Studies* **9**: 217–25.

Thomas, G. (1988a) *The Impact of the Illyrian Movement on the Croatian lexicon.* Otto Sagner, Munich.

Thomas, G. (1988b) Towards a typology of lexical purism in the Slavic literary languages. *Canadian Slavonic Papers* **30**: 95–111.

Thomas, G. (1989a) The relationship between Slavic nationalism and linguistic purism. *Canadian Review of Studies in Nationalism* **16**: 5–13.

Thomas, G. (1989b) The role of diglossia in the development of the Slavonic literary languages. *Slavistična Revija* **37**: 273–82.

Thomas, G. (forthcoming) Lexical purism as an aspect of language cultivation in Yugoslavia. In *Language planning in Yugoslavia.* Macmillan (a Serbo-Croatian version of this paper was published in *Književne novine,* No. 707, 1 December 1989).

Tolnai, V. (1929) *A nyelvújítás: a nyelvújítás elmélete es története.* Magyar Tudomanyos Akademia, Budapest.

Unbegaun, B. O. (1932) Le calque dans les langues slaves. *Révue des études slaves* **12**: 19–51.

Urbančič, B. (1972) *O jezikovni kulturi.* Cankarjeva založba, Ljubljana.

Vachek, J. (1960) *Dictionnaire de linguistique de l'école de Prague.* Het Spectrum, Utrecht.

Vince, Z. (1978) *Putovima hrvatskoga književnog jezika.* Liber, Zagreb.

Vince, Z. (1979–80) I jezična čistoća i funkcionalnost. *Jezik* **27**: 65–79.

Vitale, M. (1964) *Purista* e *purismo:* storia di parole e motivi della loro fortuna. *Acme* **17**: 187–211.

Vočadlo, O. (1926) Slavic linguistic purity and the use of foreign words. *Slavonic Review* **5**: 352–63.

Vooys, C. G. N. de (1924–7) Purisme. In *Versamelde taalkundige opstellen.* J. B. Wolters U.M. Groningen/Den Haag.

Vooys, C. G. N. de (1946) *Duitse invloed op de Nederlands woordvorraad.* Noord-Hollandsche uitgevers maatschappij, Amsterdam.

Waight, T. (1980) On the phonology of words of foreign origin. *Russian Linguistics* **5**: 75–90.

Weingart, M. (1932) Slovo o české jazykové kultuře. *Časopis pro moderní filologii* **18**: 113–32, 239–60.

Weingart, M. (1934) O germanismech. In Weingart, M. *Český jazyk v přítomnosti: úvahy a podněty z jazykové therapie a kultury.* Nakladatelství československé grafické unie, Prague, 56–62.

Weinreich, U. (1953) *Languages in contact: findings and problems.* Publications of the Linguistic Circle of New York, New York.

West, J. (1983) An historical survey of the language planning movement in Wales. In Fodor, I., Hagège, C. (eds) *Language reform: history and future.* Buske, Hamburg, vol. 2, 383–98.

Wexler, P. (1969) Towards a structural definition of internationalisms. *Linguistics* **48**: 77–92.

Wexler, P. (1971) Diglossia, language standardization and purism: parameters for a typology of literary languages. *Lingua* **27**: 330–54.

Wexler, P. (1974) *Purism and language: a study of modern Ukrainian and Belorussian nationalism (1840–1967)*. Indiana UP, Bloomington, Indiana.

Whinnom, K. (1971) Linguistic hybridization and the special case of pidgins and creoles. In Hymes, D. (ed.) *Pidginization and creolization of languages*. Cambridge UP, Cambridge, 91–115.

Whiteley, W. H. (1969) *Swahili: the rise of a national language*. Methuen.

Wolff, H. (1888) *Der Purismus in der deutschen Litteratur des siebzehnten Jahrhunderts*. Heitz & Mündel, Strassburg.

Zaidi, M. H. (1983) Word-borrowing and word-making in modern South Asian languages: Urdu. In Fodor, I., Hagège, C. (eds) *Language reform: history and future*. Buske, Hamburg, vol. 3, 399–421.

Zakir, M. (1983) Urdu between survival and reform: the Indian situation. In Fodor, I., Hagège, C. (eds) *Language reform: history and future*. Buske, Hamburg, vol. 3, 423–9.

Zvelebil, K. V. (1983) Word-borrowing and word-making in modern South Asian languages: Tamil. In Fodor, I., Hagège, C. (eds) *Language reform: history and future*. Buske, Hamburg, vol. 3, 431–40.

Index